CW01641892

Shaping the Fourth Industrial Revolution

Klaus Schwab

With Nicholas Davis

ISBN-978-1-944835-14-9

World Economic Forum
91–93 route de la Capite
CH-1223 Cologny/Geneva
Switzerland
www.weforum.org

Contents

Foreword

Satya Nadella
CEO of Microsoft

Through insightful convenings and publishing, the World Economic Forum, and its founder, Klaus Schwab, have continued to cast a bright light on both the opportunities and the challenges of the Fourth Industrial Revolution. They are right to confront zero-sum thinking about the coming wave of new technologies by pointing out that their evolution is entirely within our power.

The confluence of data with massive computational storage and cognitive power will transform industry and society at every level, creating opportunities that were once unimaginable from health and education to agriculture, manufacturing and services. My company and others are betting on the convergence of several important technology shifts – mixed reality, artificial intelligence and quantum computing. With mixed reality we are building the ultimate computing experience, one in which your field of view becomes a computing surface; your digital world and your physical world become one. The data, apps, and even the colleagues and friends on your phone or tablet will be available anywhere you want to access them—while you're working in your office, visiting a customer, or collaborating with colleagues in a conference room. Artificial intelligence will power every experience, augmenting human capability with insights and predictive power that would be impossible to achieve on our own. Finally, quantum computing will allow us to go beyond the bounds of Moore's Law—the observation that the number of transistors in a computer chip doubles roughly every two years—by changing the very physics of computing as we know it today, providing the computational power to solve the world's biggest and most complex problems. MR, AI, and quantum may be independent threads today, but they are going to come together.

Similarly, industry and society must come together to focus on empowering both people and organizations by democratizing access to intelligence to help solve our most pressing challenges. For example,

Satya Nadella is CEO of Microsoft and author of Hit Refresh: The Quest to Rediscover Microsoft's Soul and Imagine a Better Future for Everyone

if AI is one of technology's top priorities, healthcare is surely one of AI's most urgent applications. Coupled with mixed reality, the cloud and business optimization tools, AI will be central to health care transformation underway on the science bench, in the clinic and throughout medical center operations. Advancing global health through precision medicine – understanding individual variability in genes, immunological systems, environment, and lifestyle for each person – can only be accomplished through web-scale machine learning, cognitive services and deep neural networks. There is an ethical imperative to be inclusive and transparent in the design of these technologies, but there also is an engineering necessity – the products and services simply will be better as a result. Toward this end, in 2016, Microsoft, Amazon, Google, Facebook, and IBM announced a Partnership on AI to benefit people and society. The aim is to advance public understanding of AI and formulate best practices on the challenges and opportunities within the field. The partnership will advance research into developing and testing safe AI systems in areas like automobiles and healthcare, human-AI collaboration, economic displacement, and how AI can be used for social good.

Restoring economic growth and productivity for everyone is an aim we all share, and technology will play a leading role. One formula to consider is to emphasize education and new skills in combination with intensified application of these technological innovations broadly across local economies (especially in sectors where the country or region has a comparative advantage). In a digital age, software acts as the universal input that can be produced in abundance and applied across both public and private sectors and every industry. Regardless of location—Detroit, Egypt, or Indonesia—this universal input needs to turn into local economic surplus. Breakthrough technologies, plus a workforce trained to use them productively, multiplied by the intensity of their use spreads economic growth and opportunity for everyone.

Finally, trust in today's digital world means everything. In every corner of this world, we need a revitalized regulatory environment that promotes innovative and confident use of technology. The biggest problem is antiquated laws that are ill-suited to deal with contemporary problems.

The prescient topics explored in this book, coupled with the dialogue it sparks at World Economic Forum gatherings are vital contributions to understanding and solutions. The potential benefits are unprecedented, and as this book concludes, public-private leadership and partnership are essential.

Preface

Klaus Schwab
Founder and Executive Chairman
World Economic Forum

The world is at a crossroads. The social and political systems that have lifted millions out of poverty and shaped our national and global policies for half a century are failing us. The economic benefits of human ingenuity and effort are becoming more concentrated, inequality is rising, and the negative externalities of our integrated global economy are harming the natural environment and vulnerable populations: the stakeholders least able to absorb the cost of progress.

Public trust in business, government, the media and even civil society has fallen to the point where more than half of the world feels the current system is failing them. The widening gap in trust between those in their country's top income quartile and the rest of the population indicates that social cohesion is fragile at best, and very close to breaking down at worst.

It is in this precarious political and social context that we face both the opportunities and the challenges of a range of powerful, emerging technologies – from artificial intelligence, to biotechnologies, advanced materials to quantum computing – that will drive radical shifts in the way we live, and which I have described as comprising the Fourth Industrial Revolution.

These emerging technologies are not merely incremental advances on today's digital technologies. Fourth Industrial Revolution technologies are truly disruptive – they upend existing ways of sensing, calculating, organizing, acting and delivering. They represent entirely new ways of creating value for organizations and citizens. They will, over time, transform all the systems we take for granted today – from the way we produce and transport goods and services, to the way we communicate, the way we collaborate, and the way we experience the world around us. Already, advances in neurotechnologies and biotechnologies are forcing us to question what it means to be human.

The good news is that the evolution of the Fourth Industrial Revolution is entirely within our power, and we are still at its very earliest stages. The social norms and regulations governing emerging technologies are in the process of being developed and written today. Everybody can and should have a say in how new technologies affect them.

But standing at these crossroads means we bear a huge responsibility. If we miss this window of opportunity to shape new technologies in ways that promote the common good, enhance human dignity and protect the environment, there is a good chance that the challenges we experience today will only be exacerbated, as narrow interests and biased systems further entrench inequalities and compromise the rights of people in every country.

Appreciating the importance of the Fourth Industrial Revolution and shaping it for the benefit of all, rather than just those privileged enough to be wealthy or skilled, requires a new way of thinking and a broad understanding of the different technologies that will impact individuals, communities, organizations and governments.

Shaping the Fourth Industrial Revolution has been designed to empower you to engage in strategic dialogues around emerging technologies within and across the communities, organizations and institutions of which you are a member, helping you to actively shape the world in line with common human values.

This book is the product of many world-class experts from across the World Economic Forum's diverse community. Section 2, in particular, synthesizes the perspectives of leading thinkers from the Forum's Global Future Councils and Expert Network. Were it not for their generous contributions of time and knowledge, it would have been impossible to cover the breadth of subject matter to the depth required to make sense of the most impactful technology domains. I also very much appreciate the thoughtful and most relevant reflections provided by Satya Nadella in the Foreword.

My thanks particularly go to my co-author Nicholas Davis, Head of Society and Innovation, as well as Thomas Philbeck, Head of Science and Technology Studies, whose intellectual contribution, hard work and dedication were absolutely essential. Thanks, too, to Anne Marie Engtoft Larsen, Knowledge Lead, Fourth Industrial Revolution, who brought critical nuance to the issues around technology and global development.

I would also like to deeply thank Katrin Eggenberger, who once again provided invaluable support in managing the internal and external publishing of the book; Kamal Kimaoui, who expertly designed the book layout; Fabienne Stassen, whose editing skill greatly improved the text; and Mel Rogers, whose strategic mindset and values-driven leadership resonate throughout the chapters.

My experience as Founder and Executive Chairman of the World Economic Forum, the International Organization for Public-Private Cooperation, has shown that sustained and inclusive progress means working across disciplines and stakeholders to promote common visions and confront zero-sum thinking. If we are successful, we can choose the fork in the road that offers the opportunity to address the failures of past industrial revolutions, and create a far more inclusive, sustainable, prosperous and peaceful world. I hope this book, along with my 2016 book, *The Fourth Industrial Revolution*, helps guide our steps in the right direction.

Introduction

In January 2016, the publication of *The Fourth Industrial Revolution* called for all of us to take collective responsibility "for a future where innovation and technology are centred on humanity and the need to serve the public interest":

> *The new technology age, if shaped in a responsive and responsible way, could catalyse a new cultural renaissance that will enable us to feel part of something much larger than ourselves – a true global civilization. The Fourth Industrial Revolution has the potential to robotize humanity, and thus compromise our traditional sources of meaning – work, community, family, identity. Or we can use the Fourth Industrial Revolution to lift humanity into a new collective and moral consciousness based on a shared sense of destiny. It is incumbent on us all to make sure that the latter is what happens.*

The relevance of this call has only increased in the last 24 months, as research and development has further advanced fast-moving technologies, companies have adopted new approaches, and new empirical evidence has emerged of the disruptive impacts of emerging technologies and new business models on labour markets, social relationships and political systems.

This book complements *The Fourth Industrial Revolution* in two ways. First, it is intended to help all readers – from global leaders to engaged citizens – to "connect the dots", framing issues from a systems perspective and highlighting the connections between emerging technologies, global challenges and the actions we take today. Second, it enables readers to dive more deeply into the substance of specific technologies and governance issues, illustrated by recent examples and supported by perspectives from the world's leading experts.

This book highlights that:

- The Fourth Industrial Revolution represents a significant source of hope for continuing the climb in human development that has resulted in dramatic increases in quality of life for billions of people since 1800.
- Realizing these benefits requires collaborating across diverse stakeholders to overcome three core challenges: distributing the benefits of technological disruptions fairly, containing the inevitable externalities and ensuring that emerging technologies empower, rather than determine, all of us as human beings.
- The technologies at the heart of the Fourth Industrial Revolution are connected in many ways – in the way they extend digital capabilities, in the way they scale, emerge and embed themselves in our lives, in their combinatorial power and in their potential to concentrate privilege and challenge existing governance systems.
- To harness the benefits of the Fourth Industrial Revolution, we should not view emerging technologies as "mere tools" that are completely under our conscious control, nor as external forces that cannot be guided. Instead, we should seek to understand how and where human values are embedded within new technologies, and how these can be shaped to enhance the common good, environmental stewardship and human dignity.
- All stakeholders must be part of a global discussion about the ways in which technologies are changing the systems that surround us and impacting the lives of everyone on the planet. In particular, three often excluded groups need to be better represented in discussions around the governance and impact of emerging technologies: developing economies, environmental institutions and organizations, and citizens from across all income groups, generations and education levels.

In Section 1, four chapters present the challenges and principles critical to realizing a human-centred future, discuss the ways in which the technologies of the Fourth Industrial Revolution are connected, offer a framework for understanding and deepening the role of values and principles in emerging technological systems and consider the stakeholders that need to be more involved in discussions and applications of the Fourth Industrial Revolution.

Section 2, written in collaboration with members of the World Economic Forum's expert network and Global Future Councils, consists of 12 chapters, each focused on a particular set of technologies, explaining their potential impacts and why they matter for leaders today. These indicate how emerging technologies interact with one another and co-evolve as our relationship with data is transformed, the physical world is reformed, human beings are enhanced and new systems with huge power envelop us.

The book closes with a vision for systems leadership, summarizing the critical governance issues that leaders from all sectors, along with the general public, must tackle together to create an inclusive, sustainable and prosperous future.

Section 1

The Fourth Industrial Revolution

Chapter 1

Framing the Fourth Industrial Revolution

The idea that the world is entering a new phase of disruptive change has become one of the most discussed topics in boardrooms and parliaments around the world. This chapter introduces the core concepts of the Fourth Industrial Revolution, identifies three central challenges that must be managed collaboratively, and highlights four principles that citizens and leaders can draw on to guide and shape new technologies and systems as they emerge.

A mental model for shaping the future

The Fourth Industrial Revolution is a way of describing a set of ongoing and impending transformations in the systems that surround us, and which most of us take for granted every day. While it may not feel momentous to those of us experiencing a series of small but significant adjustments to life on a daily basis, it is not a minor change – the Fourth Industrial Revolution is a new chapter in human development, on par with the first, second and third Industrial Revolutions, and once again driven by the increasing availability and interaction of a set of extraordinary technologies.

The emerging technologies driving the Fourth Industrial Revolution build on the knowledge and systems of prior industrial revolutions, in particular the digital capabilities of the third Industrial Revolution. They include the 12 clusters of technologies discussed in Section 2 of this book, such as artificial intelligence (AI) and robotics, additive manufacturing, neurotechnologies, biotechnologies, virtual and augmented reality, new materials, energy technologies, as well as ideas and capabilities we don't yet know exist.

But the Fourth Industrial Revolution is much more than just a description of technologically-driven change. Most importantly, it is an opportunity to frame a series of public conversations that can help all of us – from technology leaders and policy-makers to citizens from all income groups, nationalities and backgrounds – to understand and guide the way that powerful, emerging and converging technologies influence the world around us.

To do this, the way we view and discuss the powerful new technologies that are shaping our world needs to change – we can't think of technology as a wholly exogenous force that will inevitably determine our future, nor can we take the opposite view of technology as simply a tool that humans can choose to use in whichever way we want.

Rather, we need to deepen our understanding of the way that new technologies connect with one another and influence us in both subtle and obvious ways, reflecting and amplifying human values as we make decisions around investment, design, adoption and reinvention. It is difficult, if not impossible, to collaborate on investments, policies and collective action that positively affect the future unless we can appreciate the way that people and technologies interact.

The overarching opportunity of the Fourth Industrial Revolution is therefore to look beyond technologies as either simple tools or inevitable forces, finding ways to give the greatest number of people the ability to positively impact their families, organizations and communities by influencing and guiding the systems that surround us and shape our lives.

By systems, we mean the norms, rules, expectations, goals, institutions and incentives that guide our behaviour every day, as well as the infrastructure and flows of material and people that are fundamental to our economic, political and social lives. Collectively, these influence how we manage our health, make decisions, produce and consume goods and services, work, communicate, socialize and move around – even what we consider it means to be human. As throughout the history of industrial revolutions, all these things, and many more, will fundamentally shift as the Fourth Industrial Revolution unfolds.

Industrial revolutions, growth and opportunity

Over the past 250 years, three industrial revolutions have transformed the way human beings create value and have changed the world. In each, technologies, political systems and social institutions all co-evolved, changing not just industries, but how people saw themselves, related to one another and interacted with the natural world.

The first Industrial Revolution started in Britain's textile industry in the mid-18th century, sparked by the mechanization of spinning and weaving. Over the subsequent 100 years, it transformed every existing industry and gave birth to many more, from machine tools to steel manufacturing, the steam engine and railways. New technologies led to shifts in cooperation and competition that, in turn, created entirely new systems of value production, exchange and distribution, and upended sectors from agriculture to manufacturing, from communications to transport. Indeed, the way we use the word "industrial" today is too narrow to encompass the scope of the revolution. A better framing is perhaps the way 19th-century thinkers Thomas Carlyle and John Stuart Mill used "industry" to refer to all activities that flow from human effort.

Although it contributed to the spread of colonialism and environmental degradation, the first Industrial Revolution succeeded in making the world wealthier. Before 1750, even the richest countries – Britain, France, Prussia, the Netherlands, the North American colonies – averaged growth of only around 0.2% per year, and even this was highly volatile. Inequality was higher than today, and per capita incomes were at levels we would consider to be extreme poverty today. By 1850, thanks to the impact of technologies, annual growth rates in those same countries had risen to 2-3%, and per capita incomes were rising steadily.[1]

In the period between 1870 and 1930, a new wave of interrelated technologies compounded the growth and opportunity that came from the first Industrial Revolution. The radio, telephone, television, home appliances and electric lighting demonstrated the transformative power of electricity. The internal combustion engine enabled the automobile, the aeroplane and, ultimately, their ecosystems – including manufacturing jobs and highway infrastructure. There were breakthroughs in chemistry: the world got new materials, such as thermoset plastics, and new processes – the Haber-Bosch process, synthesizing ammonia, paved the way for cheap nitrogen fertilizer, the "green revolution" of the 1950s and the subsequent spike in human population.[2] From sanitation to international air travel, the second Industrial Revolution ushered in the modern world.

Around 1950, revolutionary breakthroughs occurred in information theory and digital computing, the technologies at the heart of the third Industrial Revolution. As with the previous periods, the third Industrial Revolution was not due to the existence of digital technologies, but to the ways in which they changed the structure of our economic and social systems. The ability to store, process and transmit information in digital form reformatted almost every industry, and dramatically changed the working and social lives of billions of people. The cumulative impact of these three industrial revolutions has been an incredible increase in wealth and opportunity – at least for those in advanced economies.

Today's OECD countries, home to around one-sixth of the world's population, have per capita incomes around 30 to 100 times higher than their equivalents in 1800.[3] Figure 1 draws on data from the UN Human Development Index for OECD countries and assessments of the contribution of different technologies to growth, health and education outcomes to illustrate the extent to which different industrial revolutions have supported continually rising quality of life since the first Industrial Revolution.

Figure 1: Illustrative Contribution of Industrial Revolutions to Human Development: OECD Countries 1750-2017

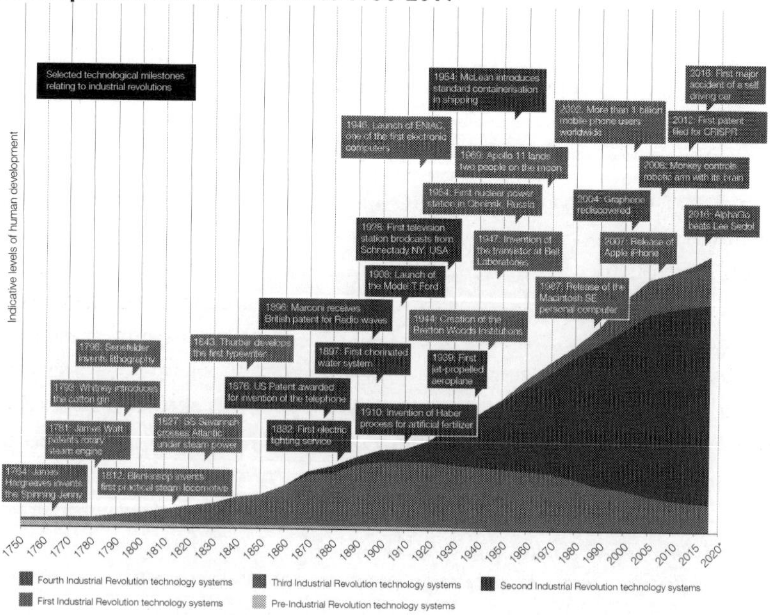

Source: World Economic Forum

Figure 1 is indicative only, based on a rough estimate of how dominant technologies, industries and institutional developments contributed to measures of human development since 1750.[4] The figure shows that, even for countries close to the technological frontier, the lion's share of human development comes from the technologies and systems developed during the second Industrial Revolution – such as electricity, water and sanitation, modern healthcare and the huge expansion in agricultural productivity driven by the invention of artificial fertilizer. This is an argument that Robert Gordon and others have made persuasively.[5]

The process of technological innovation – invention, commercialization, widespread adoption and use – has been the most powerful driver of wealth and increased well-being since the beginning of history. Today the average person has a longer lifespan, better health, more economic security and a far lower chance of dying through violence than in any prior era. Since the first Industrial Revolution, the average real income per person in OECD economies has increased around 2,900%.[6] Over the same period, life expectancy at birth has more than doubled in almost every country – from 40 years to more than 80 years in the United Kingdom, and from 23.5 years in India to 65 years today.

Future benefits and challenges

Under ideal circumstances, the Fourth Industrial Revolution offers the opportunity for those lucky enough already to enjoy the benefits of three prior industrial revolutions to continue the upward climb in human development, as illustrated in Figure 2, while also improving the lives of those who currently miss out on the benefits that the combination of technological systems and healthy public and private institutions can provide. If the technologies of the Fourth Industrial Revolution can be matched with appropriate institutions, standards and norms, people around the world will have the opportunity to enjoy more freedom, better health, higher levels of education and more opportunities to live lives they value, while suffering less from insecurity and economic uncertainty.

Figure 2: Illustrative Contribution of Industrial Revolutions to Human Development to 2050 (benefits realized)

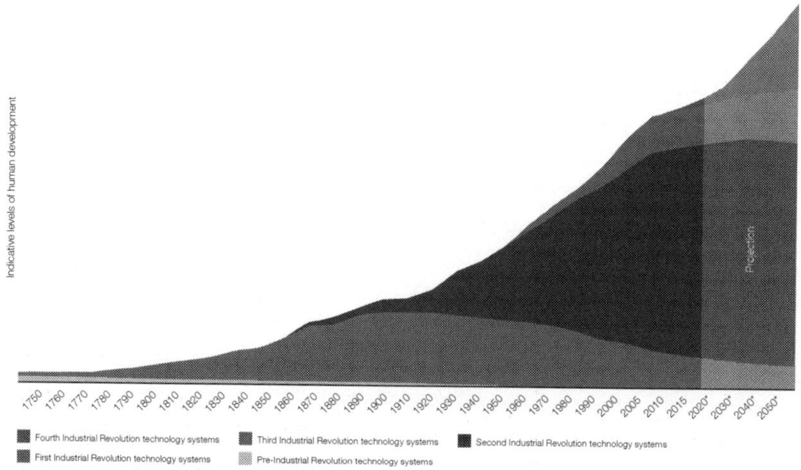

Source: World Economic Forum

Section 2 of this book highlights the potential upsides for 12 clusters of emerging technologies. To give just a few examples, quantum computing technologies offer incredible breakthroughs in the way that we model and optimize complex systems – promising huge increases in efficiencies in fields as diverse as logistics and drug discovery. The use of distributed ledger technology promises not just to dramatically reduce the transaction cost of coordinating between diverse parties – such as verifying the provenance of diamonds – but could be the driving force behind massive flows of value in digital products and services, providing secure digital identities that can make new markets accessible to anyone connected to the internet. Virtual and augmented reality offers an entirely new channel for experiencing the world around us – and could dramatically accelerate how we learn or apply skills across time and space. And if new materials can deliver a step-change in battery energy density, it would revolutionize the use of civilian and military drones and the provision of electricity services to vulnerable populations, and accelerate a wholesale change of transport systems.

These benefits seem as though they rely almost entirely on technological breakthroughs. But when and how they materialize, and who they benefit, is uncertain. The Fourth Industrial Revolution is evolving and emerging in ways that are creating new challenges and concerns for the world at a time when concerns about inequality, social tension and political fragmentation are rising, and where vulnerable populations are increasingly exposed to economic uncertainty and the threat of natural disasters. What type of thinking, and what kind of institutions, do we need to create a world where everyone has the chance to enjoy the highest possible levels of human development? To create such an equitable and inclusive future, we will have to adjust our mindsets and our institutions. After all, the experience from the previous industrial revolutions indicate that for the benefits of these new technologies to be fully realized in the coming systems upheaval, the world must meet three pressing challenges.

The first challenge is to ensure that the benefits of the Fourth Industrial Revolution are distributed fairly. The wealth and well-being generated by previous industrial revolutions were, and continue to be, unevenly distributed. While inequality between countries has reduced considerably since the 1970s due to the rapid development of emerging market nations, inequality within countries is rising. Annual median incomes declined by 2.4% in advanced economies between 2011 and 2016, and in 2015 the United States recorded a reduction in life expectancy for the first time in over 25 years, mainly as a result of a decline in the health of working class whites.[7] People can miss out on the benefits of systems for a number of reasons: because they are unavailable, unaffordable or irrelevant, because those systems are biased in overt or subtle ways, or through the operations of institutions that tend to privatize profits and concentrate wealth and opportunities. Chapter 4 looks in detail at the stakeholders of the Fourth Industrial Revolution and what is required to ensure that they all have the chance to benefit from it.

The second challenge is to manage the externalities of the Fourth Industrial Revolution in terms of the risks and harm that it causes. In previous industrial revolutions, too little effort was made to protect vulnerable populations, the natural environment and future generations from suffering as a result of unintended consequences, costs of change, second-order impacts or deliberate misuse of new capabilities.

The challenge of externalities and unintended consequences is particularly acute given the power of Fourth Industrial Revolution technologies, and the uncertainty as to their long-term impacts in complex social and environmental systems. At the most alarming level, risks range from attempts at geoengineering that could lead to sudden and irreversible damage to the biosphere, or the development of an artificial general intelligence whose goal-seeking behaviour clashes with the diverse messiness of human life. By making swathes of existing cryptographic approaches obsolete, under some scenarios quantum computing could create significant risks to privacy and security for anyone able to access new computing approaches. The widespread use of private, autonomous vehicles could increase road congestion in already crowded cities. And the rise of virtual reality may further exacerbate the challenge of online harassment, making it even more psychologically damaging.

The third challenge is to ensure that the Fourth Industrial Revolution is human-led and human-centred. Human values must be respected in themselves, rather than weighed only in financial terms. Moreover, to be human-centred is to empower, rather than to determine, humans as beings with meaningful agency in the world. This challenge is particularly critical because of how Fourth Industrial Revolution technologies differ from those of the previous industrial revolutions. As Chapter 12 explains, they can intrude into the hitherto private space of our minds, reading our thoughts and influencing our behaviour. They can assess and make decisions based on data that no human can process, and in ways no human understands. They can alter the building blocks of life itself, including human beings yet to be born. And, via digital networks, they will spread far more quickly than any previous phase of technological development.

A new leadership mindset

These three challenges – distributing benefits, managing externalities and ensuring a human-centred future – cannot be easily solved top-down through regulation or well-meaning government initiatives. Nor is it at all likely that the current constellation of international and national institutions, market structures, organized and spontaneous social movements and incentives for individuals will lead to powerful new technologies being widely available, completely free from harm and focused fully on empowering the people that use them. The world continues to struggle with a range of challenges linked to the last three industrial revolutions – median wages in advanced economies are stagnating or falling; developing economies are struggling to translate economic growth into broad-based, sustainable progress in living standards; and nearly one in 10 people lives in extreme poverty.[8] To paraphrase Madeleine Albright, we face the task of understanding and governing 21st-century technologies with a 20th-century mindset and 19th-century institutions. Institutional change is therefore critical to overcoming these challenges. But so is a mindset adapted to the 21st-century challenges we face.

Both the history of previous industrial revolutions and the dynamics of the technologies driving the Fourth Industrial Revolution indicate that four key principles are particularly useful in defining such a mindset. Think…

1. **Systems, not technologies:** It is tempting to focus on technologies themselves, when what really matters are the systems that deliver well-being. With political will, investment and cooperation across stakeholders, new technologies can enable better-performing systems to be put in place; without them, new technologies could make existing systems worse.

2. **Empowering, not determining**: It is tempting to think that technological change is impossible to control or direct and there is nothing we can do about technologies being able to influence behaviour. We should instead value human decision-making and agency, designing systems that harness new technologies to give people more choice, opportunities, freedom and control over their lives. This is particularly important given the ways in which emerging technologies advance the prospect of machines that can decide and act without human input, and influence our behaviour in both overt and subtle ways.

3. **By design, not by default**: It is tempting to dismiss any attempt to shape social and political systems as hubristic and doomed to failure, given their complexity. But we should not resign ourselves to the inevitability of default options. Design thinking – particularly employing the techniques and philosophy of human-centred design – as well as systems thinking approaches can help us to understand the structures that guide the world and appreciate how new technologies may shift systems into new configurations.

4. **Values as a feature, not a bug**: It is tempting to see technologies as mere tools, capable of being used for good or ill but value-neutral in themselves. In reality, all technologies implicitly have values baked into them, from the initial idea to how they are developed and deployed. We should recognize this and debate values at all stages of innovation, not just when they hurt someone with a voice. Chapter 3 looks closely at the role of values, and which values might be most usefully applied across the Fourth Industrial Revolution.

These four principles have emerged over the course of hundreds of conversations and interviews with scientists, entrepreneurs, civil society leaders, policy-makers, senior executives and media. Together they form a framework for evaluating, discussing and shaping the ways that technologies are influencing us today and will shape the world in the future.

Your role in shaping the Fourth Industrial Revolution

These principles are needed because the social norms, regulations, technical standards and corporate policies through which the Fourth Industrial Revolution will play out are being debated and formulated right now – all around the world, in Rwanda as much as in Switzerland or China. Evidence of the three challenges described above – exclusion, negative externalities and disempowerment – is already becoming apparent, from cases of algorithmic bias to labour market shifts that leave workers without social protection.

Given that many disruptive technologies are only just emerging from laboratories, garages, and research and development departments around the world, and that related regulations are in the process of being written and updated, there is a window of opportunity for citizens and leaders from all sectors to work together to shape the systems of the Fourth Industrial Revolution. We must seize that opportunity. If we succeed, the benefits include spreading prosperity more widely, reducing inequality and reversing the loss of trust that is dividing societies and polarizing politics. The Fourth Industrial Revolution could produce systems that support healthier, longer-lived populations with higher levels of economic and physical security, happily engaged in meaningful and fulfilling activities in a sustainable environmental context.

But how do we get there?

The first step is to connect the dots between the varying technologies comprising the Fourth Industrial Revolution. That is the subject of the next chapter.

Chapter Summary

The Fourth Industrial Revolution is a new chapter in human development, driven by the increasing availability and interaction of a set of extraordinary technologies, building on three previous technological revolutions. This revolution is only in its early stages, which provides humankind with the opportunity and responsibility to shape not just the design of new technologies, but also more agile forms of governance and positive values that will fundamentally change how we live, work and relate to one another.

Emerging technologies could provide tremendous benefits to industry and society, but experience from previous industrial revolutions reminds us that to fully realize them, the world must meet three pressing challenges. To attain a prosperous future, we must:

1. Ensure that the benefits of the Fourth Industrial Revolution are distributed fairly
2. Manage the externalities of the Fourth Industrial Revolution in terms of the risks and harm that it causes
3. Ensure that the Fourth Industrial Revolution is human-led and human-centred

As leaders grapple with the uncertainty brought about by rapid technological change, adaptation does not require predicting the future. Far more critical is developing a mindset that considers system-level effects, the impact on individuals, which remains future oriented and is aligned with common values across diverse stakeholder groups.

So, for the future, the four important principles to keep in mind when thinking about how technologies can create impact are:

1. Systems, not technologies
2. Empowering, not determining
3. By design, not by default
4. Values as a feature, not a bug

The regulation, norms and structures for a range of powerful emerging technologies are being developed and implemented today around the world. The time for action is therefore now, and it is up to all citizens to work together to shape the Fourth Industrial Revolution.

Chapter 2

Connecting the Dots

Appreciating the impact of, and finding ways to positively shape, the powerful technologies at the heart of the Fourth Industrial Revolution requires adopting a "zoom-in, zoom-out" strategy. In this context, zooming in means acquiring an understanding of the characteristics and potential disruptions of specific technologies, as discussed in Section 2. Perhaps even more important, however, is the ability to zoom out and see the patterns that connect technologies and the way they impact us.

Focusing on "systems, not technologies" can give leaders an advantageous vantage point when considering the technological changes of the Fourth Industrial Revolution, but will we be able to truly understand how technologies are transforming the systems we care about – across business, government and society – without attempting to gain a deep understanding of the different technologies themselves? This is a challenge that many of us face and that a two-pronged approach can overcome. Learning just enough about each of the technologies and attaining a "minimum viable appreciation" to be able to place them in the bigger picture is the first prong of this approach. This makes it easier to have informed discussions with experts, test ideas and explore where value can be created. Section 2 of this book is designed to provide exactly that level of understanding, by presenting succinct introductions to 12 sets of emerging technologies driving the Fourth Industrial Revolution.

This chapter deals with the second prong of the approach first, which is to "connect the dots" and appreciate the dynamics of the Fourth Industrial Revolution by looking at the trends and linkages across emerging technologies to understand how they relate to one another and will cumulatively impact our world. Essential skills must be cultivated in a fast-changing world, as the technological breakthroughs that matter today are eclipsed by further developments or applications tomorrow. This chapter examines several common aspects of Fourth Industrial Revolution technologies, allowing a look beyond the details of individual technologies to the way in which they relate to one another and combine to create similar impacts. When zooming out and connecting the dots, we see that these emerging technologies rely upon and extend digital systems, scale readily due to a foundation of digital interoperability, inhabit physical objects including us, combine in surprising and disruptive ways, and create similar benefits and challenges.

Figure 3: Time for Technologies and Applications to Be Taken Up by 100 Million Users

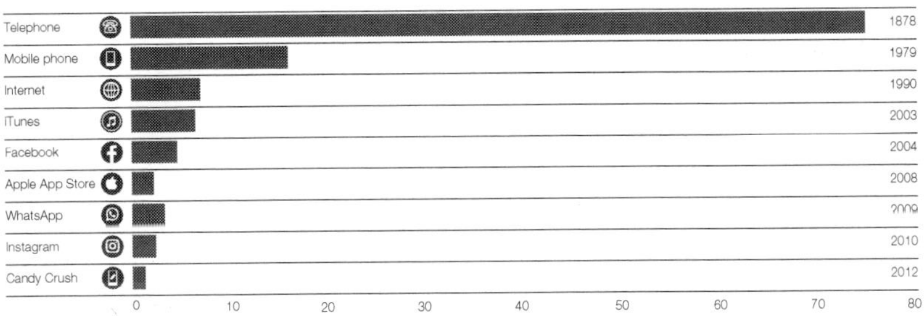

Sources: Boston Consulting Group ITU, Statista; BCG research; mobilephonehistory.co.uk; Scientific American, Internet Live Stats; iTunes; Fortune; OS X Daily; VentureBeat; Wired; Digital Quarterly; TechCrunch, AppMu.com

The clearest and most obvious aspect of Fourth Industrial Revolution technologies is that they extend and transform digital systems in significant ways. The technologies of the Fourth Industrial Revolution are connected to one another in that they all require and build on the digital capabilities and networks created by the third Industrial Revolution, just as those technologies required and built on the electricity networks of the second Industrial Revolution. None of the technologies discussed here would be possible without the advances in information processing, storage and communication that have changed the world over the past 60 years. This property of new technologies has sometimes led to the conclusion that all exciting new technologies are simply a continuation of the digital revolution. The critical difference is that Fourth Industrial Revolution technologies promise to disrupt even today's digital systems and create entirely new sources of value, turning the breakthroughs in digital technologies that organizations are struggling to make sense of today into the core infrastructure that business models will take for granted tomorrow.

We can see now that it makes no sense to think of the internet as merely an application of electricity networks, despite the fact that the majority of the internet is a phenomenon of electrical signals: the internet is a whole new ecosystem of value creation that would have been impossible to imagine with a mindset stuck in the second Industrial Revolution.

Figure 4: Artificial Intelligence M&A Activity as of March 2017

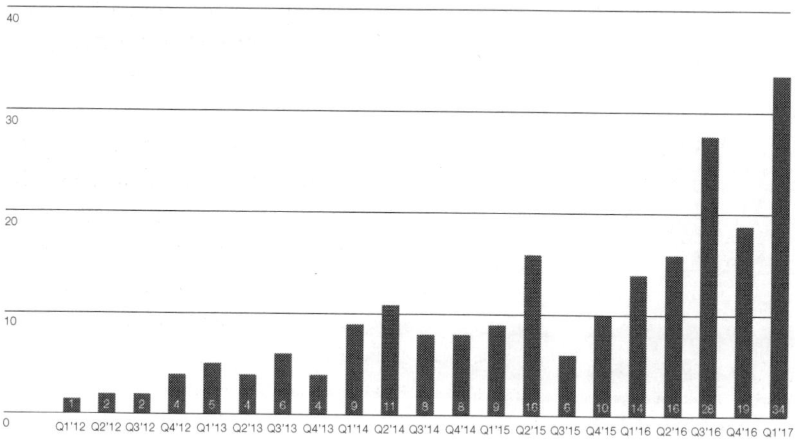

Source: CB Insights (2017)

Analogously, in the future it will make little sense to think of algorithms that independently learn from unstructured data as merely applications of digital computing power. The Fourth Industrial Revolution will give rise to ecosystems of value creation that are impossible to imagine with a mindset stuck in the third Industrial Revolution and require us to look far beyond even current digital disruptions to new sets of challenges and opportunities.

A second aspect of Fourth Industrial Revolution technologies is that they will scale exponentially, emerge physically and embed themselves in our lives. The faster a new technology scales, the more profoundly we are challenged to adapt to its disruptive impacts. And technologies of the Fourth Industrial Revolution will scale much more quickly than those of previous revolutions, because they can build on and diffuse over the digital networks of the third Industrial Revolution. Digital networks enable physical products to multiply more quickly by facilitating the transfer of knowledge and ideas; meanwhile, products or services that are themselves purely digital can be replicated at extremely low marginal cost. As Figure 3 shows, while it took the telephone 75 years to reach 100 million users, the internet garnered that many users in under a decade. As the diffusion of Fourth Industrial Revolution technologies accelerates, so will its impact on investment, productivity, organizational strategy, industry structure and individual behaviour. As Figure 4 shows, AI firms are both emerging and being acquired at exponentially increasing rates, while the use of ever-smarter algorithms is rapidly extending employee productivity, for example in the use of chat bots to augment (and, increasingly, replace) "live chat" support for customer interactions.

They may scale digitally, but Fourth Industrial Revolution technologies will not remain in the virtual realm. The third Industrial Revolution allowed physical products to seem to dematerialize, abstracting entirely into code – for example, the shift from (analogue) vinyl and cassette-tape recordings, to (digitally-encoded) compact discs (CDs), then finally to purely digital music files that can be shared online. The technologies of the Fourth Industrial Revolution massively increase the capacity for the reverse process – taking pure data and using it to create a wide variety of physical objects, actions or services. 3D printers, for example, can now produce everything from engine parts to foodstuffs to living cells; the rise of the internet of things means we can tell our virtual personal assistants to switch off the living room lights or turn up the heating; robots, drones and self-driving cars are learning to interact with the world in ever more natural ways. The phenomenon of re-emergence is becoming a common consumer experience, as companies build these new capabilities into their products and services: UPS now offers 3D printing and scanning services in almost 100 stores across the United States, targeting customers looking to build prototypes, testing jigs and creating models or personal accessories without the need for expensive computer-controlled cutting machines.

Fourth Industrial Revolution technologies will not stop at becoming part of the physical world around us – they will become part of us. Indeed, some of us already feel that our smartphones have become an extension of ourselves. Today's external devices – from wearable computers to virtual reality headsets – will almost certainly become implantable in our bodies and brains. Exoskeletons and prosthetics will increase our physical power, while advances in neurotechnology enhance our cognitive abilities. We will become better able to manipulate our own genes, and those of our children. These developments raise profound questions: where do we draw the line between human and machine? What does it mean to be human?

Another common aspect of Fourth Industrial Revolution technologies is that their power is amplified by how they combine and generate innovations. Technologies have always influenced other technologies as they are developed and commercialized, going back to steam power's influence on factory automation and the railways. Historically, there have tended to be a small number of foundational general purpose technologies that have a major impact across industries and geographies, and a larger number of more specialized technologies and applications that build on them.

Which technologies are most likely to be foundational in the Fourth Industrial Revolution? No one can predict this with confidence, but over 100 interviews with global experts in emerging technologies indicate that the foundational technologies of the Fourth Industrial Revolution are likely to be AI, distributed ledgers and new computing technologies, while both energy technologies and biotechnologies are likely to have outsized impacts in influencing other fields and domains. Also impactful but often underestimated technologies include advanced materials, which are a critical enabler across almost all fields, and the rise of virtual and augmented reality, which is creating new channels for experiencing the world. These results make sense, as it is easy to envisage how most of the other technologies would benefit from more capable algorithms, more powerful computers and physical materials with new properties. But potential interconnections and feedback loops are many and varied: for example, better AI on more powerful computers speeds up the discovery of new materials, which in turn are used to make still more powerful computers; or new materials are used to make batteries with much greater power relative to weight, unleashing new possibilities for robots and drones; and so on. The most impactful and surprising advances are likely to come from the interconnections of technologies, which means that public or private institutions unable to reform their vertically-oriented, siloed organizational structures are likely to become increasingly irrelevant.

Finally, Fourth Industrial Revolution technologies are alike in that they will create similar benefits – and challenges. One hundred years ago, as economist and author Don Boudreaux has pointed out, not even the richest person in the world could have purchased a television, a ticket for a trans-Atlantic flight, contact lenses, contraceptive pills or a course of antibiotics – all within the financial reach of an average person in an advanced economy today. It is hard to put a monetary figure on the value of these new products and services. Technologies of the Fourth Industrial Revolution will similarly vastly expand consumer choice, as well as lower costs and raise quality. And it will likewise be challenging to quantify just how much additional value this creates.

Perhaps the greatest concern related to the Fourth Industrial Revolution, however, is that the value will not be fairly shared – and that resulting increases in inequality could undermine social cohesion. One way in which the Fourth Industrial Revolution could exacerbate inequality is via monopoly power: already, for example, Google controls almost 90% of the global market share of search advertising, Facebook controls 77% of mobile social traffic and Amazon has almost 75% of the e-book market.[9] As the OECD has warned, future sophisticated self-learning algorithms may collude to raise prices in ways that make it impossible to prove wrongdoing.[10] And if it proves feasible to create an artificial general intelligence that self-improves to become a superintelligence, first-mover advantage would enable the domination of a wide range of markets.

For those who are unsettled by the potential inequalities that could be generated through Fourth Industrial Revolution technologies, it is good to know that many of these technologies provide for some form of decentralization in the way they are structured and the opportunities they create. For example, blockchain functions as a decentralized platform allowing for transparent and anonymous transactions, and 3D printing could be said, in the long run, to be democratizing manufacturing. Even biotechnologies that allow for genome editing are now available to those with modest funds. Democratization in this context means that the technologies are becoming more accessible to all as digital infrastructure spreads and knowledge is shared at a global scale. Whether or not this form of democratization is equalled by the democratization that brings access to decision-making about the technologies and their roles in industry and society is yet to be seen. Chapter 3 addresses this concern by focusing on exactly how we go about bringing societal values into the technological development process, establishing norms, and in essence democratizing the decision-making and development process that is so very often a black box.

Figures 5 and 6: Exposure to Automation of Job Characteristics, Illustrated for Selected Industries

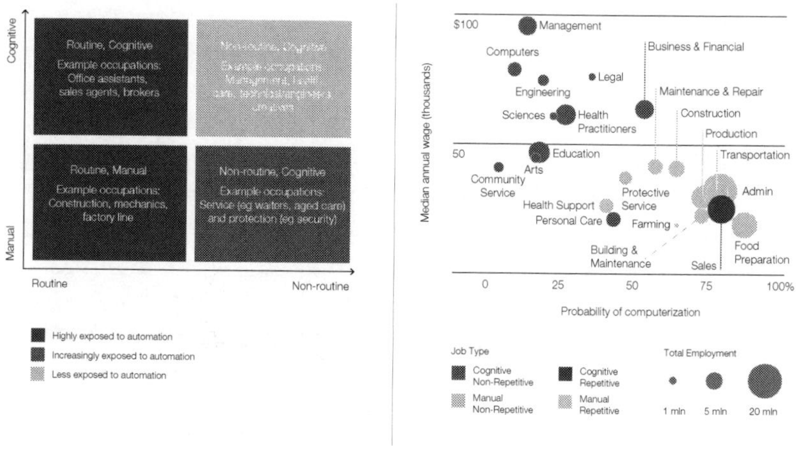

Sources: Autor, Levy and Murnane (2003); Blackrock Investment Institute (2014)

Another important and widely recognized concern is the potential impact on employment. As shown in Figures 5 and 6, a wide range of jobs are at risk of automation, far greater than in previous industrial revolutions – and rapid scaling means the job losses could accumulate quickly. Meanwhile, the rate of job creation in industries at the technological frontier is slower today than in previous decades.[11] Jobs being created in new industries demand technical expertise and non-cognitive skills, posing challenges for lower-skilled workers. In advanced economies, the majority of new jobs consist of independent contracting, part time, temporary or "gig economy" activities, which tend to lack the statutory protections and social benefits of full-time work. In the United States, for example, 94% of new jobs created between 2005 and 2015 are in "alternative forms of work", lacking social protection, labour rights or even meaningful control on the part of workers.[12] Fourth Industrial Revolution technologies therefore appear to be undermining humans' choice and ability to apply their skills and interests to meaningful work, and may lead to generations of workers living precarious and fragmented lives. Navigating these shifts will require new regulations for non-standard work, investments in adult learning and proactive employment services.[13]

Figure 7: The Varying Role of Redistribution in Reducing Inequality

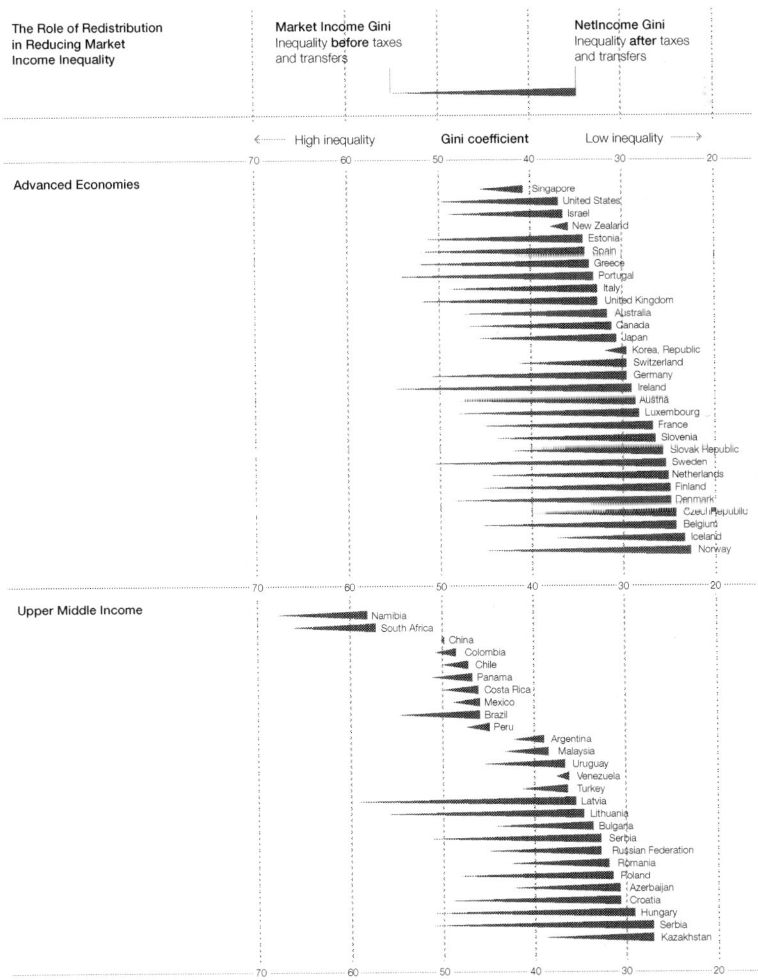

Source: World Economic Forum (2017)

It will also require new thinking about social protection systems and the role of transfers. Figure 7 shows that in most economies, transfers – most commonly through government spending and social programmes – play a significant role in shifting the distribution of market incomes. Sweden, for example, is structurally more unequal than the United States, Singapore, Mexico and Turkey – but after taxes and transfers, its GINI coefficient drops below all of these. Various new options have been proposed, such as a universal basic income – perhaps funded by a tax on robots, which is reportedly being explored in San Francisco.[14] The World Economic Forum *Inclusive Growth and Development Report 2017* argues, however, that governments should think more fundamentally about how to strengthen inclusive growth: the scope for domestic structural reforms goes well beyond taxes and transfers.[15]

Beyond the potential impacts of economic inequality, technologies of the Fourth Industrial Revolution could have significant negative externalities in a range of spheres. The following are among those mentioned by experts surveyed for *The Global Risks Report*, and explored further in the chapters of Section 2:

- Fourth Industrial Revolution technologies could democratize the ability to make massively destructive weapons – for example, bioweapons manufactured using biotechnologies.
- New materials – for example, nanotechnology – could have negative effects on the environment or human health that are not understood until those materials have already been widely deployed.
- Breakthroughs in clean energy could destabilize geopolitics by undermining the stability of fossil-fuel-producing countries.
- Attempts to tackle climate change through geoengineering could have unanticipated consequences that irreversibly damage ecosystems.
- Advances in quantum computing could render existing online security protocols useless.
- Widespread deployment of black box AI could make economic systems more fragile and volatile, and obscure lines of accountability for decisions – for example, if deployed in a conflict situation.
- Advances in neurotechnology could compromise human agency, as understanding grows about how to manipulate people into clicking links, making purchases or taking other actions.

Managing these externalities will be impossible if we rely on existing models of governance, which tend to be slow and backward-looking. For example, the US Federal Aviation Authority took eight months to grant Amazon an "experimental airworthiness certificate" to test a particular model of drone, by which time the model was obsolete; as a result, Amazon conducted its trials in Canada and the United Kingdom instead.[16] As discussed in both Chapter 3 and the conclusion, the world urgently needs new approaches to agile governance, which rethink not just the content of regulations, norms and standards, but the very mechanisms by which we produce them.

New approaches need to be found to govern technologies in ways that serve the public interest, meet human needs and ultimately make us feel part of a true global civilization. To achieve this, we will need to first address what human needs are in relation to technology, and how we might be able to align and incorporate positive human values into the technologies changing the world. This is the critical issue addressed in the next chapter.

Chapter Summary

A productive way to more deeply understand the Fourth Industrial Revolution is to take a two-pronged approach, which can be thought of as "zoom-in, zoom-out" strategy. It is important to both:

1. Gain a minimum viable appreciation of a range of specific technologies and their capabilities in order to better understand their potential and how they are being used; and
2. Connect the dots through an understanding of the relationships between technologies and systemic changes that they help catalyse

The technologies of the Fourth Industrial Revolution share some common aspects that are related to the kind of systemic changes we are seeing. Seeing the bigger, system-level picture is possible by considering four shared dynamics:

1. Fourth Industrial Revolution technologies extend and transform digital systems in significant ways;
2. They scale exponentially, emerge physically and embed themselves in our lives;
3. Their disruptive power is amplified by how they combine and generate innovations; and
4. They create similar benefits and challenges.

The benefits and challenges of these technologies relate to important issues such as inequality, employment, democracy, sovereignty, health and safety, and economic development.

Dealing successfully with the speed and scale of impact from Fourth Industrial Revolution technologies will require new, more agile models of governance which include private sector and social stakeholders as well as governments and traditional regulatory institutions. The goal is to develop more future-compatible, adaptable and multistakeholder-led forms of governance, including new norms, standards and practices.

Chapter 3

Embedding Values in Technologies

The Fourth Industrial Revolution (2016) argues that a values-based approach to a complex, uncertain and rapidly changing technological environment is essential for "the way forward".[17] This chapter expands on this idea and sets out principles and values that can help guide us forward and preserve society's role in shaping a technological future.

Technologies have undeniably contributed to the globe's overall rise in standard-of-living and well-being. They have also had troubling impacts and continue to create undesirable outcomes. Examples of the latter include the way many digital platforms are aggregating wealth in fewer and fewer hands, leaving workers more precarious and prone to abuse; how new techniques for natural gas extraction continue to damage the environment, enriching shareholders while putting the costs on marginalized stakeholders; and how investments in capital equipment may be responsible for as much as 83% of job losses in US manufacturing since 1990, and for subsequently dissolving entire communities.[18]

Many of these externalities have developed slowly over the last 30 years, but as the Fourth Industrial Revolution proceeds, bringing with it an increasing speed of change, we will have to deal with the effects of technologies that are ever more varied, complex and disruptive. Only speculation can say what their ramifications will be, but many are deeply concerned about their potential negative effects. As listed at the end of Chapter 2, the World Economic Forum *Global Risks Report 2017* revealed that experts viewed AI, biotechnologies, geoengineering and the internet of things as especially worrying.[19] *The Global Risks Report 2018* shows that cybersecurity threats to all things digital, including data, infrastructure, personal information and identities, have risen to the top of mind over the last year in response to their increasingly visible vulnerability. So, how can we tell if the technologies of the Fourth Industrial Revolution will truly improve the world and our lives? Will the economic and miscellaneous other benefits be worth the potential human costs? Do we have effective means to mitigate associated risks? And what do we really want from these technologies?

Ultimately, while any specific technology may promise convenience, entertainment, power, productivity or a combination of all four, what we want from technology, in a collective sense, tends to be the same thing we desire from a healthy economy: an improvement in human well-being. In Chapter 1, we argued that technologies should be "empowering, not determining", that the future should be "designed by and for humans", and that technologies should treat "values as a feature, not a bug". To put it simply, the clear goal for achieving well-being in the Fourth Industrial Revolution is a focus on a human-centred agenda. If the technologies of the Fourth Industrial Revolution result in a future of increased inequality, poverty, discrimination, insecurity, dislocation or environmental damage – if they result in humans being marginalized, appropriated or devalued – then things have gone terribly wrong.

Unfortunately, the feeling is growing that the world is being swept along by technological advances and economic imperatives, and losing sight of what really matters. Well-known economists, such as Erik Brynjolfsson and Andrew McAfee, have popularized the notion of the "great decoupling" of labour from productivity due to technology,[20] and the "gig" economy, enabled by technology, is expected to reach 40% of all jobs by 2020.[21] As much as 80% of the reduction of the labour share of national income in OECD countries has been credited to the effects of technology, technology is linked to increasing disparity, and the general public increasingly perceives policies as prioritizing economic growth over social cohesion and human well-being.[22] Rather than asking ourselves what outcomes we want from technological change, we keep finding that we have to react to undesirable outcomes.

Proactively taking steps towards a values-based approach to technologies can help us regain balance, rather than remaining perpetually on the back foot. First, being explicit about the political nature of technologies can help us highlight a mandate for responsible and responsive governance. Second, positioning societal values as priorities for governance can help direct how technologies are used and whom they benefit. Third, clearly identifying where and how values become part of technological systems can help raise awareness and determine the best strategies for integrating values in the development of technologies.

The politics of technologies

The relationship between technologies and values is not easy to define. Values are abstract and intangible, and differ between societies and individuals. Technologies are similarly wide in scope, encompassing everything from language to rockets that can take people into space. Given this breadth, there is pressure to find a simple way to address their relationship. Unfortunately, in a bid to simplify the discussion, two familiar and misleading perspectives have emerged. They can be described as follows:

Misleading view No. 1: Technology determines the future

This first perspective accepts that technologies influence society by incentivizing, enabling and constraining us in different ways, and characterizes technological progress as an external, almost deterministic force that cannot be changed or stopped. People who take this view often talk about technology as if it were driving history and our values in either a progressive or detrimental way and argue that there is no point trying to stop it.

Misleading view No. 2: Technology is value neutral

The second perspective denies that technologies have any meaningful influence on society in themselves, and instead characterizes them as neutral tools – it is individuals who influence society by choosing how to use them. This argument unfairly replaces the discussion of what technologies make possible and the impact they have on people with a focus solely on the moral character of the users – not the developers or diffusers – of technology.

Neither perspective is sufficient to guide the Fourth Industrial Revolution. In fact, although each contains a kernel of truth, both perspectives are extremely dangerous in an era where technologies exhibit the dynamics described in Chapter 2 – spreading more quickly, providing users with more power, and both enveloping us and embedding within us.

The first argument places technology above and outside the control of society, while the second divorces social responsibility from the influence technology exerts. They both miss the point that technologies and societies shape each other. Nuclear technologies are a good example of the danger of wholly relying on either one of these perspectives. Nuclear technologies are clearly not "mere tools" – their existence alone exerts tremendous pressures on and between societies because of the promise of nuclear-generated energy and the threat of nuclear destruction. For example, recent geopolitical tensions have heightened the awareness of nuclear dangers, and the 2017 Nobel Peace Prize was awarded to International Campaign to Abolish Nuclear Weapons (ICAN). At the same time, nuclear technologies don't have to determine humanity's fate, because societies have the ability to determine which technologies are developed, how they are developed, who has a say, and to what ends they are dedicated. Indeed, a rising number of societies are deciding against the use of nuclear power, as evidenced by the 2011 pledge by the German government to close the last of its nuclear power reactors by 2022.[23]

The way forward in the Fourth Industrial Revolution requires a more reflective and useful perspective on technologies, and the ability to have nuanced conversations about purpose, risks and uncertainties. It requires a third way of viewing technologies, which can be termed: "All technologies are political". Here we mean political in the descriptive sense. We don't mean that technologies represent governments, take a particular party line, or emanate in some way "from the left" or "from the right". Rather, we mean that technologies are solutions, products and implementations that are developed through social processes, stand in and for people and institutions, and contain within them a whole set of assumptions, values and principles that in turn can (and do) affect power, structure and status in society.

After all, technologies are tied up in how we know things, how we make decisions, and how we think about ourselves and each other. They are connected to our identities, worldviews and potential futures. From nuclear technologies to the space race, smartphones, social media, cars, medicine and infrastructure – the meaning of technologies makes them political. Even the concept of a "developed" nation implicity rests on the adoption of technologies and what they mean for us, economically and socially.

Many scientists and technologists already recognize the political aspects of technologies. For example, the Institute of Elcctrical and Electronics Engineers (IEEE) labels AI a "socio-technical system" in its Global Initiative for Ethical Considerations in Artificial Intelligence and Autonomous Systems.[24] In fact, the need to deeply think through the values of AI has led to a number of very public initiatives coordinated by academic, government and industry experts. Similarly, the Nuffield Council on Bioethics defines biotechnologies as "conjunctions of knowledge, practices, products and applications".[25] The council's explanation of this definition points out that technologies – like people – are more than the sum of their physical parts:

> *Despite the great diversity of biotechnologies, the conditions that lead to particular conjunctions coming into being in a particular social and historical context, while other possible conjunctions do not, raise common sets of issues. These conditions include both natural constraints and voluntary choices (even if those choices are not always recognised or explicit). Such choices depend on complex judgments involving values, beliefs and expectations about the technologies and their uses. How these choices are made – how different values, beliefs and expectations are drawn in, evaluated, incorporated or excluded – just as much as the nature of the considerations involved, have important ethical and political dimensions.*

When any technology is created, it contains the residue of values, goals and compromises. And the more powerful the technology, the more important it becomes to appreciate what these are.

Often, it is economics that drives choices concerning which technologies are worthwhile to pursue as well as how they are designed and implemented. These incentives can be seen through their impact on society. For example, the recent discussion around the ethics of digital content filtering (and the cost of doing it at scale) to combat "fake news" is directly related to the economic imperatives of technology companies, the design of their platforms and the techniques used to track, segment and push content to consumer groups. In the digital social media environment – just as with newspapers, television and radio – economic pressures and product management impact what billions of people know and how they know it. The open nature of the internet enables the rapid scaling of social media technologies, while simultaneously making monitoring networks for content deemed "anti-social" extremely challenging.

Understanding that technologies embody specific social attitudes, interests and goals gives us greater power to initiate change – indeed, it obligates us to take responsibility, because we cannot blame undesirable outcomes on the technologies alone, nor ignore how technologies influence the decisions we make. Accepting this means coming to grips with three responsibilities:

1. Identifying the values that are at stake with particular technologies
2. Understanding how technologies impact our choices and decision-making
3. Determining how to best influence technological development with an appropriate set of stakeholders

In the political negotiation between society, technologies and the economy, determining the amount of attention given to societal values is up to us.

Making societal values a priority

Because technologies are socially embedded, we have a responsibility to shape their development and an obligation to position societal values as priorities. Though technologies tend to transmit the values that are embedded in their design and purpose, consensus doesn't always exist on what those values should be. As John Havens of the IEEE phrased the issue: "How will machines know what we value if we don't know ourselves? ... We can't possibly increase human wellbeing if we don't take the time to identify our collective values before creating technology we know will align with those ideals."[26]

Different people and societies value different things, and there will be disagreements about the application of specific social and cultural perspectives to technologies. The fact that different cultures and types of values highlight differences in priorities shouldn't be a roadblock to thinking through a values-based approach to technologies. On the contrary, the more we think it through, the better we will become at understanding which priorities are critical for societies and how technology affects and mediates these values. In fact, it is possible to identify some values that command wide-ranging support, across the majority of cultures. In the White Paper entitled "A New Social Covenant", the World Economic Forum Global Agenda Council on Values (2012-2014) identified "a broad consensus – across cultures, religions and philosophies – on some shared, human aspirations" which together represent "a powerful, unifying ideal" of "valued individuals, committed to one another, and respectful of future generations".[27]

Agreeing on positive, unifying values is just the first step. They need to be put into practice. One way to do this is through responsive and responsible governance. In general, institutions are having a hard time keeping up with the speed and breadth of technological change. Many legal systems are ill-equipped to deal with new risks; indeed, the world is just beginning to wake up to the feasibility of a wide range of unprecedented scenarios that threaten everything from the environment to human rights. In addition, it is not particularly easy to foresee what externalities emerging technologies could have, whether due to how they are designed, used, managed or governed. Risks can and do emerge unexpectedly from the convergence of technological disciplines. Governance strategies must be flexible and become agile enough to engage and respond appropriately without roadblocks making institutions ineffective.

A New Social Covenant on Values

By the World Economic Forum Global Agenda Council on Values (2012-2014)

So this is our call: for a period of intentional, global reflection on the values we bring to the largest decisions of our time. A method to foster that reflection is the development of a New Social Covenant.

Many previous efforts have focused on individual rights – which are essential. But our focus is on what we owe to one another – both within nations and among nations.... There is great cultural diversity when it comes to values. But there is also a broad consensus – across cultures, religions and philosophies – on some shared, human aspirations.

- The dignity of the human person – whatever their race, gender, background or belief
- The importance of a common good that transcends individual interests
- The need for stewardship – a concern, not just for ourselves, but for posterity

Fostering these values is both a personal and a collective challenge. It is necessary to bring values into public life in order to bridge the gap between aspiration and practice. Discussion is not enough; we must make different decisions. And this depends on transformative values-based leadership in every field of human endeavour. We need to cultivate, encourage and honour the models, at the World Economic Forum and beyond. We must engage the people who can respond to global challenges in effective, productive, healing ways – people who will build and leave behind a more just, generous and sustainable world.

Examples of values-based governance in action already exist, however, such as the European Union's General Data Protection Regulation (GDPR), which will go into effect in the middle of 2018. This will change rules around user consent and require clear and intelligible terms and conditions. Companies that control data will have to notify users of security breaches, provide information about how their data is used, conform with "right to be forgotten" processes, allow for data portability, enlist data protection officers where necessary, and legally conform to processes that establish data protection at the design stage of technologies and services.[28]

The GDPR's emphasis on establishing privacy in the design phase of technologies illustrates a second approach to putting values into practice: trying to fold them into the processes through which technologies are developed, to ensure that their development reflects society's values rather than solely those of their creators. Rather than trying to correct for issues that have emerged from a laissez-faire perspective on technology and ethics, proactively considering ethics, values and social ramifications throughout the stages of technological development can have an important impact on how technologies integrate and support the kind of collective well-being to which societies aspire. Blockchain, the internet of things, autonomous systems, neurotechnologies and algorithms are all examples of technologies being developed by specialized communities with narrow sets of interests, sometimes in areas where values have yet to be explicitly established.

Unfortunately, folding specific values into technological development is not necessarily an easy task. It is not as simple as adding an "ethics" feature, and it can be as complex as adopting new methodologies, cultivating organizational culture, or even challenging the market mentality of the economics driving the development. Another challenge is that many technologies – especially digital ones – can be employed in multiple ways, and their risks and potential impacts are difficult to assess. Even where risks can be foreseen, not all technologies are "programmable"; for example, it is not clear how blockchain technologies could be developed to prevent their use for criminal enterprise or reduce their potential carbon footprint. Nonetheless, companies and institutions should feel an obligation to think about more than how to design and execute – they should engage in socially responsible processes from the very start. At the engineering and product development level, they should look beyond systemic incentives and technical requirements for the development or use of technologies and take a broader view of their potential impacts on society.[29]

Encoding values in technology

Making societal values a priority cannot succeed from top-down regulation. It requires flagging values as an issue and creating the opportunity for people and organizations to engage in new behaviours. It also requires inspired motivation from their leaders. It can begin in many places, as explored in the section below on inflection points, but no matter where it begins, helping to change behaviour, fostering awareness of the broader impact of technologies and setting societal values as priorities can be improved by approaching technologies in the following ways:

First, it is critical to recognize the gravity and pervasive influence of technologies. They are involved in every aspect of human life, mediating our interactions, facilitating our economies, impacting our bodies and the environment, and processing information upon which institutions and individual citizens depend. The need for a responsible atmosphere around such technologies as advanced materials and pharmaceuticals is well-established, and other technologies – from search engines, to autonomous systems, to blockchain – need a similar kind of respect. If measured by the scale of their collective impact on our lives rather than just by mortality rate, many seemingly innocuous technologies take on new significance.

Second, reflecting on and understanding personal and/or organizational purpose can provide clear perspective for engaging technologies. Scientific and technological pursuits require freedom to push boundaries, but we should also aim to contextualize new capabilities with reflection on purpose and meaning that includes the well-being of society. For example, in a famous speech in 1945 after the first use of atomic bombs, physicist J. Robert Oppenheimer offered his perspective that the purpose of being a scientist is to learn and share knowledge because of its intrinsic value to humanity.[30] Starting from this statement of purpose, he argued for the development of a joint atomic energy commission, the free exchange of information and a halt to the manufacture of bombs, all the while championing curiosity, ambition and collective responsibility.

Third, taking a stand on values and their relationship to technology is where conviction is put into action. Creating a creed for compliance with values set out by an organization can be tremendously helpful. Developing a code of ethics, or simply an organizational narrative, to reinforce a purposeful, values-based approach to technologies can help determine the culture of a company or organization, or even an entire profession or sector. The Hippocratic Oath, taken by physicians, is a model case – it focuses minds on what is at stake in research, analysis and the application of technologies, and may be one reason the biotech industry, influenced as it is by the medical sector, has seen a relatively large degree of self-reflection and restraint.

Lastly, it is essential to leverage the inflection points where values can become effective tools for shaping technologies and their development. Building on good intentions and commitments is important, but citizens and leaders can do more to leverage opportunities and raise awareness of values at critical amplifying points during the development process. For example, in ethics education, educators have successfully popularized the challenge of "the trolley problem" in order to illustrate the problematic of rational decision-making.[31]

As a device for students, this ethical conundrum makes clear that decisions difficult for humans often involve intangible or invaluable features of life. When such decisions are faced by machines, these unmeasured (and perhaps unmeasurable) criteria will have to be reduced to code. Using inflection points gives leaders the ability to emphasize the role of values in shaping technologies.

Why Values?

By Stewart Wallis, Independent Thinker, Speaker and Advocate for a New Economic System, United Kingdom

The world is facing unprecedented challenges. For the first time in human history, we are facing – or exceeding – crucial planetary ecological limits. At the same time, we must create some 1.5 billion new jobs/livelihoods by 2050 against a backdrop of both population growth and ever more rapid technological change (much of which will replace entire swathes of existing jobs). Furthermore, given current rates of decoupling from carbon and other scarce ecological resources, we face a potential conflict between the goal of job creation and that of living within safe planetary limits. Add into this mix the growing geopolitical security challenges and cross-continental movements of refugees and economic migrants; the continued rise in global inequalities of wealth and income; and the positive and negative implications of the Fourth Industrial Revolution – and it becomes obvious that we will confront either a catastrophic setback or a positive transformation in human progress. Either way, we face overwhelming system change. Many potential solutions are available, but what will determine whether or not such solutions are adopted and system change is positive will fundamentally depend on values.

Values provide us a clear destination – a "True North" – and the means of getting there. Behind the Industrial Revolution in Western Europe, there was a shift of values towards creativity, trust and enterprise. Behind the abolition of slavery and the civil rights movement, there were major values shifts. Similarly, values shifts were behind the two major changes in western economies during the 20th century: first, to Keynesianism (mid-century) and then to what is crudely called "neoliberalism" (1980s, 1990s and the first decade of the 21st century). In all of these cases, a shift in values set a goal and provided the means of achieving it, since values motivate people to act. The value shifts were accomplished by a clear, positive and strong narrative accompanied by a powerful vanguard for change. Only subsequently did changes in norms and laws lead to a wider shift in values among populations as a whole.

Given the unprecedented speed of technological and social change that will be involved in the Fourth Industrial Revolution, solely relying on government legislation and economic incentives to ensure the right outcomes is not enough. Legislation is often out of date, out of touch or redundant by the time it is implemented. The only way to ensure positive outcomes is a further revolution in values.

Recognizing that technologies have a complex impact is the easy part. This discussion is presented to the public every day in media headlines. It is more difficult, however, to find the right place to raise awareness about values and to cultivate the contextual intelligence needed in the various stages of technological development. So where in the technological development process can we take into account particular values, such as efficiency and aesthetic considerations, and align them with broader societal values, such as dignity and the common good?

The following nine inflection points is a start. Leaders – designers, entrepreneurs, policy-makers and social influencers – can leverage these points and make a difference by using them to reflect critically on values, encouraging discussion about the broader context of technological implementation, and by taking action.

Educational curricula

It's not just technologies that need attention. People need responsible development too. To their credit, in recent years, some academic accrediting bodies have made ethics a required course for engineers.[32] These curricula, however, tend to focus on issues of compliance and professional conduct, and emphasize how taking shortcuts or evading requirements can cost lives. In reaction to very public cases of fraud, MBA programmes have also begun to include courses on ethics alongside issues of corporate social responsibility and environmental awareness. Both types of curricula could benefit from more open discussion around how values are bound together with technologies, society and the economic system. For educators, cultivating awareness among students will help engineers and managers to influence others by taking a broader view of problem-solving, reflecting on their goals and putting them into context.

Fundraising and investing

Entrepreneurs and investors are the vanguard when it comes to marrying a values-based approach to technological development. Entrepreneurs are seeking to solve a problem that involves a group of people with particular needs or desires and that always necessarily affects a wider range of actors. It makes sense that thinking about broader social impact at this stage would have significant cascading effects. Investors, on the other hand, have the carrot with which to direct the development of technologies. Independent funders could do a great deal more to focus their attention on questions about social impact and create values-based investment rationales. If they found ways to positively influence and incentivize entrepreneurs to take a values-based development approach, the impact could be extraordinary.

Organizational culture

The values of entrepreneurs and organizational leaders have a tremendous influence on the workplace and how technologies are developed. Leading from the front can transform company culture and prioritize societal values. Start-ups are especially effective at setting values, because early employees tend to join due to like-minded interests or goals. One example of effective leadership comes from FIFCO, a Costa Rican alcoholic beverage producer: the CEO's values led to the firm championing moderation in alcohol consumption and ensuring none of its employees live in poverty.[33] CEOs and organizational leaders have the greatest potential impact at this inflection point and can set policies and examples to help create purposeful and socially conscious organizations.

Decision-making and priority setting

At the beginning of any institutional process, such as budgeting, determining research agendas or choosing markets, priorities are established – both implicitly and explicitly – that have clear knock-on effects. For example, the decision-making process for engineering and business projects often includes assumptions and incentives that are tied to efficiency, scalability, profit, and more. Questioning those assumptions and incentives can identify what underlying values give shape to these incentives and how an organization's or individual's choice in the development or implementation process will affect others downstream. Whether the product is a mobile phone application or secret military technology, unbundling the decision-making process can expose the values architecture of the decision-making process. Leaders can use this opportunity to reassess their alignment with the wider aspirations of societal priorities.

Operational methodologies

Since the 1970s, sociologists have been pointing out that the methods and processes by which scientists, engineers and others work in their respective laboratories expose the values embedded in their place of work. These structured values, in turn, influence outcomes in terms of their physical products and their science.[34] The discussion of processes, procedures and protocols presents another opportunity to raise values awareness in the development of technologies. Furthermore, institutional leaders can consider how the application of scientific method is performed in the workplace, or how the limitations of the technological tools and products might unknowingly influence and encode values into methods. Institutional leaders and practitioners can, through thorough examination of working environment dynamics, identify what types of values and bias are being encoded into workplace output.

Economic incentive structures

Any economic system will create incentives that influence societal values and goals. Identifying economic pressures, such as shareholder responsibility or competitive viability, can force us to think about what technologies are being used for and whether they are more aligned with incentives or values. Considering economic pressures can also highlight where incentives problematize an entire class of technologies. For example, current economic incentives often hinder the development of socially beneficial technologies – such as robotic prosthetics – which do not promise a quick return on investment or do not have large markets. By making these areas visible, we can focus attention on the question of what we really want from technologies and shape behaviour towards desirable outcomes.

Product design

From form to functionality, almost every area of product design is connected to values. Design teams have a variety of considerations, including product liability, cultural biases and the emotions a product is meant to tap into. An example of openly encouraging product designers to consider values comes from the Engineering and Physical Sciences Research Council's five principles for robotics. Three of them are explicit about the fact that robots are designed products that must take human needs into account.[35] Executives, inventors, designers and the public have roles to play in the product development cycle, and highlighting the alignment of technologies and their outcomes with societal values is an opportunity for leadership.

Technical architecture

Large-scale technical complexes that enable the deployment of other technologies – such as the internet, the military and transportation infrastructure – themselves embody values via how and where they are constructed or applied. For example, technical decisions related to infrastructure determine the rules that govern data flows, impact access to the internet, raise questions about citizens' rights and contribute to phenomena such as the digital divide.[36] Considering how technical architecture influences society during the design and construction of large systems is another way policy-makers and industry leaders can take values into account and remain attentive to societal priorities.

Societal resistance

Values are embedded in technologies through a process of negotiation. New technologies emerge from small groups that have a particular set of interests and that have knowingly or unknowingly coded a particular set of values into their technologies. Resistance arises when the attributes of the technologies impinge on societal priorities, and groups push back. If technologies receive a great deal of resistance from the public or from particular stakeholders, examining these areas of opposition can highlight the conflicts between the values of society and those that have become a part of the technologies through their process of development.

Many of these inflection points are underutilized, with almost no front-and-centre discussion about the ethical and values-related concerns connected to investors and their potential to shape values-based approaches to technological development. While investors could engage in the very early stages, it is unfortunately the final inflection point, societal resistance, that is one of the most frequent ways in which regulatory bodies are forced to address values. The very existence of societal resistance suggests that other opportunities to consider broader impact and values in the process of technological development have been missed. Successfully raising values at each of the inflection points, proactively rather than retrospectively, will provide CEOs, policy-makers, institutional leaders and others with the flexibility to influence technologies from beyond their economic roles. It gives them the opportunity to speak from their roles as citizens also.

Young Scientists' Code of Ethics

Creating a creed to establish clear values and priorities can come in a variety of formats. They can also be narrowly focused or wide in scope. For example, consider the broad scope of the code of ethics developed by the World Economic Forum Young Scientists community.

The following proposed code of ethics is interdisciplinary and global in scope. It is continuing to be developed to ensure high standards of conduct, allowing researchers to operate through self-regulation.

1. **Pursue the Truth** – Follow research wherever it leads, remain transparent in process and results, and seek verification from objective peers.
2. **Support Diversity** – Strive for an environment where the ideas of diverse groups are heard and valued on the basis of empirical evidence.
3. **Engage with the Public** – Have an open two-way communication about science and the implications of research as well as the need for research in the society.
4. **Engage with Decision-Makers** – Consult and inform relevant leaders in due time to promote evidence-based decision-making and ensure positive societal change.
5. **Be a Mentor** – Lend experience and empower other professionals to grow and realize their full research potential.
6. **Minimize Harm** – Take all reasonable precautions to minimize the known risks and hazards that are a part of the experimental process and its outcomes.
7. **Be Accountable** – Show responsibility in one's actions when carrying out research.

Moving forward with values

Emerging technologies are changing how we create, exchange and distribute not only value, but also how we derive meaning – meaning that helps us imagine our possible futures, and what possible futures are worth living. The way forward requires us to raise awareness about the politics of technology and to consider the impact of our choices at every inflection point. Advances in the Fourth Industrial Revolution call for leaders in all walks of life to cultivate a responsible relationship with technology and to consider people that will be affected by their decisions. Deliberately designing inclusiveness into the innovation ecosystems that produce technologies requires strong values from leaders, and highlights their commitment to shape a better future.

Creating new systems that provide meaningful opportunities for a growing number of people and that preserve the intrinsic value of individuals as members of society will require thinking deeply about the ways technologies subtly shift the ground from under our feet. In addition, committing to a values-based approach towards technological development may be one way to help bolster trust between the public, government and businesses. Looking forward, towards the potential futures these new technologies can help create, we must preserve the power that we have to shape technologies. For a cultural renaissance to take place, we have to voice the importance of societal values and rebalance the negotiation between society, technologies and the economy. We have to do it together and we have to do it now. Taking multiple stakeholder groups into consideration gathering their input and valuing their perspectives – is a first step towards building an inclusive and prosperous future. It is also the subject of Chapter 4.

In two or three generations' time, when today's emerging technologies have matured, our descendants will look back and either thank us for ensuring that the trajectories of these technologies supported equity, dignity and the common good, or regret that we failed them by missing our opportunity.

Chapter Summary

Two misleading views are commonly held about technologies, neither of which is helpful in guiding organisational strategy or governance in the Fourth Industrial Revolution. They are:

1. Technologies are out of our control and determine the future for us.
2. Technologies are mere tools and value neutral.

Neither of these perspectives reflects the fact that technologies and societies continuously shape each other through the politics and values they embody.

We need to shift our perspective to a more constructive view of technologies, which can allow a more human-centred approach. These are:

1. All technologies are political – they are the embodiment of social desires and compromises expressed throughout their development and implementation.
2. Technologies and societies shape each other in a reflexive way – we are the product of our technologies as much as they are products we create.

Looking at technology this way reminds us that technologies are solutions and products developed through social processes that already reflect ingrained priorities and values.

Understanding that technologies in this way entails three responsibilities:

1. Identifying the values that are tied up with particular technologies;
2. Understanding how technologies impact human choices and decision-making on a daily basis; and
3. Determining how to best influence technological development with an appropriate set of stakeholders.

This chapter identifies nine inflection points for exploring, questioning and influencing the values embedded in technologies. These are:

1. Educational curricula
2. Fundraising and investing
3. Organizational culture
4. Decision-making and priority setting
5. Operational methodologies
6. Economic incentive structures
7. Product design
8. Technical architecture
9. Societal resistance

Special Insert

A Human Rights-based Framework

The technologies of the Fourth Industrial Revolution are transforming society and reshaping our future.

As a result, there is a need for clearer articulation of ethical frameworks, normative standards and values-based governance models to help guide organizations in the development and use of these powerful tools in society, and to enable a human centric approach to development which goes beyond geographic and political boundaries.

Human rights are the "hard edge" of values and the international human rights frameworks provide a substantive basis for tackling these issues.

The Universal Declaration of Human Rights (UDHR), adopted in 1948 and signed by an unprecedented 192 countries, embraces a universal set of principles that can be applied across variable cultures. It was adopted by the United Nations at a time when the world was recoiling from the Holocaust and there was a global desire to create a new, more hopeful future for humanity. It was designed first and foremost as an expression of global values, as observed by Hernán Santa Cruz of Chile, member of the drafting sub-Committee:

> I perceived clearly that I was participating in a truly significant historic event in which a consensus had been reached as to the supreme value of the human person, a value that did not originate in the decision of a worldly power, but rather in the fact of existing.

Contributed by Hilary Sutcliffe, Director, SocietyInside, United Kingdom, and Anne-Marie Allgrove, Partner, Baker & McKenzie, Australia.

The UDHR set out universal standards that have supported efforts by states and others to develop laws and policies relating to a wide range of issues, from criminal justice to the environment, from global development to trade, from security to migration. The UDHR and the series of legally binding treaties that have elaborated on its provisions provide an essential foundation for private and international organizations and states to promote equality, fairness and justice in a people- and planet-centred innovation agenda driven by new and enhanced technologies.

Though these global rights standards were adopted by states to govern official conduct, increasingly they are being applied to the private sector. For example, global companies seeking to address labour rights issues in their global supply chains, or information and communications companies grappling with privacy and free expression issues, are being called on to address these concerns using a rights framework. Similarly, though the technology of gene editing is startlingly new and exciting, human rights standards can help us address the governance choices we face as we balance efforts to alleviate human suffering, as well as the risks and uncertainties inherent in the application of new scientific tools.

The Fourth Industrial Revolution needs to be grounded in a discussion of broader questions about the societies in which we wish to live. Today, the possibilities for human empowerment brought by technologies are immense, but we must continue to focus on the impact of technologies on people, their everyday lives, and their enjoyment of human rights.

No longer is this exclusively the domain of states and international organizations; the private sector must take a leadership role. As a starting point, private organizations and their stakeholders should review their values as against the UDHR and related human rights standards, and develop mechanisms against which they can measure and assess their conduct.

Chapter 4

Empowering All Stakeholders

To unleash the promise of the Fourth Industrial Revolution, it is crucial to ensure that the benefits are distributed fairly across all stakeholders. This chapter highlights the importance of taking a multistakeholder approach, considers three sets of often overlooked and left-out stakeholders and discusses what it will require to empower and include them. These stakeholders are developing countries still struggling to grasp the benefits of prior industrial revolutions; the environment and natural world in general, which has borne the externalities of technological change across all industrial revolutions at a cost to other species and future generations; and the majority of individuals around the world without the benefit of extremely high incomes or political power – in particular those who are often excluded or are simply overlooked.

The world is experiencing simultaneous transformative trends: urbanization, globalization, demographic shifts, climate change and increasingly disruptive emerging technologies. Developing regions that are experiencing booming youth populations will need rapid job creation at scale. Environmental changes call for faster mitigation and adaptation measures – not least in developed regions where the burden of climate change is the biggest. The impact of new technologies on wealth distribution and social cohesion is revealing that our political systems and economic models are failing to fairly provide opportunities to all citizens.

The joint impact of these trends requires that we transcend traditional boundaries and forge sustainable and inclusive partnerships. History has demonstrated that inclusivity does not occur without both intention and action. As argued in Chapter 3, technological systems alone will not provide meaningful opportunities for people broadly. Opportunities will come from engaging all stakeholders so that societal values and inclusive solutions are considered from the start. The decisions that will shape our shared future simply cannot be taken in isolation: "Decision-makers must possess a capacity and readiness to engage with all those who have a stake in the issue at hand. In this way we should aspire to be more connected and inclusive."[37] To make this industrial revolution connected and inclusive therefore requires our deliberate actions and commitment.

Including all those who have a stake in the conversation about the impact of emerging technologies on developing nations illustrates the principle at the heart of the multistakeholder approach. This principle holds that viable solutions to complex global challenges are only possible with the collaboration of leaders across business, government, civil society and academia as well as the engagement of younger generations.

The societal benefits from the emerging technologies could be truly revolutionary. Modelling the impact of self-driving vehicles in urban environments by Boston Consulting Group in collaboration with the World Economic Forum indicates that automated transport systems could in some scenarios lead to lower emissions, less congestion, faster rides and fewer deaths and injuries from accidents.[38] The rollout of new techniques within precision medicine to treat and manage non-communicable diseases could easily extend lifespans around the world by one to two years – even without considering current attempts to use gene editing techniques to slow ageing directly. Gene editing has other revolutionary abilities, one being the potential to end diseases like malaria by genetically engineering the malaria mosquito. Blockchain technology can be applied for public land registration, enabling millions of people around the world to have formal ownership over their land, which in turn can be used as collateral and thereby allow them access to financial markets. The use of virtual and augmented reality could dramatically improve educational outcomes by allowing us to develop and practise skills in safe, immersive environments.

The indirect impacts of emerging technologies are often even more important than their direct effect on productivity. The widespread availability of electricity in homes as a result of the second Industrial Revolution enabled the development of washing machines, dishwashers, electric ovens, vacuum cleaners and other home appliances that greatly reduced the time burden of cooking and cleaning. The result was not simply greater leisure time for women, on whom the burden of domestic activities still disproportionately rests today. Rather, such machines reduced the industry of domestic service, changed family structures and provided time for more productive activities outside of the home.

But how relevant are these advantages to people trapped in poverty, marginalized in their communities or living in areas underserved by the systems of prior industrial revolutions? Approximately 600 million people live on smallholder farms without access to any mechanization, their lives remaining largely untouched even by the first Industrial Revolution. Around a third of people (2.4 billion) lack clean drinking water and safe sanitation, and around one-sixth (1.2 billion) have no electricity – systems developed in the second Industrial Revolution. And while new technologies, in addition to social resistance and institutional reforms, may have liberated women in developed regions, one in five women in the Middle East and Latin America and the Caribbean continue to serve as domestic workers. More than half of the world's population – around 3.9 billion people – still cannot access the internet, one of the most transformative systems of the third Industrial Revolution.[39] In developing countries, the proportion of the offline population is 85%, compared to 22% in the developed world.[40]

If these global disparities are left unchanged, they will hinder the truly transformative potential of the Fourth Industrial Revolution. We have a choice now: to develop technologies and systems that serve to distribute economic and social values such as income, opportunity and liberty to all stakeholders, or to leave large swathes of people behind. Thinking inclusively goes beyond thinking about poverty or marginalized communities simply as an aberration – something that we can solve. It forces us to realize that "our privileges are located on the same map as their suffering".[41] It moves beyond income and entitlements, though these remain important. Instead, the inclusion of stakeholders and the distribution of benefits expand freedoms for all.

Economist and philosopher Amartya Sen argues that freedoms – freedom from hunger, the ability to go to work, the ability to participate in democratic processes, having loving relationships, etc. – serve "both as the primary end and as the principal means". Freedoms empower people and give them the capabilities to live good lives whether in a wealthy or developing society. The distribution of wealth and benefits does not need to be equal among all stakeholders, but it must be sufficient for all stakeholders to live a life they have reason to value. The multistakeholder approach is a way of organizing a conversation aimed at improving a world that works for everyone, not just the few.

Ensuring fairness in the distribution of the benefits and positive externalities of the Fourth Industrial Revolution is more than just an ethical challenge. The experience of past political revolutions teaches us that disparity has consequences. The failure of many democratic systems to address disparities in wealth or opportunity stemming from their prevailing economic models has led to entrenched social and economic imbalances that are both divisive and destabilizing. As pointed out in the World Economic Forum *Global Risks Report 2017*, today's combination of economic inequality and political polarization threatens to amplify a wide array of global risks by menacing the social solidarity on which the legitimacy of economic and political systems rests.[42]

These persistent structural divides are recognized and addressed by the UN Sustainable Development Goals (SDGs) that came into effect in January 2016. The SDGs focus on poverty alleviation, democratic governance and peace-building, climate action and resilience, reduced inequalities and economic growth. It is important that the Fourth Industrial Revolution contribute to, rather than distract from, common efforts around the distribution of opportunities for human development.

Developing economies

Economist Ricardo Hausmann and Professor of Media Arts and Sciences Cesar Hidalgo argue that it is the collective ability to make productive use of new technologies that drives human progress. Unfortunately, this ability is poorly distributed among countries:

> The social accumulation of productive knowledge has not been a universal phenomenon. It has taken place in some parts of the world, but not in others. Where it has happened, it has underpinned an incredible increase in living standards. Where it has not, living standards resemble those

> of centuries past. The enormous income gaps between rich and poor nations are an expression of the vast differences in productive knowledge amassed by different nations.[43]

Successful economies support high living standards thanks to a combination of technologies, the knowledge and capabilities to use and develop these technologies, and the existence of markets and organizations that allow knowledge held by a few to reach the many. While not every country can or should attempt to be at the cutting edge of technological progress in every area, in a global knowledge economy every country needs the capacity to absorb and adapt technologies for its national, social and economic development.

Some argue that Fourth Industrial Revolution technologies coupled with institutional reforms will enable economies to "leapfrog" previous technologically-driven approaches, allowing developing economies to advance more rapidly than traditional industrialization pathways would allow. A common example is the way in which high levels of investment in the digital technologies of the third Industrial Revolution led to the widening availability and increasing affordability of mobile phones, which meant developing countries no longer needed to invest heavily in landline telephone infrastructure to give their populations access to high-quality telecommunication networks.[44] Other promising examples of technology's impact are the use of civilian drones to deliver life-saving medicines and vaccinations, the increase in agricultural efficiency from genetically modified seeds and advanced fertilizer, and the promise to deliver low-cost, high-speed internet connectivity from new networks of low-earth satellites. However, the promise of leapfrogging in the Fourth Industrial Revolution is still just that – a promise.

One concern is that the reliance on digital infrastructure, which will accelerate and broaden the impact of the Fourth Industrial Revolution, makes closing the digital divide – both within and across countries – far more urgent. If access to high-speed digital networks and skills are a necessary precondition for the Fourth Industrial Revolution, power may flow to those whose location, educational background and income put them on the right side of a widening digital divide, while billions of others could be further excluded on the basis of income, infrastructure, language or content relevance.

A second concern regarding the mobile revolution is that this new infrastructure has not fostered innovation or development. In Africa, the services that the mobile revolution offers are mainly for consumers, not technology producers. It has been largely unsuccessful in creating formal jobs, establishing basic infrastructure for economic development or for attracting and deploying adjacent technologies.[45] For the mobile revolution to catalyse industrial development and economic diversification, it needs to go hand in hand with a "Fourth Industrial Policy" – a complementary evolution in innovation, entrepreneurship, infrastructure and industrialization policies.

A third concern is that the Fourth Industrial Revolution threatens to upend the traditional industrialization pathway to development where countries initially use an ample supply of low-cost labour to attract manufacturing, and later attracting investments and technologies. The more extreme scenarios of labour-substituting automation – high-precision factories filled with intelligent robots or the reshoring of production enabled by extensive 3D printing – seem to offer a diminishing role for low-cost, unskilled labour. So how can countries dominated by agrarian and low-industrialized economies transform themselves into knowledge-driven economies able to acquire, deploy and eventually develop new technologies in the Fourth Industrial Revolution?

Given the increasing importance of skills, fostering countries' capabilities to fruitfully employ technologies will remain a critical need and will require investments in education, skilling and national research and development (R&D). The Fourth Industrial Revolution will make closing the educational and research gap between advanced and developing countries even more important. And despite the promise of new technologies accelerating skills development, it will take commitments over decades, as well as significant resources, for the majority of developing countries to enjoy the benefits of high-quality research and educational systems.

In 2014, 263 million children and youth did not attend school globally. The highest out-of-school rates are in regions where both the need for economic and social development is greatest, and where children and youth make up the majority of the population.[46] Beyond geographical disparities the lack of educational opportunity is further exacerbated across genders. Young women are more likely to be out of school than young men, particularly in the least-developed regions.[47] For the populations of regions with the highest out-of-school rates, this disadvantaged starting point decreases their opportunities and curbs the countries' industrialization efforts.

Maintaining children in school is only the first step. Increasing diversity and economic complexity requires stable, accredited educational institutions and sufficient research funding. Today more than half of the world's indexed journals are published in the United States and United Kingdom, not surprisingly as these two countries are home to the world's leading universities.[48] And while the location of a publication reveals little about the author's origin or intention, having the majority of new knowledge published and created in the West can be limiting for the dissemination and capture of it elsewhere. This speaks to the responsibility western countries have in working with other regions to capture and relate local knowledge. Furthermore, while North America and Western Europe dominate global R&D investment (as well as the share of GDP devoted to R&D – visible in Figure 8), an incremental shift is taking place towards East Asia and the Pacific.[49] But the rest of the world's regions have a negligible share. These persistent disparities in education and R&D funding leave developing countries at a severe disadvantage in knowledge production and technology development as the Fourth Industrial Revolution unfolds.

Yet increased education and R&D investment in developing economies can make everyone better off. The diversity of thought in global research would be greatly expanded by developing the contribution of knowledge within a wider set of cultures, and new sources of expertise. This is the goal of projects like Meta, the Canadian start-up acquired in January 2017 by the Chan Zuckerberg Initiative. Meta seeks to use "AI in the service of the scientific ecosystem", creating tools to make sense of the vast amount of research produced around the world every day. This goes beyond simply the ability to read or search scientific journal articles, many of which sit behind paywalls: Meta is leveraging the technologies of the Fourth Industrial Revolution to make sense of data, find patterns and unearth insights across scientific disciplines in real time.

But investments in R&D are also insufficient. To touch and improve people's lives requires the robust commercialization of knowledge – allowing ideas and technologies to be protected, diffused and deployed across society and industries. For the commercialization of knowledge through patents, the West has historically also dominated. And while Asia is making rapid progress, Latin America and Africa continue to lag the rest of the world.

Figure 8: Regional Averages for the Share of GDP Devoted to R&D Activities

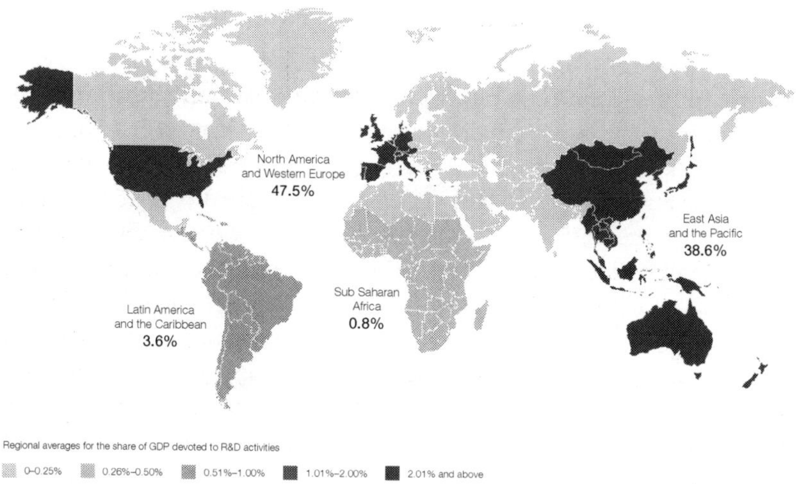

Source: UNESCO (2017)

The regions of the world that register significantly fewer patents create less wealth, which impacts global inequality – as does the constraint on industrialization that results from developing countries needing to purchase expensive patented technologies.

Poor education, low levels of R&D and the lack of commercialized new technology together lessen developing regions' ability to steer the direction of development. Certain developing countries are *de facto* largely being excluded from shaping how technology and knowledge affect their own societies, not to mention the global unfolding of the Fourth Industrial Revolution. As advanced economies have a first-mover advantage to lead in the development, design and use of technologies, the negotiation of the balance between technology, society and economy is at risk of being biased by Western values and dominated by the incentives of Western economies. Unless we act, the result is a future by default and not by design, where technologies are determining and not empowering.

We are a long way from having the political will and adequate institutions to deliver on all these challenges. Massive efforts will be required to distribute technologies and spur education and skills faster and more effectively than in previous cases of industrialization. Yet standing at the cusp of the Fourth Industrial Revolution, these needed efforts present us with robust opportunities to take responsibility and to use emerging technological systems for inclusivity, the expansion of freedoms and the distribution of benefits across all stakeholders globally.

To manage the risks and successfully harness the technologies of the Fourth Industrial Revolution for the economic and social development of developing countries, we need a new, more inclusive and deliberate approach: a multistakeholder process where development experts, technology creators, global businesses, governments, civil society, international organizations and affected populations all participate. Designing the future for the majority of the world's population cannot be left to any one group, as it risks being distorted by its biases and either hindering leapfrogging or seeing the benefits of new technologies delivered to only a narrow few. The broad, global commitment to the SDGs is one step on this path. Real success will involve responsible and responsive leadership from local and international stakeholders.

The environment

The unparalleled wealth generated by nearly three centuries of industrialization has not only been unevenly spread among people, but has come at a significant cost to Earth's natural systems; climate, water, air, biodiversity, forests and oceans are all under unprecedented, severe and increasing stress. Species are going extinct at up to 100 times natural levels.[50] In 1800, only 3% of the world's population of 1 billion lived in urban areas. Today, more than 50% of the world's 7.4 billion inhabitants live in urban areas.[51] Of these, more than 92% experience air pollution above levels deemed safe by the World Health Organization.[52] By 2050, there will be more plastic than fish in the oceans by weight.[53] Global CO_2 emissions have risen 150-fold since 1850.[54] And at the current rate of emissions, the risk that the world will be between 4°C and 6°C warmer by 2100 than it is today is real,[55] which could irreversibly alter the otherwise stable climatic system that we have enjoyed for the last 10,000 years.[56]

Climate change is, in fact, already disrupting national economies and affecting lives, with high costs for people, communities and systems, including costs associated with uncertainty and volatility. With many regions still industrializing and the world's population set to increase by 1 billion people over the next 15 years, climate-related disruptions are expected to soar, including geopolitical instability, mass migration, interrupted food production and increased security threats.[57]

Figure 9: Climate Change Trends

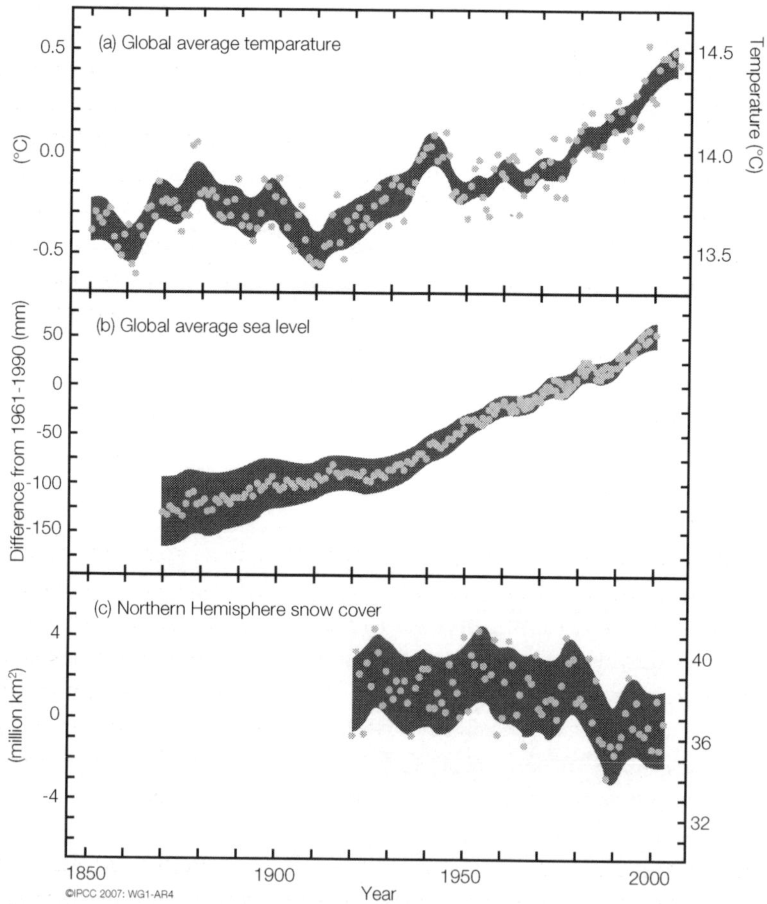

Source: Intergovernmental Panel on Climate Change (IPCC 2014)

In the Fourth Industrial Revolution, a number of challenges will need to be addressed, some relating to the environmental impact of digital technology itself, including ever-expanding mountains of e-waste that are releasing toxic chemicals into the environment. Furthermore, carbon emissions are growing, stemming from the increasing number of data centres that have high power consumption rates and are necessary for well-distributed digital infrastructure. Other challenges relate to the principles guiding technological development and deployment. What we do in the next years and decades to overcome these challenges will determine not just the livelihoods of future generations, but the planet's ecosystem for thousands of years to come.

The technologies of the Fourth Industrial Revolution present us with an opportunity to manage the externalities of the previous industrial revolutions by embarking on a more sustainable path, that of protecting our global commons. Most of the world's households will have at least one 3G cell phone by 2030. The use of distributed ledgers such as the blockchain for mobile carbon trading could give each individual an equal quota consistent with the Earth's planetary boundaries. The use of a blockchain could also be used to manage water allocations and deforestation. In fact, the Government of Honduras is already exploring the potential for distributed ledgers to help with land rights allocation.

Advances in satellite imaging are helping deforestation, which accounts for approximately 15% of global greenhouse gas emissions.[58] Drones are being used to monitor forest fires, crop harvests and water sources, and even to aid in planting crops. While farmers can plant around 3,000 seeds per day by hand, tests in which drones fire seed pods into the ground suggest they could plant more than 30,000 seeds per day.[59] Satellites are also contributing to ocean management and protection. Satellite-interfacing sensors and data-processing tools are increasing visibility of how ships use the oceans. Networks of nanosatellites will soon be able to take high-resolution snapshots of the entire earth every day. Fleets of drone ships could help to track the health of our oceans and monitor the harvesting of ocean resources.[60]

The accessibility and availability of technologies mean that environmental management can no longer be driven just by experts; it is becoming more horizontal and democratized with a wider range of actors able to engage by simply having a smartphone in their pocket. The result is that current systems of environmental management are good, but not sufficient to handle the pace and scale of disruptive change that the Fourth Industrial Revolution is expected to introduce. To fruitfully address the impending disruptions, the current economic model must be reconfigured to incentivize both producers and consumers to reduce resource consumption and encourage sustainable products and services. This requires new business models in which the currently hidden costs of environmental impacts are bundled into prices, incentivizing more sustainable production and consumption. Such a reconfiguration further calls for a fundamental shift from short-term thinking to long-term planning and a move away from the linear economic model of take-make-waste towards a circular economy, where the industrial system is restorative or regenerative by intention and design. This reconfiguration will incur short-term costs, but doing nothing will be costlier.

The Fourth Industrial Revolution is only just starting to unfold, and hopeful signs are already appearing: twice as much is being invested in renewables as fossil fuels.[61] But the world needs to make a choice. We can either continue in the vein of the first three industrial revolutions, leaving environmental considerations on the periphery of priorities, or take leadership in harnessing the Fourth Industrial Revolution to solve environmental problems through deliberate choices and collaboration among stakeholders – including ways to funnel financing into solutions that not only have commercial value but also serve the public good. We must avoid the tendency of past industrial revolutions to treat the natural world as a sink for the costs of emerging technologies. This will not be easy, yet leaders have no other choice than to manage the externalities of the Fourth Industrial Revolution so unintended consequences are carried collectively rather than concentrated on vulnerable populations or, via environmental damage, on future generations. Given the fragility of the earth's biosphere after three previous industrial revolutions, the cost of failure is simply too high.

Society and citizens

In addition to their geopolitical and environmental impacts, technological revolutions can affect the social landscape by altering the skills needed to be deemed successful. For example, the third

Industrial Revolution improved the lives of knowledge workers, making them better off than the factory workers who had seen their living standards increase during the second Industrial Revolution. The famous elephant graph by economist Branko Milanovic (Figure 10) shows how the distribution of global income changed between 1988 and 2008: the benefits bypassed not only the very poorest but also those around the 80th percentile globally, the lower-middle class in advanced economies. There, many industrial workers have joined "the precariat", facing lives of insecurity and stagnating wages. Now, increasing automation has the potential to change who benefits once again.

New forms of automation, including robots and algorithms driven by recent advances in AI, are not just replacing factory workers but increasingly accountants, lawyers and other professional workers. In 2000, Goldman Sachs' New York office employed 600 traders. In 2017, only two equity traders were left, supported by automated trading programs.[62] The same trend can be seen across dozens of Wall Street trading firms.[63] This shift seems likely to result in a further concentration of wealth in the hands of owners of capital and intellectual property. As seen in recent elections in the United Kingdom and United States, if these societal shifts and their impact on individuals are not addressed, they can result in resentment, fear and political backlash.

Beyond the immediate economic challenges, there are also challenges to the role that work has played in providing meaning for individuals, families and communities. For the past 250 years community, identity, purpose and agency have been closely linked with our roles as labourers and productive members of society. Current disruptions are forcing political leaders to rethink the paradigm that shapes the relations between individual, society and economic activity. This includes considering reforms for reshaping the social contract between individual and society.

The discussion of a universal basic income (UBI) is one example of this conversation. It is a radical idea being tested across the world from Finland to Kenya and California to India. Beyond rational and distributive arguments, the primary justification for UBI is social justice: as income increasingly goes towards land, natural resources and intellectual property – all parts of society's collective wealth –

everybody should have a modest share of this collective wealth in the form of an unconditional basic income. UBI is not presented here as a panacea, but its radical nature has spurred an important debate, one that must be taken broadly with regard to economic and social reforms, and that dares to rethink how the economic system itself can work for all stakeholders in the Fourth Industrial Revolution.

Leaders also need to pay attention to the way the Fourth Industrial Revolution will impact different genders in various ways. In the first and second Industrial Revolution, women were pushed into the homes diminishing their political and economic influence. As women entered the factory work in the 19th century, the result for the majority was a life of hardship, which led to greater organization and protests around women's rights and later campaigns for universal suffrage and political representation. The overall result has been increased female economic and societal participation and progress. Yet the gender gap still exists. Across the world men are more economically and politically empowered than women. And in almost half of the 142 countries scored in the World Economic Forum *Global Gender Gap Report 2016*, the gender gap is increasing.[64] Unfortunately, it is possible that the skills bias of the Fourth Industrial Revolution, which favours a small proportion of highly technical workers and business owners, could contribute to this growing divide.

Figure 10: Change in Real Income between 1988 and 2008 at Various Percentiles of Global Income Distribution (calculated in 2005 international dollars)

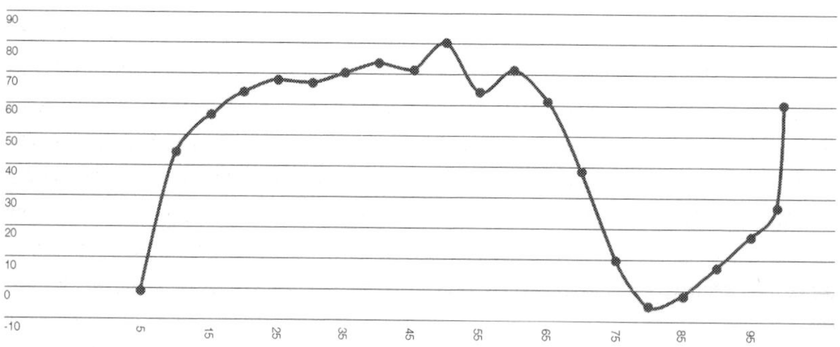

Source: Milanovic (2016)

Women account for fewer than 30% of those employed in scientific research, with an even smaller representation in STEM fields.[65] Less than 25% of IT jobs are held by women, and the proportion is even lower among tech entrepreneurs.[66] Women are 50% less likely to use the internet than men, a gap that looks to be growing wider in some developing economies.[67] Across nearly all parameters, the gap is widest between men and women in developing countries, leaving women there at a further disadvantage. This gap deprives women from fully participating in and shaping the Fourth Industrial Revolution. More specifically, it leaves millions of good ideas and input out of the conversation, holding back much needed knowledge production. For this reason, we need to address and prioritize gender equality across political, economic and social spheres. Unleashing women's potential in the Fourth Industrial Revolution is unleashing society's potential.

In addition to the opportunity to address the gender gap, the Fourth Industrial Revolution gives us the possibility to include people who have historically been marginalized or persecuted, whether because of their gender, race, age, sexual orientation or disabilities, or because they do not identify with the gender of their birth. Emerging technologies can transform the way we perceive gender, age and the body itself. People with disabilities stand to benefit from technologies that can augment human capabilities, making the idea of disability increasingly obsolete.

As robots and enhancement technologies become more commonplace in society, they could help dispel stereotypes. But this is not inevitable: it depends on the values from which we develop and deploy the technologies as discussed in Chapter 3. Already our programming of and interaction with machines is being impacted by existing prejudices, such as sexism and racism.[68] Thus, while humanoid robots in theory could transcend categories such as race and gender when designed, most often we see customer service robots designed around female characteristics whereas industrial robots are more often modelled around male characteristics. This hinders us from using new technologies to dispel century-old stereotypes and open up a more inclusive mindset towards traditional categories. Whether new technologies perpetuate existing stereotypes or increase the well-being of all individuals and the community as a whole will reflect conscious choices made during their development.

Responsible and responsive leadership to include all stakeholders

How the Fourth Industrial Revolution unfolds will depend on whether we make conscious choices or act with recklessness towards the growing economic, environmental and social challenges. If we are to truly feel part of something much larger than ourselves – a true global civilization – with a shared sense of destiny, all stakeholders must be included in the course we chart. We share a responsibility to empower and ensure equal opportunities for the growing populations in developing countries, particularly the youth who are still struggling to grasp the benefits of prior industrial revolutions. We must act as stewards, and provide future generations with a healthy planet, and we must seek to share the benefits of this technological age among all citizens regardless of age, income, race or beliefs.

Solving our shared challenges requires radical thinking. Labour-displacing technologies, severe climate change, increasing concerns over inequality and prospects of economic insecurity are eroding the models and paradigms on which our societies and economies rest. Leaders across all sectors and in all countries must take responsibility for spurring the conversation about what necessary social and economic systemic changes we must undertake and whether to do so in a revolutionary or incremental fashion.

Chapter Summary

A multistakeholder approach is essential for guiding the Fourth Industrial Revolution toward a sustainable and inclusive future.

The multistakeholder principle holds that viable solutions to complex global challenges are only possible with the collaboration of leaders across business, government, civil society and academia as well as the engagement of younger generations.

Including developing countries in the Fourth Industrial Revolution requires:

- Local and regional conversations on what the future should look like and how to harness the benefits of the emerging technologies for the local population; and
- Local, regional and global policies around innovation, infrastructure and industrialization which empower all citizens to harness the benefits and opportunities of the emerging technologies.

Protecting the environment in the Fourth Industrial Revolution entails:

- Designing and deploying emerging technologies not merely to avoid harm, but with the proactive, future-oriented goal of maintaining and improving the natural world; and
- Reconfiguring economic models around the use and impact of technology to incentivize both producers and consumers to reduce resource consumption and encourage sustainable products and services.

Creating a prosperous, inclusive and equitable Fourth Industrial Revolution for society and citizens means being conscious of the choices we make in technological systems which will inevitably impact economic, environmental and social systems. This means having the courage to confront existing economic and political paradigms and reshaping them to empower individuals regardless of ethnicity, age, gender or background.

Section 2

Technologies, Opportunities and Disruption

Section 2

Overview

In Section 1, we covered the dynamics and challenges of the Fourth Industrial Revolution and discussed the imperative for a human-centred values-based approach that is inclusive of all stakeholder groups. In Section 2, we dive deeper into the extraordinary technologies and the conditions that are producing them and that are working together to fuel this new era. The scale, scope and speed of change these technologies bring will impact far more than industries. They have the potential to change the course of history, and they will affect every aspect of our lives.

Created in collaboration with the World Economic Forum Global Future Councils and Expert Network, the next 12 chapters provide insights into the technologies that will push and shape the Fourth Industrial Revolution as it gains momentum and propagates globally. The four subsections – Extending Digital Technologies, Reforming the Physical World, Altering the Human Being and Integrating the Environment – organize discussion of the technologies around key themes that highlight how the technologies are affecting the world and signalling the beginning of a new era. These chapters aim to provide the reader with "the bigger picture", following Chapter 2's strategy of "zooming in and zooming out" by supplying a broad view of the technologies' potential and providing examples of the technologies in use.

Each of the 12 sets of technologies in these chapters are spawning novel categories, innovative processes, and amazing products and services in addition to altering value chains and organizational structures. Digital technologies, for example, are expanding their footprint in the material world through cloud computing technologies that network robotics, genetic sequencers, wearables, drones and virtual and augmented reality devices. Artificial intelligence platforms are powering applications across industries and augmenting the decision-making capabilities of companies. In addition, advanced materials continue to "upgrade" our physical world through the products they enable.

The effects of these innovative engineering capabilities, scientific applications and infrastructure developments are rippling outward across stakeholder groups. They are affecting industrial capabilities, social relationships and political strategies. It is clear to both the public and private sectors that managing their impact is of critical importance to successfully navigating the next decades. Seeing "the bigger picture" is the key to managing them well, and each chapter in Section 2 seeks to broaden the understanding of their capabilities and to help the reader to "zoom out". In addition, to help the reader "zoom in", each chapter provides examples of where and how the technologies are being used and speaks to their specific potentials. Expert perspectives on the technologies are also incorporated throughout the chapters through special supplements.

The choice of 12 categories of related technologies is by no means exhaustive, as there are so many individual technologies; it is difficult to keep them all within view. Many more technologies can be imagined, coming from just over the horizon. The selection presented in Section 2 has been chosen because it represents those technologies that are most visible at this early stage. And early as it may be, we can see that they will interface with human biology, intelligence and experience, as well as our environment, and their effects will be wide-ranging and hard to predict. They will impact our personal lives, how we work, raise children and socialize. They will impact broader areas, such as our rights and interactions with our communities and nations. They will restructure what's possible, what's permissible and what's necessary in our lives. For these reasons and more, keeping a watchful eye to make sure our steps forward with technology remain human-centred is of the utmost importance.

2.1 Extending Digital Technologies

The digital revolution, which we call the third Industrial Revolution, brought us general computing, software development, personal computers and a connected world via widespread digital infrastructure and the internet. Most of the computing technologies with which we are familiar, however, represent the advances along just one classical approach to the computing process established in the 1940s. Researchers and entrepreneurs today are working on other possibilities for computing that will expand our capabilities and widen our expectations in relation to the storage, manipulation and communication of information. The chapters in this section address new computing technologies, blockchain and distributed ledger systems, and the growing internet of things, and provide examples of how innovative digital, quantum and embedded computing approaches could transform the future.

2.2 Reforming the Physical World

In the Fourth Industrial Revolution, technologies are harnessing expanding bandwidth, the growing availability of cloud services, and the increasing speed and power of graphics processing to move beyond the screen and into industrial production, city transportation infrastructure and interactive devices. Just as the electrical grids and mechanical control mechanisms from the second Industrial Revolution provided a foundation for the development of digital technologies, digital infrastructure is providing a foundation for reconstituting the technologies that provide the materials of our lived environment as well as those with which we will interact in both industrial and social spaces. The three chapters in this section include discussions of artificial intelligence and robotics, advanced materials, additive manufacturing and multidimensional printing, and drones. We are now confronted with a future where digital agents and actors will cross the boundary between software and artefact, inspire new functional capabilities and even move independently among us.

Chapter 8	Artificial Intelligence and Robotics
Chapter 9	Advanced Materials
Chapter 10	Additive Manufacturing and Multidimensional Printing
Special Insert	The Upside and Downside of Drones

2.3 Altering the Human Being

The lines between technologies and beings are becoming blurred, and not just by the ability to create lifelike robots or synthetic organisms. Instead, it is about the ability of new technologies to literally become part of us. Technologies already influence how we understand ourselves, how we think about each other, and how we determine our realities. As the technologies in this section give us deeper access to parts of ourselves, we may begin to integrate digital technologies into our bodies. The metaphor of the "cyborg" may seem to have lost its ability to shock, but the future may see curious mixes of digital-and-analogue life that will redefine our very natures. The chapters here cover biotechnologies, neurotechnologies and brain science, and virtual and augmented reality devices. Perhaps more than any other set of technologies in the Fourth Industrial Revolution, these will challenge us ethically. These technologies will operate within our own biology and change how we interface with the world. They are capable of crossing the boundaries of body and mind, enhancing our physical abilities, and even having a lasting impact on life itself. They are more than mere tools, and demand special consideration for their ability to augment or intrude upon human beings, human behaviours and human rights.

Chapter 11	Biotechnologies
Chapter 12	Neurotechnologies
Chapter 13	Virtual and Augmented Realities
Special Insert	A Perspective on Arts, Culture and the Fourth Industrial Revolution

2.4 Integrating the Environment

The Fourth Industrial Revolution will be dependent on technologies that enable infrastructure development, perform global systems maintenance and open up new pathways for the future. The technologies covered by these chapters are expanding their capabilities to do just this. Energy capture, storage and transmission capabilities, especially those based on sustainable materials and practices, stand ready to reduce fossil-fuel dependence and provide low-cost, distributed power for people and their technologies. Geoengineering, though still highly speculative, is forcing us to consider what goes into managing a climate and what way we can best confront the global challenge of rising atmospheric temperatures. Space technologies surround us, monitor the planet and its ecosystems and provide a frontier for science, exploration and technological innovation. Each of these connects us and the planet and the wider universe beyond, and each requires an understanding that the environment – land, air and space – is a shared multistakeholder responsibility. The potential of these technologies to have such dramatic impact will require collaborative efforts and important decisions to be made about our collective future.

Extending Digital Technologies

Chapter 5

New Computing Technologies

Digital computing capabilities were the general-purpose technology behind the third Industrial Revolution, thanks to exponential reductions in the size and cost of transistors since their invention in 1947. New computing technologies will continue to be important because ubiquitous, robust, efficient and low-cost digital capabilities are an essential backbone for the technologies and systems of the Fourth Industrial Revolution, and because of the prospect of radically different approaches to computing with new opportunities and challenges for the future.

At the heart of advances in computing lie innovations in materials, assemblies and architectures that we use to process, store, manipulate and interact with information. These cluster into fields, such as centralized cloud computing, quantum computing, neural network processing, biological data storage, optical and mesh computing. These approaches are leading to software development and new forms of cryptography. They are creating and solving cybersecurity challenges, enabling natural language processing and promising huge efficiency gains in areas such as healthcare applications and the simulation of physical and chemical processes. New computing technologies can solve some of the trickiest challenges we face. But without agile governance approaches to ensure that their benefits are shared and their impact on security managed, they may also drive significant risks.

Extending the democratizing impact of Moore's Law

Moore's Law, named after Intel Co-Founder Gordon Moore, is based on the observation that the number of transistors per square inch has doubled approximately every 18 months to two years since the mid-1960s. This means that computers have become smaller and faster at an exponential rate, reducing costs at around 30% per year. Without Moore's Law, we would not benefit from mobile consumer computing, which relies on very small processors and storage. We would also not see mobile telephony and, according to Pew Research Center investigation, its impact, which is currently responsible for

Written in collaboration with the World Economic Forum Global Future Council on the Future of Computing a global median of 43% of people reporting owning some type of smartphone.[69],[70] Nor would researchers, technology entrepreneurs and corporations have access to the incredible speed of today's fastest computers at negligible costs, factors behind both innovation and productivity increases.

But as stunning as the cost reductions and performance increases have been, we need them to continue, even as Moore's Law becomes untenable. Over 4 billion people around the world have no access to the internet, yet the use of digitally-enabled information technologies is a powerful driver of economic opportunity.[71] Maintaining Moore's Law poses a challenge. For several years, chip manufacturers and material scientists have been concerned that the reduction in transistor size is now facing physical limits. The increase in speed and decrease in power usage (known as Dennard's Law) for transistors already ended nearly a decade ago. Today, transistors are already smaller than viruses; 14 nanometres (nm) is currently the smallest commercial standard. Smaller chips (10nm) will come into production in 2017, with plans for an Intel plant to produce 7nm chips within the next five years. For comparison, a human hair is 50,000nm in diameter.

Five nanometres may represent the physical limit for transistor size in silicon, due to the interference of quantum tunnelling effects – where electrons can pass directly through thin materials – and other forms of current leakage that can damage chips or make them highly inefficient. As the International Technology Roadmap for Semiconductors (ITRS) put it: "The semiconductor industry is running out of horizontal space."[72] Stacking transistors vertically is one solution, but new problems arise with this approach, such as managing performance-degrading heat produced by denser chips. New materials, though, may solve these size-limitation challenges and reduce the transistors still further.

Researchers at Berkeley have created a working transistor with a 1nm wide gate, using carbon nanotubes and molybdenum disulfide.[73] But sooner or later doubling the number of transistors per square inch will become physically impossible. Even before that happens, such results may become commercially impossible. Rock's Law, a complement to Moore's Law, predicts that the cost of the factories needed to make new, smaller chips doubles about every four years, as machines need ever-greater precision and lower error rates. As Peter Denning and

Ted Lewis have noted, Rock's Law implies that the size of the market for each new generation of chips must be at least double the existing market to make the new fabrication facility economically viable.[74] The need for greater investment, when coupled with the steep changes in complexity of chip manufacturing, has recently extended the two-year pattern of density doubling to around 2.5 years.[75]

If exponential growth in computing power is to continue, it will require a broader focus on improving systems rather than simply continuing to reduce transistor size. In 2016, the Institute of Electrical and Electronics Engineers (IEEE) recognized this need for a new approach: for years they have guided chip investment by publishing reports focused on transistor reduction; in the future, they will refocus on developing an "International Roadmap for Devices and Systems" intended to "create a new 'Moore's Law' of computer performance, and accelerate bringing to market new, novel computing technologies".[76] New ways of increasing performance and efficiency are being sought through novel materials, new architectures and a systems approach to computing. This means that more people and organizations will be able to benefit from ubiquitous, low-cost computing.

One pathway to continuing the acceleration of performance is to move to more specialized processors, like the early days of computing, when chips were custom-designed for specific purposes. Since the 1970s, digital computing has been dominated by standardized, mass-produced, general-purpose microprocessors programmed for almost any purpose.[77] But for data-intensive functions where the same operation is performed over and over, standard central processing units are relatively inefficient. Today the second most common microprocessor, after the central processing unit, is the graphics processing unit, a specialized circuit to handle the display of information on screens – an intensive task for rapidly creating and updating three-dimensional images.

The rising importance and applicability of machine learning has created the demand for new types of customized computing architectures. Google, one of the world's largest purchasers of chips, designed large numbers of tensor processing units, application-specific integrated circuits designed for deep learning algorithms. It claims its tensor processing units powered its AlphaGo program, which beat world champion Go player Lee Sedol in a five-game series in 2016. New memory and processing structures are leading to a new class of microprocessor known as "AI accelerators", with architectures optimized for operations performed by the artificial neural networks at the heart of many machine-learning approaches. These offer advantages in the speed, cost and energy-efficiency required for large-scale applications of artificial intelligence (AI) algorithms.[78]

Pathways for increasing supply and performance are, however, just one place to look for managing the problems we're facing. We don't just need more power, more computing speed or more transistors; we need to be able to address the demands that are coming from the proliferation of devices and data. We need to be able to use computing capabilities in situations and contexts that are meaningful and in real time. For example, cloud-based applications can function across the globe in seconds, but for AI to work in conjunction with people and serve major needs such as public safety or traffic systems, computation that may involve exabytes of data will have to function at millisecond or microsecond speeds. Critical components of the problems we are trying to solve are not related to volume, but rather to speed, latency and energy.

At the most radical end, however, breakthroughs in physics and materials science are realizing not just specialized, more efficient processors based on digital computers, but new forms of computing, the most promising and disruptive of which is quantum computing.

Quantum computing – disruptive in theory, challenging in reality

Once we build stable, high-powered quantum computer models, this technology has the potential to be one of the most disruptive examples of Fourth Industrial Revolution technologies. But there is still some way to go. Quantum computers rethink computing by leveraging the strange laws of quantum mechanics. Instead of using transistors designed around binary units representing either 1 or 0 (bits) that classical computers use to store information and perform operations, quantum computers employ quantum bits, or qubits. Unlike bits, which are limited to being either 1 or 0, qubits exist in superposition, with a probability of being in either state until measured; this enables them to simultaneously simulate multiple states.

Another strange property of matter at the quantum level is entanglement, which means that multiple qubits can be connected so that measuring the quantum state of one qubit provides information about the others. Thus, quantum computers can employ quantum algorithms that create probabilistic shortcuts, thereby providing acceptable answers to difficult kinds of mathematical problems that would require inordinate amounts of time for classical, digital computers to solve. One example is finding the prime factors of large numbers. Many current encryption techniques work only because classical computers cannot do this quickly. Other examples include solving optimization problems with large numbers of variables, useful for a huge range of operational efficiency and logistical challenges, or searching through large, unstructured databases.[79]

Quantum computers can also model other quantum systems, such as the behaviour of atoms and other particles, much more accurately and in unusual conditions, like those inside the Large Hadron Collider. Using quantum simulation, quantum computers will easily be able to perform with calculations of, for example, molecular interactions intractable for classical computers. These calculations are key in creating even smarter materials, clean energy devices and new pharmaceuticals. Realized quantum computing will, therefore, power many fundamental technologies and systems of the Fourth Industrial Revolution.

There is, however, an important caveat. While quantum computers have existed in theory for over 30 years, since Richard Feynman first proposed them in 1982, their most disruptive potential is still only conjecture because building a universal quantum computer remains extremely difficult in engineering terms. Creating and maintaining qubits require stable systems under extreme conditions – for example, maintaining component temperatures very close to absolute zero.[80] Today's leading quantum computers either have very few qubits (IBM's quantum computer has five qubits) or few uses (such as D-Wave's quantum annealing approach), most of which are limited in their power and the types of problems they solve. Still, progress is occurring rapidly enough to demonstrate the practical potential of quantum computers. The theoretical aspect also continues to advance, with new ideas being proposed for quantum algorithms and in the emerging field of quantum machine learning.

When the physical, engineering aspects of quantum computing are solved, further challenges will arise, the most significant of which are trust and security. Current classical computers would need over 13 billion years to crack the 2048-bit certificate secured by Transport Layer Security, used by our web browsers to connect to our bank or email accounts on the internet. But a quantum-gate computer utilizing mathematician Peter Shor's algorithm, which was developed in 1994, would be able to do this kind of calculation quickly enough to render useless many current cryptographic approaches.[81] We would need to rethink the standards currently used to secure our online transactions and other means of keeping information safe. This would require us to further develop current approaches that are not susceptible to being cracked by quantum computers and to look for ways to harness quantum effects to create new forms of quantum cryptography.

Quantum computing is unlikely ever to make classical computers irrelevant. Exploiting quantum effects offers fewer significant advantages for much of the world's day-to-day processing needs than it does in the specialized areas of maths and chemistry. Moreover, our current understanding of physics makes it difficult to imagine quantum computers ever becoming cheaper and smaller than classical computers. For all its potentially transformative impact, harnessing the strangeness of quantum effects is – at least perhaps until the fifth Industrial Revolution – likely to remain a specialized and higher-cost area of computing.

The wider impacts of ever-smaller, quicker computers

As Mark Weiser wrote in 1991, "The most profound technologies are those that disappear. They weave themselves into the fabric of everyday life until they are indistinguishable from it."[82] The democratizing march of Moore's Law means that digital computers are losing their status as discrete objects: computers today are more than just an important part of new cars, consumer electronics and most home appliances. They are now integrated into textiles and clothing and are being built into the infrastructure that surrounds us – in roads, street lights, bridges and buildings.[83] We live in a computer-built world.

Thanks to new sensors and machine-learning algorithms, we can access computers through novel channels. Voice command and natural language capabilities free us from screens and keyboards. Sensors that capture body language and hand and eye gestures enable computers to read both conscious and unconscious intentions to control computers and other devices, such as wheelchairs and prosthetic limbs. Facebook announced in April 2017 that a team of 60 researchers, including machine-learning and neural prosthetic experts, is working to enable its users to dictate commands or messages to a computer by thought alone.[84] These recursive techniques to access computers will provide new ways to multitask or process information from the world around us.

Computers are also physically becoming part of us. External wearable devices, such as smart watches, intelligent earbuds and augmented reality glasses, are giving way to active implantable microchips that break the skin barrier of our bodies, creating intriguing possibilities that range from integrated treatment systems to opportunities for human enhancement.

Biological computing could soon allow us to replace specialized microchips with custom-designed organisms, a key aspect of a new cultural form of expression and consumption called "biohacking". Researchers at MIT have demonstrated that sensors, memory switches and circuits can be encoded in common human gut bacteria, indicating that our biomes could, for example, be purposefully designed to detect and treat inflammatory bowel disease or colon cancer.[85]

Such potential benefits come, however, with challenges and risks. The increase in possibilities for the two-way flow of information between us and our environment highlights the challenge of continually expanding bandwidth, as well as improving compression technology. The vast amounts of data created in a digitally-driven world require new approaches that offer dense, long-term storage. One solution is using DNA to store information. In 2012, Harvard's George Church demonstrated the possibility of storing data on DNA at more than 100,000 times the density of the best flash memory options available. It was also stable at a wide range of temperatures: according to Church, "You can drop it wherever you want, in the desert or your backyard, and it will be there 400,000 years later."[86]

In some ways, particularly under extreme conditions, ubiquitous computing could make the world more fragile. Relying on systems that require always-on computing raises the risk that power outages could create severe challenges. Even worse, the lower our familiarity with more primitive, manual fallback systems, the more negative consequences those crises could have. Ever more ubiquitous computing is sure to have social impacts, too. Already, smaller and faster computers have changed human behaviour: the mere presence of a mobile phone on a table means, for example, that people are less likely to feel connected to their conversational partner or to remember the details of their interaction.[87] Social media use is also correlated with declining empathy among young people.

Environmental externalities will become a bigger issue as computing technologies continue to spread. Data centres in developed economies already account for around 2% of electricity use. In the United States, that amounts to 70 billion kilowatt hours, more than the entire country of Austria in a year. Acting as stewards for the planet means that, as researchers and firms develop new materials to support future waves of computing innovation, we should commit to market mechanisms that support increasing the sustainability and energy efficiency of computing methods and hardware. As new types of processors are developed, the sustainability of resources should be a central goal.

With sustainability in mind, it is important to think about the limitations on the systems we are currently constructing. Though "the cloud" is less than a decade old for wide consumer use, the trajectory towards larger and more efficient centralized data centres as well as concerns about security and privacy mean thinking more creatively about how and where we store data and the costs associated with it. If an important use of data is to have real-time insight and decision-making, mesh computing – distributed computing across many devices on a network – may prove to be a more agile solution. While data centres can maintain archives, mesh computing may bring much needed analytics and swift decision-making closer to the action, without incurring scalability costs needed at centres for ever higher levels of efficiency.

Also of importance should be equality of access. The frontier of new computing development and adoption tends to occur in developed economies that possess large, wealthy consumer markets, abundant human capital and the ability to raise investment for technology development. However, ensuring that the Fourth Industrial Revolution is able to benefit the largest number of people requires the development of affordable computing technologies, as well as those that operate well in a wide range of environments, including places where power is intermittent, temperature shifts are significant, and even where radiation is a challenge.[88] One example is the Raspberry Pi, a low-cost, high-performance computer designed to make computing more relevant and accessible to people around the world. It has sold more than 12 million devices since being launched in 2012.[89]

Designing computers that can be used in a wide range of conditions is only a small part of the broader challenge of shaping the distribution of benefits that flow from new computing technologies. Innovative technologies tend to accrue their benefits to first movers. Special efforts are required to ensure that economically, socially and physically vulnerable populations can access new tools as they emerge. This must be addressed so they can share in the economic benefits created by new general-purpose technologies. It is not just a question of fair taxation but also of competition policy and consumer rights: being at the frontier of advances in computing technologies can enable "super-platforms" to wield outsized power over their value chains. For example, the ability to use specialized processors and access huge amounts of data allows price discrimination among consumers, ultimately putting disadvantaged competitors out of business.[90]

Finally, as emphasized in the preface, trust in both institutions and in technology is under threat. As computers become indistinguishable in the daily lives of more and more people around the world, securing these approaches and protecting privacy are vital to restoring trust between citizens, governments and corporations.

Five key ideas

1. Moore's Law (the consistent reduction in transistor size and cost) is closing in on physical limitations at the atomic level, while Dennard's Law (the increase in speed and decrease in power usage of transistors) has already ended. Material science is working to find solutions, but straightforward linear processing is approaching physical limits and will need to be augmented by new forms of computing.
2. Major issues facing computational needs are concerned with more than processing power (numbers of transistors); they are concerned with speed, proximity, latency and energy requirements that require new ways of thinking about computing – thus, the attractiveness of potential alternatives, such as quantum computing, photonics and mesh computing.
3. The proliferation of smaller, quicker computers means devices are saturating our urban environments, consumer products, homes and even our bodies. Connected to the internet, these devices will become a part of a global network (see Chapter 7: Internet of Things).
4. Data centres are becoming centralized spaces for our data and currently provide access to archived data and computing power. In the future, our needs for responsive computing may require more locally accessible distributed computing across devices, to ensure speed and time relevance. This could mean a big shift where computational power lies and is utilized.
5. The bigger challenge for new computing technologies is maintaining a wide perspective on how they will impact our societies and communities. Accessibility, inclusivity and concerns about security, privacy and authority will need to be given as much thought as the technologies themselves.

Chapter 6

Blockchain and Distributed Ledger Technologies

Satoshi Nakamoto, the person or persons who published a paper detailing the foundations of distributed ledger technology in October 2008, may one day become a household name, famous far beyond the technologically savvy. His, her or their anonymous publication of a deeply transformative payment technology based on a blockchain, a groundbreaking combination of mathematics, cryptography, computer science and game theory, was the first step in the rise of digital currencies and the creation of entire new systems of storing and exchanging value in both our digital and real economies.[91]

By the 2030s, versions of distributed ledger technologies or "blockchains" may well change everything from online financial transactions to the way we vote and how we tell where goods are produced. Imagine the impact of nearly 10% of global GDP being stored and traded in currencies outside the sovereignty of nation states or the automated, transparent and real-time collection of taxes across all parts of the economy. The widespread implementation of blockchain technology could very well be a turning point in history, but both the technology itself and the ability of organizations to adopt it are at early stages. Disagreements about the structure of blockchain networks, the fact that transactions may run afoul of national data transmission regulations and many other issues, stand in the way of realizing their benefits. Collective governance, stakeholder engagement and solving a number of "offline" coordination challenges are key priorities if this revolutionary technology is to realize its potential to redefine both transactions and trust.

An architecture of trust

As the phrase "distributed ledger technology" implies, at the centre of blockchain technology is the ability to create and exchange unique digital records without requiring a centralized, trusted party. By using a clever combination of cryptography and peer-to-peer networking, it guarantees that information stored and shared between a group of people is both accurate and transparent – with a number of added

Written in collaboration with Jesse McWaters, World Economic Forum, and the World Economic Forum Global Future Council on the Future of Blockchain bonuses, such as the ability to see every prior state of a record and the opportunity to create programmable records – so-called "smart contracts".

This is revolutionary for four reasons. First, blockchain technology helps overcome the double-edged sword of the digital economy – the fact that digital objects can be copied exactly and transmitted at almost no marginal cost to multiple people simultaneously. This is valuable for sharing information but is problematic when transmitting something of unique value or guaranteed provenance – whether a unit of a digital currency, a document that contains indispensable information or perhaps a piece of art, where knowing who holds the original is important. Blockchains enable the creation and transfer of verifiably unique digital objects, without the risk of false copies or double-sending, creating what has been called "the internet of value."[92]

The second revolutionary aspect is that distributed ledger technologies allow transparency, verification and "immutability" without requiring anyone to trust a single central third party. This is important because situations abound where it is extremely difficult to trust, agree on or set up a third party to record the details of transactions, or assert the source or ownership of a valuable asset.

The third important attribute is that distributed ledgers allow for programmable actions – transactions that can be executed (and then traced and verified) without human intervention. This ability goes far beyond algorithmic trading or automated online transfers. Smart contracts on a blockchain can be designed to transfer any piece of information or asset under any set of specific circumstances, from an insurance contract that pays out when rainfall levels exceed a certain amount, to automatically distributing royalties or rewarding multiple parties for different amounts of work on a project. Importantly, the code that executes the smart contract is in itself stored on the blockchain, is available for inspection and runs for everyone without delays.

Fourth, digital ledgers can be designed to be inclusive. Blockchain transactions are by nature simultaneously transparent, secure and traceable. If desired, they can also be anonymous. At least for the user, making a transaction requires little bandwidth and requires only basic software, storage and connectivity. This means that individuals and small contributors who normally would be excluded from markets can become market players as producers, shareholders, beneficiaries or consumers of any asset capable of being tracked and traded in a digital form.[93]

These characteristics mean that blockchain offers the world an unprecedented opportunity to distribute the rewards of economic activity with a far lower threat of capture or hidden costs being imposed by centralized, monopolistic or rent-seeking intermediaries. Possibly the use of distributed ledgers could allow individuals to recapture some of the value created by their personal data, or at least ensure greater transparency and security in a world where people's data is both a significant asset and a potential liability.

Navigating the wild west of blockchain

Primavera De Filippi, Faculty Associate, Berkman Center for Internet & Society, USA, compares blockchain in its current form to the internet in the early 1990s, when technologists and businesses had no inkling of its potential and value, or any understanding of its myriad uses. For De Filippi, blockchain's most transformative role is as a tool against exploitation, with the ability to influence a new social contract adapted to societies and economies increasingly dependent on and enveloped by technology.

But despite its advantages and the hype that surrounds the value of cryptocurrencies, blockchain is neither a panacea nor without significant challenges. Some of these challenges can be seen in the experiences of bitcoin, the largest cryptocurrency and the first and most famous use of blockchain. As bitcoin grows and scales, so do the demands on the network, which has led to disagreements among participants about whether to shift key aspects of the bitcoin blockchain (such as the size of what constitutes a "block") to increase the efficiency of transactions. Without any form of central governance, the bitcoin chain could "fork" – with different groups of participants adopting alternate pathways depending on their interests.

Setting up a blockchain requires overcoming significant coordination challenges. As Behlendorf points out, a working blockchain still requires an initial group of diverse stakeholders to trust that their interests are better served by a distributed ledger than by any alternative, including not transacting at all.[94] This means agreeing on a wide range of technical approaches and committing resources to shift to a new technology and way of working.

When Are Blockchains Useful?

According to Brian Behlendorf, Executive Director, Hyperledger Project, distributed ledgers could be particularly useful when:

- There is demand or unmet potential for a transaction to occur between two or more parties
- Performing these kind of transactions is inefficient or impossible, perhaps because:
- Many, diverse parties can't agree on a trusted third party to act as an efficient, centralized intermediary for exchange
- Monopoly power, rent-seeking, corruption, lack of transparency or institutional inefficiency mean the transaction costs are significant and/or uncertainty is distributed throughout the system
- Individuals or groups are excluded from an existing platform because of the cost of verifying or managing their participation
- The asset being transacted can be easily forged or duplicated, such that participants do not trust each other not to cheat

Building a working blockchain system for a specific use is not straightforward. Before individuals or organizations can start transacting on a distributed ledger, potential participants must agree on a number of issues including, but by no means limited to:

- The parameters for value – what is the unit of value that is being represented on the ledger?
- The technical architecture – is a private blockchain piggybacking on a public one? By what means does the ledger securely validate transactions? How and at what rate are new tokens of value generated?
- How do participants validate the "starting conditions" of the chain?

If the digital transactions relate to physical objects, how are the physical objects securely identified, tagged and linked to digital tokens?

The coordination problem is compounded in scenarios where distributed ledgers become widely adopted; it would naturally be desirable for blockchains to be interoperable across networks so it would be possible to connect a cryptocurrency chain with a carbon credit network and a forestry contracting ledger. But that would require standards across multiple applications – standards that presently do not exist.

Distributed ledgers can also have environmental externalities. The most common way that a blockchain achieves its goal of immutability is known as "proof-of-work", where network participants compete by expending large amounts of computing effort, and therefore energy, to securely validate transactions in return for the possibility of a reward. Under this model, employed by both the bitcoin and Ethereum cryptocurrencies, more transactions mean more energy is needed to verify them and the greater the environmental impact – another example of a not-so-hidden transaction cost in a Fourth Industrial Revolution technology.[95]

There is also the fact that secure, anonymous, programmable networks could lower the cost of criminal activity. The same protocols that allow for smart contracts to protect the interests of individuals through encryption also allow consortiums to perform illicit activities, such as illegal drug trading, human trafficking, fraud, and more.[96] Another issue is the accessibility of the technology itself. While bitcoin "wallets" are becoming easier to access and use, few mass or widespread incentives exist for individuals and organizations to accept the switching costs of moving to blockchain-enabled platforms. The lack of abundant platforms and intuitive applications, though they are not far away, poses another barrier.

A Technology for Trust

By Carsten Stöcker, Head, Blockchain Competence Team, innogy, Germany, and Burkhard Blechschmidt, Head, CIO Advisory, Cognizant, Germany

Historically, trust was added on to products or transactions as they flowed through the manufacturing supply chain. Physical, or electronic, records trailed every object to prove its origin, destination, quantity and history. Producing, tracking and verifying all this information imposes a massive "trust tax" of time and effort on banks, accountants, lawyers, auditors and quality inspectors. Important information could be lost, inaccessible or even intentionally hidden.

As the Fourth Industrial Revolution unfolds, blurring the line between the physical and digital worlds, blockchain is emerging to allow digital product memories to follow physical objects and guide them through the entire supply chain. When combined with cryptographically secure tagging, blockchain will create truly unique IDs and immutable records to make it easier and less expensive for suppliers and customers to transact with one another in a verifiable way.

Blockchain-enabled "distributed trust" will drive entire new manufacturing business models such as:

- Secure marketplaces for designers to publish, and be paid for, their work in the form of protected manufacturing design files
- Marketplaces of digital product memories enabling manufacturers to reduce the cost of quality control, regulatory compliance, warranty or recall actions
- Data services using blockchains to sell data-driven insights in areas such as product design, marketing, supply-chain orchestration or manufacturing
- "Asset-less" enterprises that rely on third-party manufacturers, verifying their work with blockchain-enabled transparent and credible supply-chain data

Potential winners in this new world include:

- Product and service providers in geographies with weak rule of law and intellectual property, as blockchains make it easier to protect their data and financial transactions even in the absence of strong governmental institutions
- Smaller product designers, raw material suppliers and service providers that would otherwise find it too expensive or time-consuming to ensure trust with larger, geographically dispersed counterparties
- Aggregators and sellers of blockchain-protected data on manufacturing or operations that can help maximize the value of products produced within blockchain value chains
- Service providers for decentralized autonomous manufacturing organizations enabled by blockchain; such services could include robotic manufacturing, shipping and financing
- Micromanufacturers specializing in high value make-to-order products

Potential losers include:

- Any supply-chain player with higher hidden costs and inefficiencies or lower quality whose traditional, cumbersome, opaque trust mechanisms can be replaced by blockchain
- Intermediary business service providers that provide "matching" or "marketplace" services, such as e-commerce aggregators
- Lower-skilled workers, both on the assembly line and in supporting clerical jobs, as blockchain and new technologies such as 3D printing and advanced robotics automate the routine assembly and tracking of products and contracts
- Higher-skilled workers, such as vendor managers, accountants, warranty managers and lawyers, as blockchain technology automates complex negotiations, tracking and verification processes
- Financial, auditing and related institutions, as payment, risk management and quality assurance move to the blockchain

As a consequence, the intersection of blockchain-enabled distributed trust with a variety of Fourth Industrial Revolution technologies will radically transform entire ecosystems.

Early blockchain adopters face challenges with this still-evolving technology in areas such as systems integration, business cases, standards and regulatory compliance. Many are developing cross-industry partnerships and actively building ecosystems while demonstrating "applied ecosystem leadership" to inform cost-effective, low-risk innovation.

The permanent and transparent nature of blockchain records means they would be well-suited to creating secure digital identities, potentially revolutionizing everything from healthcare records to voting and the delivery of government services. But, as argues Catherine Mulligan, Co-Director, Centre for Cryptocurrency Research and Engineering, Imperial College London, we should pause to consider the risks before rushing in this direction: the information in an undeniable ledger could be grossly misused by a malevolent government with access to private keys.[97]

Perhaps most challenging, conceptually, is the loss of central authority. This challenge is more than institutional. It is deeply psychological and attached to systems of human order. Decentralizing trust by relying on a complex set of algorithms is as radical as the shift from human deduction as the ultimate source of knowledge to reliance on modern scientific instrumentation. It took society centuries to adapt to the latter, though economic incentives may catalyse the former. Ultimately, with blockchain, trust will have to lie with the mathematicians and the infrastructure rather than with politicians and individual, recognizable institutions. This raises existential, in addition to political and technological, challenges.

A technology built for more than just business

African diamond-producing nations convened in Kimberley, South Africa, in May 2000 to stop the proliferation of conflict diamonds. They succeeded through extensive agreements, and by implementing strict policies and certifications on participating members, requiring nations to establish legislation and institutions to support the process. In 2015, however, the London-based start-up Everledger was founded with the idea of supporting the Kimberley process, combatting fraud in the diamond supply chain using a combination of blockchain and machine vision.

Some of the most revolutionary and valuable uses of blockchain are in the physical world. The potential upside of solving supply-chain tracking issues in everything from endangered fish to high art makes the use of distributed ledgers very attractive. For example, blockchain could potentially crush the global counterfeiting market, estimated to total as much as 2.5% of world trade.[98] Linking physical objects to a digital ledger means overcoming the last-mile challenge of secure tagging. Innovative combinations of machine vision, biometrics, 3D printing and nanotechnologies promise tagging and tracing options that mean secure and transparent supply chains may be within grasp, particularly for industries focused on high-value goods.

While blockchain is taking small steps into the physical world, it is taking large steps in its native digital habitat. As the basis for bitcoin and other cryptocurrencies, blockchain has enabled billions of dollars in currency and exchange, though not without some volatile valuation adjustments. In June 2017, more than $700 billion had been transacted through the bitcoin blockchain. Blockchain applications have a large market in the financial industry, with many prospects for profitable applications as well as the opportunity to extend financial inclusion by offering people access to financial markets and services without the need for a bank. Here, the last-mile problems faced in the application to physical goods are confined to the usability and accessibility of applications and clients, as well as the stability of the platforms themselves.

Blockchain will have much of its impact through the combinatorial power of the Fourth Industrial Revolution. As suggested by the supply-chain discussion above, the combination of blockchain with the internet of things (IoT) has exciting prospects. Marketplaces are being designed with end-to-end services completely secured through blockchain, from proof of production feasibility, to contractual agreements, to file transfers and trade finance. This is occurring with all the players and consortiums tied in. With services such as these and real-world verification componentry, such as cameras, printers and sensor readers, dropping steadily in price, we may see such marketplaces open in the near future.

While cryptocurrencies, funds, exchanges and asset management still comprise a significant proportion of players in the distributed ledger ecosystem, significant activity is taking place in identity management, government and legal technology, energy, logistics and even tokens that reward attention flows for advertising purposes.[99]

For most businesses, the impacts of blockchain are desirable: access to new markets, secure and programmable transactions, and less attention on routine oversight and audit tasks. For society, the outcomes are mixed. As Peter Smith, Chief Executive Officer, Blockchain, USA, said, "Blockchain can benefit individuals by giving them more secure, collaborative ways of generating and transferring value. But implementing it across industries could lead to millions of job losses, as the intermediaries that sit between transactions today are made obsolete."[100] In a dynamic economy, the net benefit of course could be positive: blockchain could unleash a world of microtransactions and opportunities to create value that more than compensate for the loss of intermediaries. Furthermore, in a future where an increasing amount of work is performed by algorithms and robots, distributed ledgers could become the basis for radically revised social protection systems.

Given the potential impact of blockchain technology, weighing the trade-offs and determining regulatory action should be a subject for multistakeholder dialogue. While the technology is still young and the market relatively small, heavy or premature regulation could hinder its potential. Nevertheless, a number of risks and challenges need to be addressed. These critical issues will likely be topics for the coming years:

- Significant legal ambiguity exists around blockchain-based transactions, particularly the liability framework and the mechanisms of recourse in case of conflicts and unexpected problems, such as service interruptions, or unintentional actions, such as "fat-finger" trading errors.[101]

- The rollout of new infrastructure based on blockchain will require effective governance frameworks. Applications for financial, real-economy and humanitarian purposes will highlight different concerns over the technology's implementation. The replacement of data infrastructure will require regulators to consider how blockchain adoption will impact current risks, and think about the unintended consequences of its regulation across the system.

- No standards yet exist to facilitate technical and data interoperability across various blockchain technologies or implementations. If this is not rectified, the risk remains that blockchain will be unable to achieve its promise of replacing data silos and improving operational efficiency.

- For applications in the physical world, current last-mile problems require convoluted solutions to enable the verification of goods and services. These foster interlopers and corruption, which counteracts the purpose of using blockchain for supply-chain verification. Industry leaders, with local support and regulators, can help devise solutions for these unique and contextual challenges.

- Data regulations at the national level can conflict with the required transmission of data that is part of the blockchain process. This data could concern payments or non-financial data, such as various business-related information or restricted personal information, like healthcare data. Identifying these areas and working towards adequate solutions will be a challenge given the unique decentralizing nature of the blockchain.

Five key ideas

1. Blockchain technology is a form of distributed digital ledger that makes it possible to share digital records and information securely and with confidence that there aren't multiple copies of those unique records, thus preserving the value of the digital object or information.
2. Blockchain technology is a decentralizing force because no central authority is responsible for maintaining the system. Instead, collaborative incentives require various parties to act in good faith and make it mathematically improbable that the system can be hacked.
3. Blockchain technology is useful for the creation of cryptocurrencies, digital identities, tracking physical objects with the use of encryption and digital identifiers, and other areas where the provenance of virtual or physical objects needs to be authenticated. The verifiability of these assets enables whole new way for us to relate to the data we create as users of digital devices, services and applications.
4. Blockchain technologies can help distribute benefits to those who are traditionally excluded from economic rewards, such as individuals and small groups that would otherwise have to create consortia in order to engage in larger business process.
5. Some challenges that need to be addressed are legal ambiguities, blockchain related infrastructure, lack of standards, last-mile problems for physical goods, and national and cross-border data regulation issues. For example, cryptocurrencies are still in their early stages and there are unresolved externalities, such as environmental impact, their use by criminal organizations and general dispute resolution.

Chapter 7

The Internet of Things

In the next decade, more than 80 billion connected devices around the world will be in constant communication with people and with each other. This vast web of interaction, analysis and output will remould the way objects are produced, anticipate our needs and provide new perspectives on the world. At the same time, distributed systems will challenge how we create, measure and apportion data and value. Thanks to the ubiquity of sensors, the world will change in other ways, too. Supermarkets, for example, will no longer have check-out facilities, and fast-food restaurants will have less than half the staff they had 10 years before. As business models take advantage of the internet of things (IoT) to optimize their operations and create a "pull economy", the world around us will continuously anticipate our needs by analysing our patterns of behaviour. In this future, we will become more conscious of the value of our data and more concerned about our digital security; data flows will become overwhelming and cybersecurity threats part of daily headlines.

Yet there is much potential for good. IoT is already helping track water levels in developing nations, and can animate medical technologies in remote areas through satellite coverage. Public crime is likely to decrease due to the convergence of sensors, cameras, AI and facial recognition software. Trust in technological systems could increase as IoT helps decentralize and democratize economic production, providing many people around the globe with new and creative opportunities. However, to provide the expected value to society and industry, IoT must contend with the lack of security protocols, bandwidth limits, cultural acceptance hurdles, and missing agreements on how to parse the value of data and collaborative opportunities. It's far from a fait accompli. It will require collective effort and cooperative governance for the investments to pay off.

Written in collaboration with Derek O'Halloran, World Economic Forum.

Enveloping the world

IoT is a core infrastructure element of the Fourth Industrial Revolution. It consists of a range of smart and connected sensors that gather data, and process and transform it according to need; it then communicates data to other devices or individuals to meet the goals of a system or user. IHS, a London-based market analytics company, forecast that the number of IoT devices will grow from an estimated 15.4 billion devices in 2015 to 75.4 billion in 2025.[102] This fivefold increase will drive deeper connectivity in every part of life, link together global economies in novel ways and likely encompass a burgeoning machine-to-machine economy as well.

The impacts will be large and will subject current service and manufacturing industries to the type of upheaval that the media industry experienced between 1995 and 2015. Principles of jurisdiction and complex data traffic laws must be addressed so that the end goal can release vast amounts of value, accruing first in factories and the manufacturing sector, where operational efficiency is an understood quick fix, and the potential for better asset utilization and productivity is significant. The value of these shifts has been estimated as representing up to 11% of the world economy.[103] Work by the World Economic Forum and Accenture indicates that most of this value will be generated in industrial applications, dwarfing the consumer side in business and socio-economic impacts; as much as $14 trillion could be added to the global economy by 2030, while supporting 12 of the UN Sustainable Development Goals (Figure 11).[104]

Delivering this value is possible because of IoT's three core capabilities. First, it enables rich data to be combined with smart analytics, which provides new sources of contextual data reflecting events in the wider environment. It also provides device performance data, helping firms and individuals anticipate how assets are performing and where opportunities to extend value exist. It will also deliver user-impact data, showing the effects of how, when and why people take actions. This enabling capability will reshape what we know and prioritize how we make decisions.

Figure 11: The Internet of Things Offers a Potential Economic Impact of $4 Trillion to $11 Trillion a Year in 2025

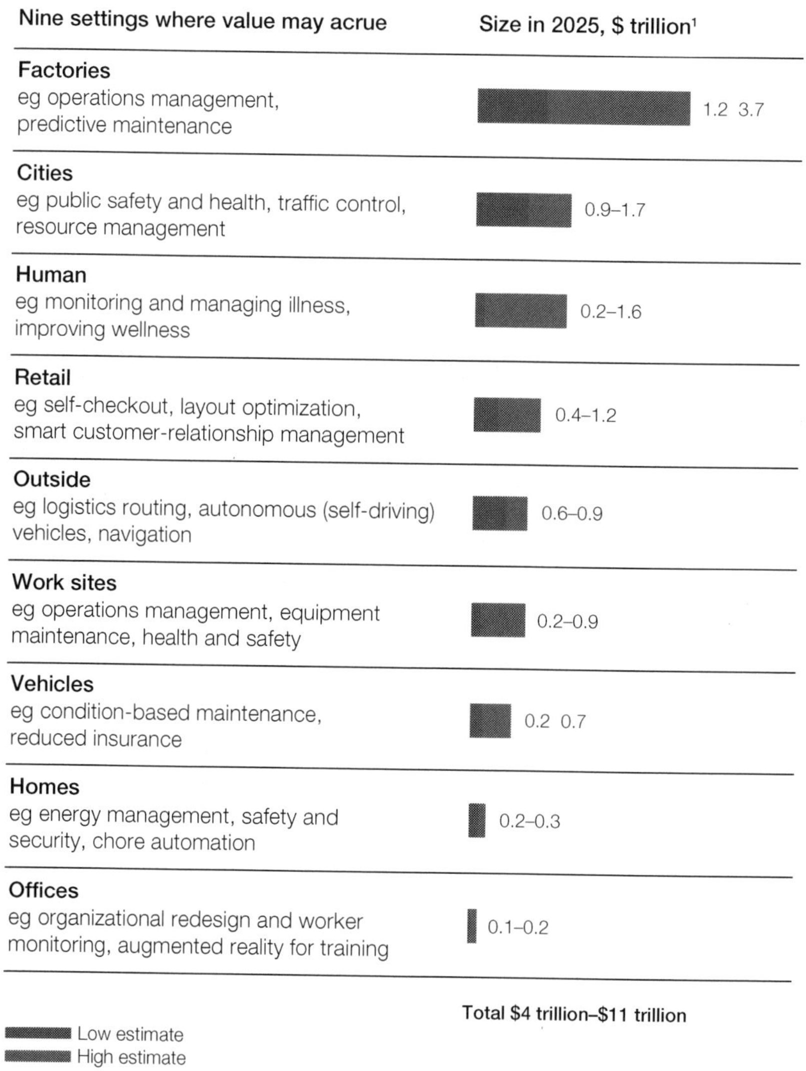

Source: McKinsey Global Institute (2015)

The second core capability comes from these devices communicating and coordinating in ways that enhance efficiency and productivity. Both end-to-end automation and new forms of human–machine collaboration will streamline routine tasks and enhance individuals' ability to apply creativity and problem-solving skills to higher-value challenges. The ability to expand from an administrative and task-oriented mindset can shape more synthetic perspectives as people become accustomed to considering peripheral input in the shaping of products, services and ideas.

The third capability is the creation of intelligent-interactive objects that provide new channels for delivering value to citizens. As a distributed network of sensors and devices, synergistic opportunities exist for other distributed technologies, such as cloud AI, blockchain, additive manufacturing, drones, energy production, and more. With these new technologies converging, the decentralization of value creation and exchange will mimic the infrastructure that enables it, and the outcomes of this economic reformatting are likely to surprise us. For this reason, IoT will ultimately challenge existing institutions and conceptual frameworks on how to think about the nature of products, services and data, as well as how to think about the definition of their value in a way that works for business.

Thus, these three capabilities will create the impetus for changes to business models and structural shifts across a wide range of industries, including manufacturing, oil and gas, agriculture, mining, transportation and healthcare. As discussed in the World Economic Forum report, *Industrial Internet of Things: Unleashing the Potential of Connected Products and Services*, its pathway starts with firms improving their operational efficiency, and progresses through the creation of new products and services. This leads to an "outcome economy", followed by an "autonomous, pull economy" (Figure 12).[105] This process will also be applicable to sensors in the environment, helping create a proactive management of resources. For example, system-wide issues, such as power usage and emissions, can be optimized through incentives sent to citizens in real time to shape behaviour for optimal traffic routing and energy consumption.

The diffusion of IoT requires the development and deployment of four different layers: first, the devices that sense, communicate and (in some cases) perform an action, such as moving an object or opening a door; second, the communications infrastructure that connects these devices together; third, a secure data management system that gathers and distributes the data generated by the devices for use by the fourth layer: the applications that process the data and deliver bundles of services to meet the needs of organizations or individuals.

Figure 12: The Adoption and Impact Path of the Industrial Internet

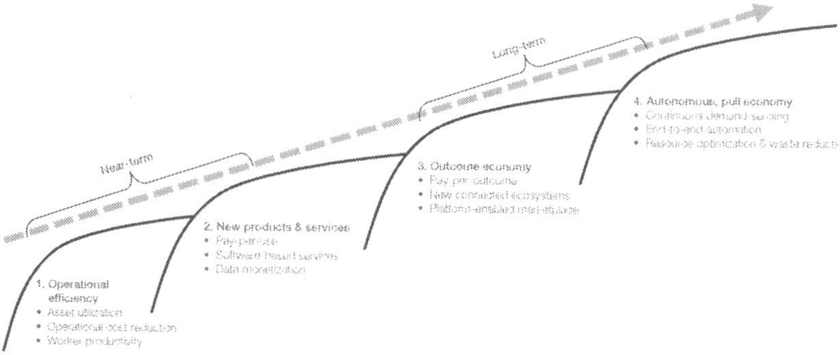

Source: World Economic Forum (2015)

Data management and application layers are often overlooked. These are critical, though, because value flows when data is transformed into valuable inputs or actionable insights rather than when objects are connected. A McKinsey analysis demonstrates that the average oil rig has 30,000 sensors, yet only 1% of the data is analysed and used.[106] Likewise, many other industries suffer from a glut of data and a dearth of creative mechanisms to interrogate it. Inexperienced with so much data, many companies struggle to understand what they should be looking for or even what questions to ask beyond the linear expansion of previous metrics.

With new networked devices, identities, goods and services on offer in the Fourth Industrial Revolution, businesses and consumers may have to learn new ways to remunerate each other for data usage, as well as learn how to disaggregate the components of value with transactions and collaborations. In such a new arrangement, consumers could become partners, even though negotiations will be difficult. Legal challenges are certain to arise, and societal stakeholders will be responsible for defending consumer rights and space for privacy in this deeply connected future. If the medium is the message, then IoT, like the World Wide Web, is a harbinger of shake-ups far beyond the business world.

Revolution, Not Evolution: The Promise, Challenge and Opportunity of IoT

By Richard Soley, Chairman and Chief Executive Officer, Object Management Group, USA

In writing about new technology interruptions over the past 40 years, I cannot count the number of times I have said, "evolution, not revolution". Expert systems, distributed computing, object technology, graphical modelling, semantic modelling – they've all presented challenges but, more importantly, opportunities. But the "old" models of computation didn't change – the architectures were rather the same, software improvements were gradual, and the total outcome, while worth the investment, was measured in tens of percentage points. Evolution, not revolution.

This time it's different. While the components of IoT transition may not be particularly new, the outcomes are distinctly different, both from a qualitative and a quantitative viewpoint. IoT is essentially the practice of gathering thousands or millions of sensor data points, real-time integration and predictive analysis of that data, and either delivery of decision support to decision-makers or direct control of real-world actuators. In the presence of ubiquitous communications (via the worldwide internet), with remarkable, inexpensive computational power and storage (again via the internet and through cloud computing), combined with advances in the real-time analysis of huge amounts of data (so-called "big data"), the impossible becomes possible – and begets revolution.

It's unfortunate that nearly all discussion of the IoT revolution revolves around refrigerators and light bulbs – consumer technology. While those changes will happen (and will highlight better than ever the lack of trust, privacy and security on the internet), they ignore the much larger opportunity – the "internetization" of industry, a revolution equal in impact to the electrification of industry a century ago. Like electrification, the application of IoT to industry will not be held to just manufacturing and production (though it has appeared there first); rather, it's easy to see how IoT will impact every major industry: healthcare; financial systems; transportation; energy production, transmission and distribution; agriculture; smart city services; the list is endless. Rather than focus, as too many presenters do, on the number of devices that will be connected to the internet, it's much more valuable to understand what will be done by those connected devices.

In particular, there are entirely new business models to be discovered:

- The most obvious, often called the "outcome economy", is the transition to the purchase of outcomes by the hour, or by the metre, or by the litre – rather than the purchase of machinery to deliver the same. Airlines have for decades moved from owning airplanes to leasing them; they are starting to lease jet engines as well, leaving the care and maintenance of those huge but delicate pieces of machinery in the hands of those who know them best – the manufacturers. Airlines get higher efficiency and dispatch reliability for the engines; jet engine manufacturers get a new service income stream. By maintaining connection to the equipment (and its enormous stream of performance data, and many other of the same engines elsewhere), they can offer better service, higher efficiency and lower prices all at once. Better, faster, cheaper – choose all three this time.

- Entirely new and unexpected opportunities are discovered in the strangest places when previously unconnected streams of data become connected. In a provincial ambulance management system, a pattern of drivers' use of the equipment was discovered that made it possible to optimize routes, minimize the time to access the services and return to the hospital, and at the same time make the drivers happier with the time off between emergency calls. Lives may also have been saved. But nobody could see the opportunity until the location data for the ambulances was connected with emergency call data and geographic data for coffee shops. There are surprises everywhere.

Winners in this world will be:

- Those who try early to overcome the challenges of data collection, analysis and management. In every real IoT project or test bed we've seen, there have been unexpected positive results that could not have been predicted.

- Those who connect seemingly unrelated streams of data in real time to find unexpected correlations and opportunities. The cost of entry is rather low when computational power is abundant and inexpensive; it pays to look for opportunities.

- Most importantly, those who realize that their industries are facing disruption, and want to take part in that disruption rather than waiting to be disrupted –potentially catastrophically. We are already seeing major disruption, to the extent of societal change, in transportation and manufacturing.

The losers in this new, revolutionary world will be those who stand by and wait for disruption, fail to see the new business models emerging and ignore progress. The big changes aren't to the information and communications technology (ICT) world this time – they're to the industries that depend on ICT. And today, that's every industry.

Challenges, risks and dangers

For IoT to achieve its promise, several challenges need to be met. The most commonly identified barriers inhibiting the adoption of the industrial IoT by businesses are a lack of standards, which is to say a lack (or potential lack) of interoperability, and security concerns (Figure 13). Without the equivalent of something like a World Wide Web Consortium to set standards and protocols, the potential of the IoT is threatened. Less obvious barriers, although equally challenging, relate to how firms manage new business models created around data analytics and services attached to connected assets.

Several risks associated with IoT systems exist that affect not just the companies employing the systems, but users and the public. For example, a risk occurs when individuals and firms become reliant on IoT systems in ways that encourage the loss of important skills, as well as encourage new fragilities to emerge when connectivity and power conditions are not met. More complex, tightly coupled systems are more exposed to "normal accidents".[107]

Cybersecurity is a standout risk. Hacking risks apply to both companies and stakeholders linked to data travelling between devices and networks. The World Economic Forum Industrial Internet Survey revealed that 76% of business respondents believe the likelihood of such attacks against their IoT systems is "very or extremely high".[108] Even more worrisome, perhaps, is that IoT is not just a target for cyberattacks but can also be used to perpetrate them. Some of the largest cyberattacks recorded occurred in 2016 and involved hacked IoT devices, such as security cameras and other monitors, which sent traffic to cripple websites.[109]

The challenge of cybersecurity in IoT, therefore, requires the management of multiple risks, including stopping the use of insecure devices to attack third parties; preventing individuals or smart systems from wresting control of IoT devices or systems with the intent to intimidate, steal, harm or ransom; and securing the stability of essential private and public services. Security issues are also linked to concerns with data privacy and cross-border data communication. This need will require policy-makers across jurisdictions to find a balance between protecting consumers and enabling companies. Procedures and protocols for sharing and storing data will be a critical topic if global data flows are to create the full spectrum of IoT potential.

Figure 13: Key Barriers in Adopting the Industrial Internet

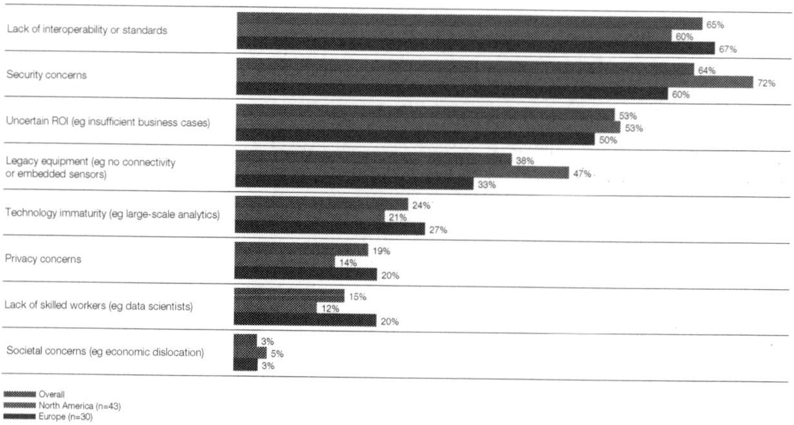

Source: World Economic Forum (2015)

As well as the rise of secure distributed ledgers such as the blockchain, innovations in IoT architecture encourage opportunities to find this balance in new ways. For example, Sensity Systems (a Verizon company), worked with Genetec to design smart city security systems to manage both security and privacy concerns. Their IoT devices achieve this by performing data processing "on the edge" of the network. This means that a compromise was reached. Sensitive video data remain on the device unless device-side algorithms determine that a threat has been detected in the video feed. If not, authorization sends the video to security agents. This type of compromise lowered bandwidth needs, while avoiding the vulnerability of centrally-stored, wide-ranging data.

As with other emerging technologies, such as AI and robotics and blockchain, a critical concern involves the social impact on employment and skills. In particular, IoT's potential for disruption will transform organizations and industries. In combination with AI and robotics, IoT is likely to reduce demand for routine, manual work, as well as to place increased scrutiny on workers (Figure 14). This reduction, though, will create increased demand for creative and problem-solving skills linked to programming, design and maintenance. Social and ethical discussions of the IoT should focus on an empowering and integrated digital-human workforce, with value delivered through augmentation rather than replacement. Curiously, each of these technologies alone may reduce employment opportunities, but together may enable new and prosperous opportunities for individuals. The future will reveal the truth.

The IoT will integrate us deeper into our symbiosis with the digital infrastructure, products and communications that mediate our lives. It will envelop the physical environment and find its way into the deep cracks of societal interactions, as well as affect the relationships between stakeholder groups. It will become indispensable and yet, like mobile technologies today, will also create demands on each of the stakeholder groups. The following are a few of these demands:

- In many business scenarios that utilize the IoT, data is multiuse, meaning it can render value to multiple parties in a variety of contexts. Contextual questions about who owns the data, who profits from its use and how it can be valued properly will all need some form of resolution, depending on the business models employed.

- In some IoT scenarios, the potential outcomes of data usage could be valuable for environmental and social benefit, such as in the reduction of waste or energy usage. However, in some scenarios, the optimal benefits for society fail to equate to the maximal benefits for businesses. Policy-makers and societal stakeholders need to consider how we value the utilization of the infrastructure and machine-to-machine communications in areas where productivity isn't the biggest or most important outcome.

- To reduce *ex post* conflict, businesses will need to learn how to approach collaborative opportunities (e.g. using mobile applications data for the determination of insurance premiums) and clarify business cases. The value created in this way across a distributed system through the sharing of data will require disassembling the value that is created and apportioned to the requisite actors. Frameworks and best practices for fair outcomes should be a topic that includes societal stakeholders.

- Technology, especially the internet, has had a tremendous impact on social life, economic opportunities, wages, the availability of knowledge, communications, and more. Technologized living has accelerated in the age of social networks. There is some concern that such life will become even more demanding with further entrenched technological pressures. Stakeholders will most likely be faced with similar questions posed by users of the internet; whether it should be a public good, who has access and how to create fair practices that do not exploit people are questions that must be addressed.

- IoT is likely to create volatility in a significant portion of the world's economy, just as the internet did in the media, entertainment and travel industries. Policy-makers and businesses will need strategies to manage the fallout. Learning from best practices in earlier industry transitions will require collaboration from industry and governmental stakeholders.

Figure 14: Workforce Impact of the Industrial Internet

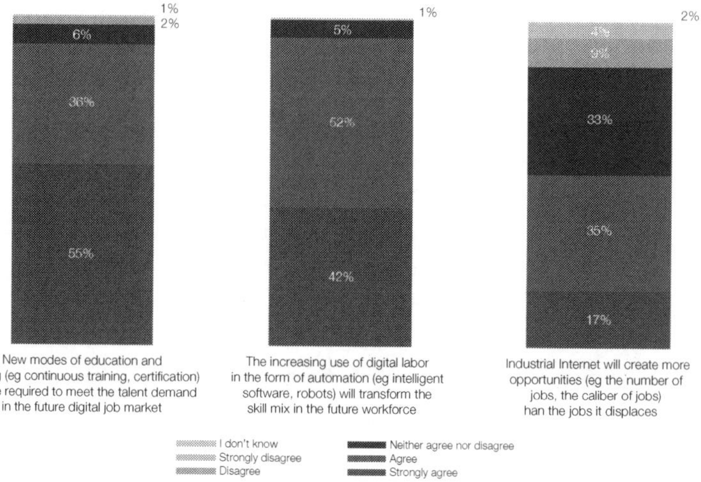

Source: World Economic Forum (2015)

Five key ideas

1. IoT consists of a range of smart and connected sensors that gather and communicate data to other devices or individuals across the internet for a wide variety of uses. IoT will enhance human and machine interaction, and the machine-to-machine data economy will grow larger than that of the human-to-human. Tens of billions of devices will be added to the IoT over the next decade and, through industrial applications, their interaction could add as much as $14 trillion to the global economy by 2030.
2. The distribution of sensors and devices means challenges to cross-border data issues, such as privacy, ownership, availability, and more. Policies and regulation concerning global IoT data flows will be a major challenge of the Fourth Industrial Revolution.
3. IoT is about much more than just smart appliances that are connected to the Internet and the services they provide. The real value in IoT development lies in data collection, analysis and management, finding unexpected correlations and opportunities, and anticipating disruption trends.
4. The use of sensors to return close to real-time data could help create a pull economy with positive outcome spirals due to optimization and incentives for consumer and citizen behaviours. This means that IoT could be instrumental in addressing systemic problems, such as efficient energy usage, traffic systems, global emissions, among others.
5. A critical concern for IoT involves the social impact on employment and skills as it combines with AI and robotics and reduces the need for routine or manual labour. The major risks from IoT systems, however, are generally thought to be cybersecurity-related hazards, due to unsecured devices, the lack of standards and cross-border data concerns.

Special Insert

Highlight on Data Ethics

Data, algorithms, their sciences, technologies, uses and applications provide huge opportunities to improve private and public life, as well as our environments. Unfortunately, such opportunities are also coupled with significant ethical challenges. Three elements are particularly relevant: the extensive use of big data; the growing reliance on algorithms to perform tasks, shape choices and make decisions; and the gradual reduction of human involvement or even oversight over many automatic processes. Together, they pose pressing issues of fairness, responsibility, equality and respect of human rights, among others. These ethical challenges can be addressed successfully. We can and must take advantage of the great opportunity to foster the development and applications of digital solutions, while ensuring respect for human rights and for the values supporting open, pluralistic and tolerant information societies.

Striking a robust and fair balance will not be an easy or simple task. But the alternative, failing to advance the ethics of the science and the technology of our informational environment, would have regrettable consequences. On the one hand, overlooking ethical issues may prompt negative impact and social rejection, as was the case, for example, in England, with the failure of the NHS care data programme. On the other hand, overemphasizing the protection of individual rights and ethical values in the wrong contexts may lead to regulations that are too rigid. This in turn can cripple the chances of harnessing the social and human usefulness of digital solutions. The European Parliament's Committee on Civil Liberties, Justice and Home Affairs (LIBE) amendments, initially proposed to the EU General Data Protection Regulation, offer a concrete example. To avoid both extremes, adopting a four-stage scale is recommended: looking at the technical feasibility, environmental sustainability,

Contributed by Luciano Floridi, Professor of Philosophy and Ethics of Information, University of Oxford, and Director of the Digital Ethics Lab, Oxford Internet Institute, United Kingdom, and Mariarosaria Taddeo, Researcher, University of Oxford, United Kingdom.

social acceptability and human preferability as the necessary guiding features for any digital project with even a remote impact on human life and our planet. This ensures that the risks are minimized and the opportunities are not missed.

How can we deliver this balanced approach? In the last few decades, we have come to understand that it is not a specific technology (computers, tablets, mobile phones, internet protocols, Web applications, online platforms, cloud computing, and so forth) that represents the correct focus of our ethical strategies. It is the data that any digital technology manipulates. That is why labels such as "internet ethics", "roboethics" or "machine ethics" miss the point, anachronistically stepping back to a time when "computer ethics" seemed to provide the right perspective. Before concerning any specific digital technology, ethical problems, such as privacy, anonymity, transparency, trust and responsibility, concern the life cycle of data, from collection and curation, to manipulation and use. That is why we need data ethics, to navigate between the risk of social rejection and too strict regulation, to reach solutions that maximize the ethical value of data and algorithms to benefit our societies, all of us, and our environments.

Data ethics is the branch of ethics that studies and evaluates moral problems related to data, algorithms and corresponding practices. Its goal is to formulate and support morally good solutions (e.g. right conducts or right values) by developing three lines of research: the ethics of data, the ethics of algorithms and the ethics of practices.

The ethics of data narrowly construed looks at the generation, recording, curation, processing, dissemination, sharing and use of data. It is concerned with moral problems posed by the collection, analysis and application of large data sets. Issues range from the use of big data in biomedical research and the social sciences to profiling, advertising and data philanthropy, as well as open data in government projects. One major concern is the possible reidentification of individuals through the data-mining, -linking, -merging and re-using of large data sets. There is also a distinct risk to so-called "group privacy", when the identification of types of individuals, independently of the deidentification of each of them, may lead to serious ethical problems, from group discrimination (e.g. ageism, ethnicism, sexism) to group-targeted forms of violence.

Trust and transparency are also crucial topics in the ethics of data, in connection with an acknowledged lack of public awareness of the benefits, opportunities, risks and challenges associated with data science and technology.

The ethics of algorithms focuses on software, AI, artificial agents, machine learning and robots. It addresses issues posed by the increasing complexity and autonomy of algorithms, broadly understood. Algorithms create ethical challenges in the form of AI routines and smart agents, such as internet bots. This is especially relevant in the case of machine-learning applications. Crucial challenges include the moral responsibility and accountability of users, designers and data scientists with respect to unforeseen and undesired consequences as well as missed opportunities. Unsurprisingly, the ethical design and auditing of algorithms' requirements and the assessment of potential, undesirable outcomes (e.g. discrimination or the promotion of antisocial content) is attracting increasing research.

Finally, the ethics of practices is interested in responsible innovation, programming, hacking, professional codes and deontology. It addresses the pressing questions concerning the responsibilities and liabilities of people and organizations in charge of data processes, strategies and policies, including data scientists. Its goal is to define an ethical framework to shape professional codes about responsible innovation, development and usage, which may ensure ethical practices fostering both the progress of data science and technologies, and the protection of the rights of individuals and groups. Three issues are central in this line of analysis: consent, user privacy and secondary use.

These distinct lines of research – the ethics of data, algorithms and practices – are closely related. They form the conceptual axes that define the three-dimensional space within which ethical problems can be identified and plotted. For example, analyses focusing on data privacy will also address issues concerning consent, the auditing of algorithms and professional responsibilities. Likewise, the ethical auditing of algorithms often involves analyses of the responsibilities of their designers, developers, users and adopters.

Data ethics must address the whole conceptual space and hence the three axes of research together – after all, most problems do not lie on a single axis – though priorities and focus may change depending on the issue. For this reason, data ethics needs to be developed from the start as a macroethics, that is, as an overall "geometry" of the ethical space that avoids narrow, ad hoc approaches and addresses the diverse set of ethical implications brought about by the information revolution within a consistent, holistic, inclusive and multistakeholder framework.

Special Insert

Cyber Risks

Ten years ago, you would have been hard pressed to find a board proactively discussing cyber risks unless the organisations had recently been a victim of a known, successful attack. A 2008 survey by Carnegie Mellon University's Cylab found that 77% of US board members rarely or never received reports from senior management regarding privacy and security risks. And when it came to reviewing cybersecurity resources, roles or top level policies, more than 80% of board members reported that these were rarely or never discussed.[110]

In 2015, however, a survey of 200 directors by NYSE found that cybersecurity issues were more firmly on board agendas, following a series of high-profile company breaches. 80% of responding directors stating they discussed cyber risks at most or all meetings, with brand damage, corporate espionage and breach costs being the top three concerns.[111]

Governments have also become highly sensitized to the risks of criminal or malicious attacks on digital systems. After the development of specific government policies to cyber risks by eight OECD countries between 2009 and 2011, the OECD reported in 2012 that cyber security policy was becoming "a national policy priority supported by stronger leadership".[112] Governments' awareness of cyber risks has become even more acute since then, given rising concerns around protecting critical national infrastructure and guarding against the influence of foreign actors in democratic processes. And, in a context of more restrictive regulation around civil society activities and polarised political environments, civil society organisations are increasingly paying attention to their exposure to cyber-attacks.

Written in collaboration with Jean-Luc Vez and Ushang Damachi, World Economic Forum

Yet World Economic Forum research shows that, while awareness of cyber risks has increased, many organizations feel they are far from adequately equipped with the tools to manage cyber risks, and leading practices in this domain "have not yet become part of the standard set of board competencies".[113]

Closing this gap between awareness and ability to respond is a critically important task – for individuals as well as for businesses, governments and civil society organisations.

Cyber risks are increasing rapidly as three interconnected trends expand the scope of the digital domain. First, the number of people using the internet around the world has risen almost 1,000% percent since 2000.[114] Between 2018 and 2020 another 300 million users are likely to be added.[115] Perhaps an even more important trend is the number of devices being connected to the internet: an estimated 20 billion phones, computers, sensors and other devices were linked to global digital networks in 2017 and IHS Markit projects another 10 billion by 2020. Third, as more people use digital systems more intensively, the amount of data in digital form produced, processed and communicated is rising exponentially – market intelligence firm IDC predicts a tenfold increase in "the global datasphere" between 2017 and 2025, a 30% yearly growth rate.[116]

More users, more objects and more data results in greater reliance on digital systems. Indeed, as IDC put it, digital data and operations are rapidly moving from becoming background issues to "life-critical … essential to our society and our individual lives". Ensuring that these systems are able to perform their functions in the way they were intended is therefore a task of both rising importance and increasing difficulty.

To respond effectively to cyber risks, we suggest four strategies, which are as much shifts in the way of perceiving the challenge as they are areas in which to invest.

1. *Redefine the goal: from cybersecurity to cyber resilience*

First and foremost, both individuals and organisations need to think beyond the focus of securing the perimeters of IT systems, which the concept of "cybersecurity" tends to invoke. We should be shifting mindsets to encompass interdependence and resilience, in order to be prepared for the multiple ways in which cyber risks can emerge and affect operations. In this context, cyber resilience can be thought of as the ability of systems and organizations to withstand cyber events, measured by combining the time to failure and the time to recovery.[117]

As the framework in Figure 15 indicates, cyber risks put both assets and values at risk, and are result from the intersection of threats and vulnerabilities. Cyber resilience is therefore a strategic issue, which need to be to be incorporated into overarching business models as well as across operations.

Cyber resilience also enlarges the time horizon for preparing for the inevitability of cyber-attacks. Changing from a perimeter-based approach requires careful thinking in advance about actions required before, during and after a cyber-attack, particularly who should be informed both inside and outside an enterprise.

Figure 15: Cyber Risk Framework

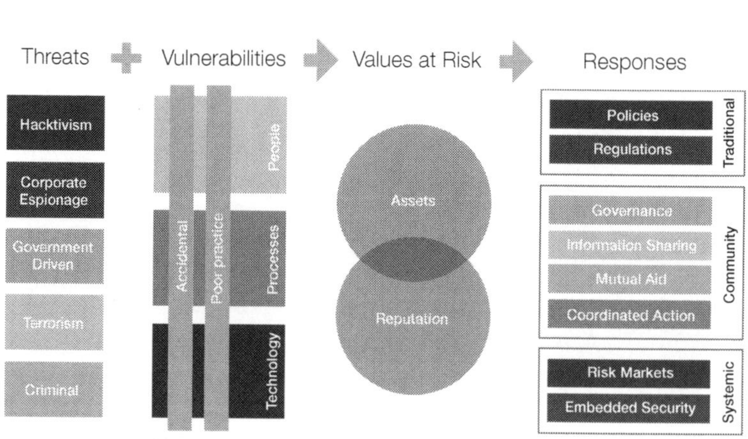

Source: World Economic Forum

When focusing on systems which relate to data, rather than digital operations, organisations and individuals need to be resilient to at least three different cyber risks: the confidentiality of data; its integrity; and its ongoing availability to ensure business continuity. While the leaking of private information as a result of data breaches are the most discussed type of cyber risk, attacks which deny availability to systems or data through deletion or ransom , such as the WannaCry attack which crippled large parts of the UK's health system in May 2017, are increasingly common. And just as concerning is the prospect of data or wider systems that have been compromised and altered.

Things become even more complicated when we consider the integration of data with digital operations and digitally-connected systems that perform physical services or that manage infrastructure. In these cases, organisations must also content with the threat of losing control of essential system functions which could be life threatening, as demonstrated in 2015 by hackers who were able to remotely control the transmission and brakes of a Jeep Cherokee[118]. Another challenge is the fact that connected systems might create new channels for intrusion in other parts of a business or operation. One such case was the 2013 breach of US retailer Target's payment systems, which was traced to stolen credentials provided to subcontractors managing the company's heating and air conditioning systems.[119]

2. *Redefine the adversary: From hacker to criminal organisation*

The most common depiction in popular culture – and therefore in the mental models of most people – of a person trying to access a secure system normally involves a sole, scrappy "hacker" interested in glory or revenge. However such an image may raise doubts in people's minds about the true threat of cyber risks today.

While talented, solitary hackers undoubtedly exist, more common and concerning are cyber risks created by talented individuals operating within structured criminal organisations, which are likely to have staffing, research and operational budgets that dwarf the resources their targets have prepared for defence. Furthermore, these organisations tend to be focused on the financial rewards that a security breach brings – from holding a company to ransom, to selling data, providing system access to others for a fee, or using the system to perform other actions beneficial to the attackers or their clients.

It's therefore important to shift the common image of the source of cyber threats towards adversaries who are well-financed, systematic, motivated, innovative and persistent.

3. *Rethink attack vectors: from technical exploits to human behaviour*

Hand in hand with the "sole hacker" image is their reliance of technical skills to bypass system security remotely, which gives the impression that the main line of defence for cyber risks lies with IT departments and their implementation technical barriers such as firewalls and strong password systems.

However, the easiest way to gain access to secure systems is simply to ask. An estimated 97% of malware attacks try and trick users into giving access to their systems, with only 3% aimed at exploiting a technical flaw. More than 84% of hackers rely on such social engineering strategies as their primary strategy for accessing systems.[120] The fact that most hacks operate in this way contributes to the fact that many go unnoticed for long periods of time. Chris Pogue, Chief Information Security Officer at Nuix, claims that data breaches take an average of 250-300 days to detect.[121]

Given the fact that both threats and vulnerabilities exist within and outside organisations, managing cyber risks therefore becomes a task and responsibility of all staff members. In turn, response strategies shifting toward training employees how to avoid phishing and other social engineering attacks, implementing endpoint security to limit access and deploying systems that look to detect and quarantine abnormal user and network activity.

4. *Cyber resilience as a common activity: from individual to collective risks across industries and organisations*

Resilience is influenced by system-level effects, as well as being a property of individuals or organizations. As the world becomes more interconnected, cyber risks become truly systemic. It is not just the possibility of contagion between companies and nations that creates systemic risk, but the world's mutual reliance on shared, critical global services which underpin global trade, finance, security and transport.

Conversely, there is significant opportunity for a more multistakeholder and cross-community approach to increasing resilience to cyber risks. More regular exchanges of critical information on cyber activity and attacks across industries and sectors, as well as between government, industry and civil society, would enable earlier intervention when an attack occurs as well the ability to reduce contagion risks. Mutual investment in cyber skills would also assist entire sectors given the shortage of expert employees able to provide strategic and operational capabilities relevant to cyber resilience.

Efforts are ongoing to support international, multistakeholder conversations around cyber resilience, such as the Forum's Global Cyber Centre, a Geneva-based public-private platform aimed to strengthen cyber resilience around the world. Other examples include INTERPOL's Global Complex for Innovation in Singapore, which has begun work on establishing an information-sharing platform, Europol's Joint Cybercrime Action Taskforce, and national initiatives include the UK's Cybersecurity Information Sharing Partnership (CiSP), which works to enhance awareness on cyber information and threats for UK businesses. However, working across sectors and countries requires overcoming the inherent suspicion between public and private actors, as well as between sovereign states which are reluctant to share details of their offensive and defensive cyber capabilities.

These are barriers which need to be overcome. The scale of the threat of cyber risks in a world reliant on "life critical" digital systems requires investment and action at all levels – from individual education and new behaviours, to organisational investment and new board responsibilities, to national and international cooperation and more agile governance models.

Reforming the Physical World

Chapter 8

Artificial Intelligence and Robotics

Artificial intelligence (AI) is already reinventing the digital economy and will soon reconfigure the physical one. The early 21st-century goals for AI include helping autonomous machinery to navigate the physical world, and helping humans and computers to interrelate. In the future, AI systems could manage systemic challenges, such as global emissions of CO_2 *or global air traffic control functions, tackling complex issues at scales beyond human capability. Experts predict that even science fiction scenarios of smart operating systems or empathetic digital assistants might become reality. Someday, perhaps, robots could oversee many basic policing duties. AI is already monitoring data from sensor networks and video streams and can alert security officials to suspicious patterns. Meanwhile police have deployed robots for search and rescue, and have also used them to kill an armed gunman.*[122]

AI will change the world in profound ways, and these changes are not without risks. For example, robots controlled by AI will have a difficult to predict reshuffling impact on skills and employment, creating heavy strains on society. Furthermore, the workings of machine-learning algorithms remain opaque to most people, and these mechanisms may reflect socially undesirable biases that need to be rectified. Long-term forecasters warn not to underestimate existential threats if we fail to align the values of AI with human value. They also warn about cybersecurity risks that may occur if criminals trick, hack or confuse AI applications. Researchers are therefore currently calling for the discussion of ethical frameworks and values to guide the development and deployment of AI and robotics. Whatever the future holds, AI will be with us, and the relationship we build with it will have lasting consequences.

Integrating AI into a human world

No combination of technologies has captured the public imagination quite like AI and robotics. A conference at Dartmouth college

Written in collaboration with the World Economic Forum Global Future Council on the Future of Artificial Intelligence and Robotics.

launched the field of AI in 1956, and the first factory robot arrived in 1961. Within a decade, popular culture had envisioned myriad new gadgets and beings that would make our lives easier – such as Rosie the Robot, the household helper in The Jetsons – as well as frightening technological scenarios that would pose new threats – such as Stanley Kubrick's hauntingly disobedient HAL 9000 in 2001: A Space Odyssey.

Today, AI is rapidly improving at performing cognitive functions we associate only with humans, such as general learning and high-level reasoning. Machine-learning techniques are beating humans at games once thought to require human intuition. Computers have arguably already passed a simple version of the Turing test that examines if a machine could be indistinguishable from a human: in 2014, a chatbot masquerading as 13-year-old Eugene Goostman persuaded more than 30% of its interlocutors that it was a real person.[123]

Breakthroughs in materials science and sensor technology have improved the perception and locomotion, as well as cognition, of machines. Flying robots, also known as drones, and industrial robots like those that assemble car parts independently of humans, use AI to perform complex navigation and interaction functions. Self-driving robots, also known as autonomous vehicles, have surpassed previous unassailable challenges, such as navigating the highway system with driverless trucks.[124] Humanoid robots are also entering service as personal assistants and companions, bridging the gap between science fiction and reality.

Around the world, more graduate programmes are dedicating curricula to robotic engineering and AI research.[125] By deriving insights from data sets too large for human-level synthesis, AI applications are tackling such problems as climate modelling and nuclear scenarios, and managing large-scale sensor networks. They are also gleaning new, financially significant information from publicly available data. For example, Orbital Insight has applied machine learning to low-resolution US Landsat and EU Sentinel satellite coverage. This allows them to identify objects with greater precision and speed and to provide information about subjects such as trade, emissions, infrastructure and oceanic indicators – all with clear value to industry, society and government. AI applications are not only informing decisions but making them: some expect AI to become commonplace in the management of hedge funds, and at least one investment firm already has an AI board member.[126]

Figure 16: Race for AI: Major Acquirers in Artificial Intelligence, 2011-2016

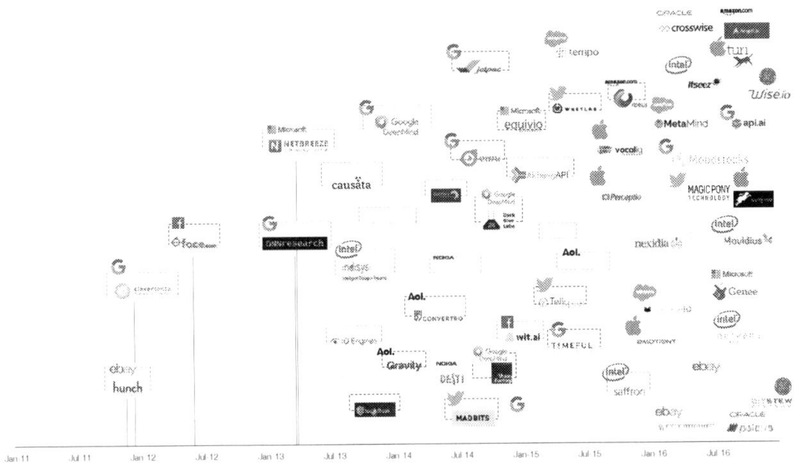

Source: CB Insights (2017)

The better AI applications become at making decisions, the better the robots governed by these decisions will work alongside human beings, and vice versa. If Rosie the Robot is ever to become a reality, machines need to learn from observation and decipher human values. Issues of trust become paramount, as robots learn to carry out service roles, teach students, fly aircraft, perform surgery, and conduct search and rescue operations. As we become accustomed to AI in our daily lives, such interaction may become a mediating layer through which we interpret the world around us, much as a pilot trusts her instruments in inclement weather. And at the extreme end of the spectrum, but not unrealistic or unfeasible, the potential for AI along with robotic applications to be weaponized by both states and individual actors is of clear concern, with various international groups seeking the practical and ethical boundaries of such development. On its current path, the combination of AI and robotics will migrate into positions of power, responsibility and accountability and will, thus, require extensive governance.

Recognizing that AI will have a large and disruptive impact on society, the planet and the economy, some of the leading corporations in the field, Microsoft, Amazon, Facebook, IBM, Google and DeepMind, have joined in a "partnership on AI to benefit people and society". They aim "to study and formulate best practices on AI technologies, to advance the public's understanding of AI, and to serve as an open platform for discussion and engagement about AI and its influences on people and society."[127] In fact, the creation of teams and ethics divisions within companies has begun to gather momentum, as evidenced by DeepMind.[128] This astute move hopes to persuade the public that industry understands its responsibility. They are attempting to demonstrate this responsibility with the billions of dollars invested and the hundreds of companies acquired over the last five years (Figure 16), embracing the concerns of thinkers such as Stuart Russell about the implications of increasingly intelligent AI.[129]

An Intelligent Artificial Intelligence

By Stuart Russell, Professor of Computer Science, University of California, Berkeley, USA

AI research is progressing rapidly, with new capabilities arriving at an increasing rate and leading to further increases in R&D investment. Few in the field believe that there are intrinsic limits to machine intelligence, and even fewer argue for self-imposed limits. Thus, it is prudent to anticipate the possibility that machines will exceed human capabilities, as Alan Turing did in 1951: "If a machine can think, it might think more intelligently than we do … [T]his new danger … is certainly something which can give us anxiety."

So far, the most general approach to creating generally intelligent machines is to provide them with our desired objectives and with algorithms for finding ways to achieve the objectives. (We can preprogramme the behaviours instead, but that means the humans have to do all the mental work, which both misses the point of AI and is simply impossible even for tasks as simple as chess.) Unfortunately, as King Midas found out to his cost, we do not know how to specify our objectives in so complete and well-calibrated a fashion that a machine cannot find an undesirable way to achieve them. This is the value alignment problem: if a sufficiently capable machine is given objectives that are misaligned with our true objectives – even in the sense of being merely incomplete – then it is as if we are playing chess against the machine, with the world as the board and humanity as our pieces. Turing suggested "turning off the power at strategic moments" as a possible solution, but a superintelligent machine is likely to have taken steps to prevent that – not from any survival instinct, but because it cannot achieve its given objectives if it's dead.

We have to assume that a sufficiently capable system will solve whatever decision problem it is set up to solve; the trick is to define the problem in such a way that the solution the machine finds is provably beneficial. This sounds like an oxymoron, but it is in fact possible. The key idea is that the machine's objective is to maximize the true human objective, but it doesn't initially know what that is. It is precisely this uncertainty that avoids the single-minded and potentially catastrophic pursuit of a partial or erroneous objective. The machine's initial uncertainty can be gradually resolved by observing human actions, which reveal information about the true underlying objectives. In some cases, at least, the human is probably better off with such a machine than without it. It is even possible to convince a machine to allow itself to be switched off (so perhaps Turing was right after all): a rational human would only do that if the machine were likely to do something harmful to the human's true objective – which is, by definition the machine's objective too, so it gains by being switched off in that case.

These ideas provide a glimmer of hope that an engineering discipline can be developed around provably beneficial systems, allowing a safe way forward for AI. Needless to say, there are complications: humans are nasty, irrational, inconsistent, weak-willed, computationally limited and heterogeneous, all of which conspire to make learning about human values from human behaviour a difficult enterprise. On the other hand, near term developments, such as intelligent personal assistants and domestic robots, provide a very strong incentive to understand value alignment: assistants that book employees into $20,000-a-night suites and robots that cook the cat for the family dinner are unlikely to prove popular.

AI will soon be learning on the job

AI research has its hurdles. Current benchmarks are set by brute-force pattern matching, and slight changes in input signals can wreck machine-learning models. It may be that current approaches are not structurally sound enough to address the biggest challenges facing AI, such as solving the "common sense" problem or replicating situational awareness. Researchers would like machines to take appropriate action based on situational context and to generalize without having to train through vast data pools, but this is not yet possible. New technologies, such as quantum computing, may be able to change how AI applications interrogate problems and learn from feedback loops, potentially mimicking human cognitive appreciation of the world. If so, they could bring economic benefits by eroding human error and taking over synthetic tasks that lead to fatigue.

Even without such breakthroughs, progress is quick and hopes are high. Robots are being developed to travel to Mars, to assist nurses and even to build themselves.[131] Swarms of tiny robots, controlled by AI in the cloud, may someday feed data via AI applications to centralized servers capable of coordinating tasks and deploying resources. AI is already advancing into knowledge-based professions, such as journalism, medicine, accountancy and law. Even if it does not altogether replace lawyers or doctors, AI applications that can synthesize and analyse case studies and diagnostic images will change these professions. And while AI is busy improving itself, robotics' industry spending is set to exceed $135 billion in 2019, nearly double its 2015 figure.[132] Not only will vehicles lose their drivers, the vehicles themselves are likely to be built by robots, especially since the automotive industry is the number one buyer of automated robots (Figure 17).[133]

Figure 17: Number of Multipurpose Industrial Robots (All Types) per 10,000 Employees in the Automotive and in All Other Industries, 2014

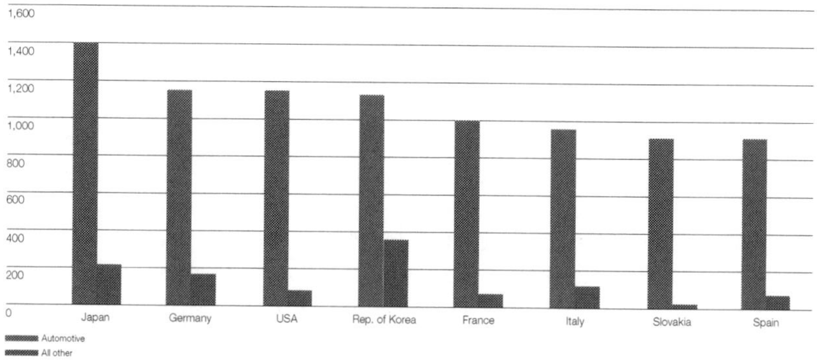

Source: Pittman (2016)

In many areas of the economy, increased automation may create new types of jobs while rendering others obsolete. Automated trucking, for example, is likely to lead to job losses across the logistics industry.[134]

The impact of AI and robotics on labour markets is expected to grow, both in developing and developed regions. In the United States, estimates range from 10% to nearly 50% of US jobs at risk of computerization.[135,136] In China, Foxconn replaced 60,000 workers in factories with robots over the course of two years.[137] Automation could undermine industrialization in developing countries by undercutting their labour cost advantage: production once offshored by developed countries is now being reshored.[138]

The ramifications for the global economy are immense and unpredictable. Economists are busy modelling potential automated post-work economies, and educators are forecasting the skill sets that will be needed by the workforce of tomorrow.[139] The need for multistakeholder cooperation and collaboration has never been higher; policy-makers, business leaders and civil society leaders will need to find compromises between economic and social desires to achieve this goal. Leaders and policy-makers will also need to address the security vulnerabilities of AI. While they offer immense opportunities for society, specialized AI applications are also vulnerable to being tricked, hacked or confused. Efforts will be needed to ensure that decisions made by machines are programmed in a secure manner, resistant to being subverted or exploited through cyberattacks.

Underlying this crucial problem is another with wider implications: the ways in which machine-learning algorithms make decisions often remain opaque to their human creators, which raises questions about the acceptability of delegating authority to them. In the human world, justification and trust are deeply linked. Even if, for example, AI is better than humans at predicting which prisoners will reoffend or which borrowers will default on a loan, we may feel uncomfortable allowing machines to make such decisions, if they cannot explain their reasoning. This is especially true when algorithms show bias after examining data sets that reflect human bias. They can spot helpful patterns, but without machine understanding, we may feel that the decisions are flawed. The most pressing issues for stakeholders to consider include:

– Ethical standards: The creation of principles and guidelines is needed for ethical standards and normative expectations of autonomous processes and machines. Various bodies and groups, such as the UK Engineering and Physical Sciences Research

Council (EPSRC), have proposed "principles of robotics", but no overarching, or global, set of standards exists.[140]

- AI and robotics governance: The lack of general expertise about AI research and applications creates a foresight challenge for policy-makers. In addition, it is difficult to determine which institutions should be making AI policy formation decisions. Recognizing these factors creates spaces for innovative governance procedures and the potential creation of new types of committees, agencies or advisory groups, whose authority has not yet been cemented.

- Conflict resolution: Currently, no established frameworks or best practices exist for resolving conflicts associated with AI applications and systems. Various difficulties regarding how to anticipate the potential conflicts complicate the development of these frameworks. For example, AI research is not regulated, although products that employ AI applications may be, thus placing regulatory burden at the product level.

How deeply AI becomes integrated into the economy, the labour market and other challenging areas, such as our bodies, is a conversation that is still in its early stages. Thinking ahead and assembling a wide range of perspectives on the impact of AI and robotics are critical for anticipating potential outcomes and encouraging diverse points of view.

Ten Things Everyone Should Know About AI Today

1. Artificial Intelligence changes over time. AI today most often refers to machine learning – software approaches that range from linear regression models, to decision trees, Bayesian networks, artificial neural networks and evolutionary algorithms. In the 1960s, robot mobility was an AI milestone. Today, defeating the world's Go masters is the latest grand achievement. Our perception of what artificial intelligence is and can do shifts every time a major milestone is passed.

2. Artificial General Intelligence doesn't exist, but we are already surrounded by "narrow AI". Today's AI systems are getting rapidly better at specific, well-defined tasks, but still lack the broader context and common sense that humans take for granted. Meanwhile, Google's search algorithm, the conversational capabilities of Apple's Siri and

the way your smartphone predicts the next word you'll type are all driven by task specific narrow AI. Other important but less visible applications of AI include choosing which online advertisements to display, supporting cybersecurity, controlling industrial robots, driving autonomous vehicles, summarizing text and diagnosing certain diseases.

3. AI, robots and humans work better when they work together. Human chess players in collaboration with AI chess programmes consistently beat both other humans and other computers working on their own. Intelligent robots also benefit from collaboration with humans – Carnegie Mellon's CoBot programme uses collaborative robots that guide visitors to meetings and perform tasks like fetching documents. The CoBots proactively ask for help from humans to do things like pick up objects, call a lift, or find their way home if they get lost.

4. AI systems need our help in setting goals. We may be worrying too much about the prospect of an "artificial superintelligence" in the near future, but there's no doubt that AI systems can have harmful or unintended consequences if we don't take care when orienting them towards particular goals. As Stuart Russell states elsewhere in this chapter, the key to success is in training an AI to observe people and align its objectives with human objectives and values.

5. Many of today's AI systems act as black boxes. We don't yet understand fully how some of the most popular machine-learning algorithms, such as artificial neural nets and deep learning approaches arrive at their conclusions. Unpacking their processes is technically possible, but the AI will likely modify its approach for the next decision. This means it is difficult to verify results, and in some ways limits the ability for humans to learn from machines as they make independent decisions.

6. AI resources are open and available today. Much of the most innovative work in machine learning is being done by university research departments and entrepreneurs around the world. A significant proportion of this knowledge is open source, and for good reason; without transparency, it won't be easy for us to isolate problems and make critical adjustments. It only takes minutes to find a cloud-based, AI-driven "bot" that can help with custom natural language processing or image recognition.

7. Using AI requires individuals to get their data in order. While a number of AI systems help people make sense of data from outside

their organization, to apply machine learning to proprietary data means making sure it is organized and protected appropriately. Data management is one of the biggest challenges for many organizations. Luckily, some AI systems are being developed to help search and discover data in company systems and servers, as well as organize it to achieve this prerequisite.

8. Even the smartest AI systems can be biased and fallible. The accuracy and usefulness of any algorithms depends on both how they are designed and the nature of the data they are trained on. There are numerous cases of powerful algorithms displaying bias or producing highly inaccurate responses thanks to misspecification or unrepresentative training data.

9. AI and robotics will transform tasks rather than make humans obsolete. With notable exceptions (such as delivery drivers and check-out assistants), a very small proportion of occupations are fully automatable. Instead, as analysis by AlphaBeta has shown, the biggest impact of AI and robotics on the future of work will be the automation of a range of repetitive or technical tasks, freeing up people's time for more interpersonal and creative work.

10. The impact of AI and robotics depends on how we adopt them. The way that AI and robotics systems are applied by organizations to real-life problems is the primary driver of their impact. This means that, as AI and robotic systems become more powerful and capable, the decision-making processes for boards and managers in determining where and when to use them also rise in importance.

Five key ideas

1. AI has improved rapidly in recent years due to machine-learning techniques that take advantage of the increase in available data, sensors and processing power. Machine learning has reached a level where it is capable of mimicking close to (or better than) human-level interaction in constrained scenarios involving areas such as gameplay, customer service queries, medical diagnostics and the navigation of autonomous vehicles.
2. Robotic potential has increased in the last decade as AI has begun to power new physical systems. Humans and machines, working together, will likely begin to take over and reduce the number of roles traditionally needed for educated or skilled persons, such as doctors, lawyers, pilots and truck drivers. This is creating concern about the

role of human expertise and to what extent human intelligence and judgement will be needed for many tasks that could be given over to automated systems.

3. Companies are putting AI to work to gain insights from large caches of freely available data, such as satellite data, and innovative entrepreneurs are creating new sources of value from this data. AI, as a generator of new insights from freely available data, is an important new contributor to economic and scientific knowledge, and could be very beneficial for policy making related to areas such as environmental monitoring and protection.
4. Ethical concerns about AI and robotics are a particularly high priority for many people and organisations, as AI is capable of having an impact everywhere from the labour market to vehicle navigation to decisions about creditworthiness. These ethical concerns are often related to transparency issues, consent and forms of bias embedded in the algorithms that power the AI.
5. AI and robotics will require collaborative governance as issues involving conflict resolution, ethical standards, data regulation and policy formation become priorities at the global scale. For example, robots controlled by AI, such as lethal autonomous weapons, are of deep ethical concern to international organizations that see their potential for harm in both global conflict zones and in domestic scenarios.

Chapter 9

Advanced Materials

Materials are the building blocks of innovation in the Fourth Industrial Revolution. Over the next 20 years, the ability to manipulate the material foundations of many technologies, beginning at the atomic level, may help solve some of the world's most daunting challenges. Thanks to the virtuous feedback loop of innovation created by the application of materials science in the miniaturization of computing technologies, computing technologies are helping scientists in a variety of fields to create new products that range from synthetic organisms to graphene batteries.

The potential for sensors to transform heat waste into electricity, or for nanobots to deliver drugs that repair cellular damage, or for materials science to solve myriad challenges can only be realized through careful assessment and investments with a long-term vision. Just as new materials and nanotechnologies can be used beneficially, nanopollutants can cause devastating ecological damage, nanosensors can create serious privacy and security risks, and new martial capabilities can be used to enhance explosives and chemical weapons. Common frameworks for governance, as well as greater research on the ecological implications of materials, are needed if industries, societies and the environment are to maximize the benefit of how we manipulate the physical world and minimize the unforeseen harm.

Convergence, cost and reducing timelines

Advanced materials science will impact most, if not all, aspects of the Fourth Industrial Revolution (Figure 18). They are crucial for technologies ranging from energy generation, transmission and storage to water filtration and consumer electronics. They may not be visible in all cases, but they will, quite literally, create a different material world. They will reorder supply chains, transform the environment and change consumption. Industries require these materials to satisfy increasingly demanding performance

Contributed by Alán Aspuru-Guzik, Professor, Department of Chemistry and Chemical Biology, Harvard University, USA, and the World Economic Forum Global Future Council on the Future of Advanced Materials.

requirements. The world needs the manufacturing processes for these materials to be sustainable to meet the greater global challenges for human civilization. Furthermore, converging technologies and sciences will help deliver the greatest possible gains from advanced materials and nanotechnology. For example, the development of AI and robotics platforms, combined with the development of mature start-up ecosystems, may rapidly accelerate innovation in this space.

Ideally, the components of advanced materials would be sourced in an ecologically responsible manner, be composed of earth-abundant raw materials and be manufactured using green processes well-integrated in a circular economy. They would also feature low toxicities with minimal damage to the environment. However, market incentives alone – including consumer demand and reputational risk – may fail to force manufacturers of new materials to accept responsibility for their environmental impacts.

As new materials are introduced into the market, strategies for their effective recycling, repurposing and reuse will need to be implemented. Besides consumer drivers and reputational hazards, government regulation will be crucial to making manufacturers responsible for the environmental impacts. Luckily, to meet our sustainability goals, other technologies of the Fourth Industrial Revolution provide innovative solutions in this governance space. For example, the integration of materials with blockchain technologies could aid in the implementation of a global database for trusted materials sourcing and recycling provenance records. In addition, databases can foster connectivity among different industry players so that they are able to add value and recyclability opportunities to the waste of others.

Another issue requiring attention is the profitability of new technologies. The requirements for higher performance and reduced cost in the manufacturing of materials are affecting the bottom line. For example, humanity has never stored energy at the scale needed for mass utilities. Terawatts of energy storage will be required for the renewable energy transition due to the intrinsic intermittency of these energy sources. One innovation to cut the costs of mass energy storage is the flow battery. These are promising candidates for energy storage, but the cost of high-performing membranes and electrolytes would need to be reduced by 50% for them to be competitive in most energy markets. Some flow batteries, however, involve transition metals, such as vanadium, that are not earth-abundant enough to store energy required for a widespread clean-energy scenario.

Figure 18: Examples of Products from Chemistry and Advanced Materials Used in Key Technologies

		Growth rates for key innovations	Examples of relevant products from chemistry and advanced materials
MOBILITY	Electric vehicles	Annual sales of electric vehicles 2020: 4.9 million	Plastic, composites and battery technologies
	Drones	Market size for drones* 2015: $10.1 billion 2020: $14.9 billion	Plastic, composites and battery technologies
MOBILE AND SMART DEVICES	Smartphones and tablets	Mobile devices in use 2015: 8.6 billion 2020: 12.1 billion	Substrate, backplane, transparent conductor, barrier films and photoresists
	Flexible displays (e.g. wearable devices, VR, TVs)	Market for AMOLED** displays 2016: $2 billion 2020: 12.1 billion	Substrate, backplane, transparent conductor, barrier films and photoresists
CONNECTIVITY AND COMPUTING	High-speed internet	Fixed broadband speed 2015: 24.7 Mbps 2020: 47.7 Mbps	Ultrapure glassis chlorosilane
	More efficient and smaller integrated circuits	Processor logic gate length 2015: 14mm 2019: 7mm	Dielectrics, colloidal silica, photo resists, yield enhancers and edge-bead removers

* Defence, commercial and homeland security sectors
** Active-Matrix Organic LED

Source: World Economic Forum (2017a)

Materials discovery, development and implementation have traditionally been capital intensive. They have also involved long timelines, with a new materials technology typically reaching the market after 10 to 20 years of basic and applied research. Here, too, other Fourth Industrial Revolution technologies could help. Platforms that use AI and large-materials databases coupled to robotics promise a holistic accelerated process of the discovery of materials. Knowledge transfer across industry verticals is yet another challenge and opportunity to advance materials discovery. The transformation of current materials discovery pipelines into these integrated platforms requires buy-in from government, industry and start-up stakeholders. Continued research and long-term investment, as well as multistakeholder dialogues, will be needed to push the industry forward.

The Expanding Application of Advanced Materials

By Bernard Meyerson, Chief Innovation Officer, IBM Corporation, USA

To assert that advanced materials are the stuff of life probably badly understates the reality. It is clear from a historical perspective that advancements in materials have been transformational, as evidenced by the nomenclature for societal descriptors, such as the Stone Age, the Bronze Age and the Iron Age. The evolution of tooling alone made possible in each era revolutionized life on the planet, but as of late the pace of that evolution has accelerated dramatically.

To put things in perspective, materials advancements in just one system, semiconductors, have revolutionized modern society. The pervasive deployment of computing and communications technologies has resulted from a greater than millionfold improvement in semiconductor technology over the past four decades. In roughly 40 years we have gone from sending men to the moon employing ~4,000 bytes of computer memory to smartphones routinely accessing 64 billion bytes of data, driven by tremendous advancements in the underlying materials science. A challenge is that no such trend continues forever, and discontinuities in long-established trends can be highly disruptive.

Steady advances have reduced the dimensions of semiconductor materials in transistor layers to mere atoms in thickness. At such dimensions, quantum mechanical behaviours emerge, rendering the material useless for next generation applications. As such, advanced materials R&D seeking alternative paths forward is a major focus of the impacted industries. Recognizing the enormity of this challenge, it is already possible to see dramatic shifts as to where further progress in information technology will be derived and the skills required in that pursuit.

Virtually no endeavour developing advanced materials lacks societal impact. In fact, the societal impacts and interdependencies of such efforts are quite remarkable. Consider the challenge of providing potable water for a global society that is growing by several billion individuals in the coming two decades. As present aquifers and reservoirs are exhausted, energy intensive water sources, such as desalinization, become vital means to supplement existing supplies. Purification via reverse osmosis, which underlies this process, will demand ever more efficient membrane materials if this option is to scale adequately.

However, even with significant membrane improvements, this effort will demand vast new energy resources. Once again, advanced materials will be called upon to address this challenge.

The ability to generate power without adding to global warming requires dramatic advances in materials associated with energy production. Renewable energy via photovoltaics, solar thermal, wind power and the like can all benefit from advancements in their respective material systems. Perhaps more importantly, the ability to efficiently store and release such energy, through materials greatly enhancing battery technologies, makes such renewable sources more practical in displacing traditional generation capacity. In a parallel vein, advances allowing the encapsulation of nuclear fuel could potentially enable economical nuclear reactors utilizing gas cooling that are inherently safe given fuel containment and the option of resorting to passive air cooling in the event of a failure.

The global challenges we face as society deals with ever-expanding demands on our natural resources in the face of diminishing availability require that we continue to innovate in numerous technical and societal areas offering the potential to mitigate emergent issues. Advances in materials are one of the options providing great promise in developing solutions to our most pressing issues.

Inspiration, collaboration and capital investment

Collective benefits from materials science and nanotechnology will require collaborative efforts. The formation of a multidisciplinary workforce for the discovery, production and integration of advanced materials will necessitate support from academia, government and industry. International coalitions around these topics are critical to driving the advanced materials agenda forward. Thankfully, examples of collaborative efforts already exist in this space, for instance research projects such as the Materials Genome Initiative, as well as concerned international coalitions such as Mission Innovation, a 23-country coalition developing an advanced energy materials discovery platform.

To accelerate the discovery and implementation of new materials, the chemical industry is already taking a cue from other innovation models. For example, in the software industry, the combination of large industry players with sophisticated venture capital and start-up ecosystems has catalysed a virtuous cycle of development and growth. The start-up scene in new materials is less vigorous – but that could change with materials incubators that offer appropriate infrastructure and incentives. Investors aware of the longer-term nature of this area of science and technology must recognize this potential. With the right support, young companies could coexist with large multinational consortia, abiding by the appropriate interaction cultures and mechanisms.

Such a development sandbox could lead to mutually beneficial, yet disruptive innovation outcomes, creating materials functioning as the foundations for new technologies and industries. In the far future, when technologies such as long-distance human space travel and nuclear fusion are commonplace, materials with unprecedented requirements, such as resistance to high levels of radiation, will drive these applications. In space colonies, for example, in situ manufacturing from raw sources would require the development and deployment of miniaturized modular factories as transformational to humanity then as 3D printers are today.

As the Fourth Industrial Revolution unfolds, our world will continue to need solutions to material problems, and material problems will need solutions delivered by collaborative leaders with a long-term perspective and creative minds, individuals who can focus on the imposing priority of risk mitigation.

Figure 19: US National Nanotechnology Initiative Funding Has Exceeded $1 Billion for More than a Decade

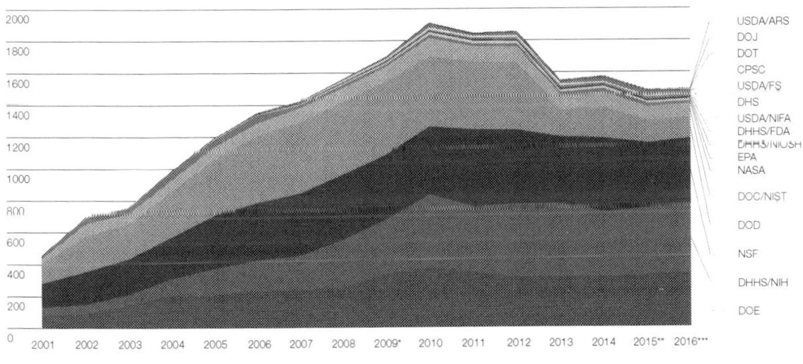

* 2009 figures do not include American Recovery and Reinvestment Act funds for DOE ($293 million), NSF ($101 million), NIST ($43 million), and NIH ($73 million).
** 2015 estimated based on 2015 enacted levels and may shift as operating plans are finalized.
*** 2016 Budget.

Source: US National Nanotechnology Initiative (2017)

In the early 2000s, nanotechnologies received much attention, focused on the potential risks of nanoparticles, nanopollutants and the infamous "grey goo". Since then, government funding has increased across differing government organizations (Figure 19). Attention to nanotechnology and stakeholder concerns has led to international policy recommendations, such as the International Risk Governance Council's policy briefings in the cosmetic and food industries. Currently, however, the broader discussion includes new risks to privacy from nanobots and nanosensors that can infiltrate secure areas, as well as risk to safety from nanomaterials used to create explosives and chemical weapons. Add irreversible damage to human health and the environment from other products containing engineered materials and plenty of concerns demand our attention.

The variety of fields in which advanced materials and nanotechnologies could be applied makes creating a one-size-fits-all policy framework nevertheless difficult. Industry dependency on materials leaves no alternative but to tackle the relevant issues. Among those concerns that coalitions of stakeholders need to consider, to manage risks and inspire innovation in materials development, are:

- Lack of consensus on the problems that can be solved through technology application versus through incentive structures and behavioural change. Given that nations at different stages on the development curve may tolerate risks unevenly in pursuit of economic advantage, aligning priorities at the international level is critical. Stakeholders should work together to establish international communication and global governance.

- Limited knowledge about the ecological effects of new materials and nanotechnologies, or their impact on health-related issues, presents problems for the creation of standardized policies. Increased research, longitudinal studies and institutional principles that prioritize health and safety for people and the environment would help assuage fears regarding the potentially harmful application of nanotechnologies.

- Intellectual property hurdles impede efforts to incentivize information sharing that would provide a better understanding of what is occurring in the field. Without clear information about what is accomplished, creating effective policies that concern safety and risk mitigation also becomes difficult. Reducing the legal obstructions for sharing would have the added benefit of helping spur innovation.

- As the economic feasibility to scale production of advanced materials and nanotechnologies becomes a challenge, the potential for widespread environmental or health-related externalities to affect cross-border relationships increases. Cooperative and collaborative international leadership will be needed to manage the application of these transformative technologies.

Five key ideas

1. Advances in materials science are upgrading the capabilities of the technologies that order the world and impact our lives. Components of advanced materials will become parts of technologies in every industry and will need to be sourced in an ecologically responsible way. Manufacturers will have to accept responsibility for environmental impacts instead of passing responsibility down the value chain.
2. The materials development timelines from investment to market are typically very long (in the order of decades) and capital intensive. Investment in developing databases and the integration of machine learning can help accelerate the timelines, but a lack of long-term thinking around investment threatens the innovation cycle.
3. The convergence of technologies, and the resulting innovation opportunities, means that collaborative efforts from experts, government and industry will be needed to push the agenda for advanced materials forward. For example, opening up funding and employing other technologies such as distributed ledgers, could help create and maintain databases for sourcing trusted materials and improve provenance records.
4. The risks involved with advanced materials and nanotechnology, and the need for multistakeholder collaboration, highlight the variety of issues involved and mean that a one-size-fits-all framework is unlikely to be the best strategy. The reaction to nanotechnologies – the investment, oversight, policy recommendations – is a good case study for thinking about how society, experts and regulators have approached similar challenges.
5. Major issues facing advanced materials include the lack of consensus on the problems, limited knowledge about the ecological effects, intellectual property hurdles, cross-border application risks and knowledge transfer impediments to scaling.

Chapter 10

Additive Manufacturing and Multidimensional Printing

In today's wealthiest societies, people source their goods and food from all over the world through physical supply chains. 3D printing could change all that. In the future, we may revitalize the local production of personal consumption goods, such as clothing, electronics and tools, as well as industrial products and spare parts. Many geographically and culturally specific designs for products may still be sourced digitally from all over the world, but the goods themselves could be made in our own towns or regions. The supply chain and the physical movement of goods are what might suffer, along with the logistics companies and hubs that have facilitated global trade over the last centuries. Unlike technologies in previous industrial revolutions, this technology has the potential to reduce the exchange of physical goods while adding to our productive capabilities.

3D printers remain niche these days, though they are rapidly progressing towards the mainstream. As bandwidth expands, data regulations catch up and heavy file size transmission issues become less problematic, they will enable new opportunities for product design and personalization, from fashion items to medical implants. Products may become digital recipes with various vendors providing competing versions. But this scenario of radical democratization of production also creates risks. At the very least, it would challenge current regulatory frameworks and undermine the industrialization model in low-income countries dependent on low-cost labour for economic development. At most, it could dissolve supply chains and make internet service providers direct competitors with shipping companies. In either case, advances in 3D printing will bring serious challenges and require the full attention of industries and governments.

Decentralizing and disrupting manufacturing

The terms "3D printing" and "additive manufacturing" (AM) describe any process of creating a physical object through the continual addition of layers of material – in contrast with conventional

Contributed by Phill Dickens, Professor of Manufacturing Technology, University of Nottingham, United Kingdom.

manufacturing processes in which physical shapes emerge either by removing material, as in machining, or changing the shape of a set volume of material, as in injection moulding of plastics or casting of metals. These terms, however, do not fully capture the technology's cutting-edge capabilities, such as the bioprinting of organic tissues or 4D printing, in which objects change in post-production over time.

3D printing processes have existed for more than 25 years. They have attracted more attention recently, however, because they have become smaller, cheaper, better and more versatile. Products now have very complex material properties, detailed surface finishes and machining accuracy. While many still associate 3D printing with small plastic objects, we can now print materials such as metal, ceramics and concrete, as well as advanced materials, which include graphene (thin, strong and flexible), cemented carbide (which can withstand enormous forces in mills or drills, for instance) and ecological bio-based material (alternatives to plastic, and food materials such as pasta).[142] Multimaterial 3D printing already exists and will likely become common.

3D printing facilitates the production of economically much lower volumes, and manufactures closer to the customer, providing faster delivery times and lower shipping costs. This could reverse the trend of separating processing from consumption, which started with the first Industrial Revolution, when steam power reduced the cost of transporting goods. It continued through more recent advances in containerization and technological coordination, enabling offshoring production within labour-rich economies in today's developing countries. With its current growth trajectories, 3D printing could disrupt the entire production system – manufacturing, shipping, logistics, transportation, infrastructure, construction, retail and aerospace companies – with vast impacts on governments, economies and labour markets in both developed and developing countries.[143]

The progress of 3D printing will correspond with other advances in Fourth Industrial Revolution technologies. It will increasingly enable the manufacturing of bespoke smart components for cyber-physical systems, with intelligence built in through sensors, actuators and power sources to generate and collect data. Meanwhile, new computing technologies, nanotech, advanced materials and biotechnology will contribute to the development of 3D printing technologies, creating opportunities for visionaries to determine their use in future manufacturing facilities.

3D printing is not yet mainstream. It currently represents only about 0.04% of global manufacturing, and less than 1% of all manufactured goods in the United States.[144] However, the industry is growing fast. According to Gartner, half a million 3D printers were shipped globally in 2016 – double the figure of 2015 – and by 2020, that figure is expected to jump to 6.7 million.[145] Wohlers estimates the AM industry's annual growth rate at over 25%.[146] PricewaterhouseCoopers found in 2016 that 52% of US manufacturers expected 3D printing to be used for high-volume production in the next three to five years, and 22% predicted a disruptive effect on supply chains in the same time frame.[147] This means that the growth trajectory of 3D printers will reflect the archetypical hockey stick growth pattern, wherein growth moves rapidly from horizontal to vertical.[148]

Mass customization – from fashion items to printed organs

3D printing allows unprecedented design freedom, but it can be employed at almost every point of the value chain (Figure 20). Companies such as Boeing and GE are manufacturing new parts that reduce the need for assembly. Parts can be built lighter, with the reduction of extraneous material and with lattices used to reduce weight or increase heat transfer. Quality control is also changing. Rather than sampling from large production runs, as each layer is deposited, online control systems monitor the part interior for shape, tolerance and material properties. Maintaining the integrity and security of the digital templates used for distributed manufacturing becomes extremely important.

The combination of low volumes and design freedom makes product customization more viable. Personalized fashion items are becoming more common, while the medical uses of personalized 3D printing include customized dentistry and in-the-ear hearing aids and orthopaedic implants. Indeed, 3D printing is likely to revolutionize the entire health industry. As the population ages, and the technology becomes available, we may see the printing of pharmaceuticals in the home. We can already print pills with multiple active ingredients that can be released in a controlled sequence and at a controlled rate. Governments and drug companies will need to consider new regulatory issues and business models.

Figure 20: Where Additive Manufacturing Is Applied in Production

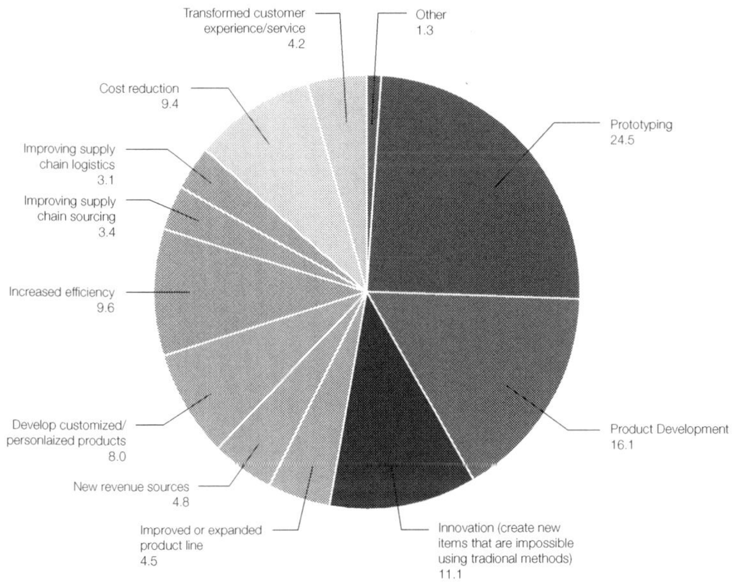

Source: Gartner (2014)

Bioprinting, the printing of living tissue, is also advancing steadily. Entire organs will likely be printed on demand in the future. This will raise ethical and social issues as the technology will initially probably be affordable only to a wealthy minority, widening inequalities in health and longevity. Even more so, the potential for consumers or criminals to hack the human genome will require extensive study and regulation. When the public wields digital-driven analogue tools to transform the human body into a work of art, or a production machine, or even a weapon, society must face critical issues related to our biology as material objects.

Industrialization in the 21st century

3D printing is set to transform production and consumption systems, as well as global value chains. It is a technology being pioneered by companies based in the Global North, with most 3D printing production kept in-country. In 2012, for example, 40% of 3D printing systems were installed in North America, 30% in Europe, 26% in Asia-Pacific and only 4% in other locations.[149] In some cases, impacts of 3D printing could be relatively modest, complementing current value chains by applying the technology at various stages of production. In others, it could be far more disruptive, with 3D printed products completely replacing low-skill, labour-intensive and low-value added functions.[150] If this results in the large-scale reshoring of production to advanced countries, developing economies could find industrialization strategies based on labour-intensive low-cost manufacturing rendered obsolete, leaving them with growing populations of unemployed youth.

The current legal and regulatory frameworks supporting the production, distribution and use of goods and services must also be revisited. For example, if products are 3D printed locally by a 3D printing shop or by an individual consumer, who bears the liability for product defects: the supplier of the digital template for the product, the manufacturer of the 3D printer or the person who does the 3D printing?[151] What intellectual property regimes should govern the ownership and cross-border transmission of the data needed to 3D print a product? How should value added tax and tariff systems adapt?

A final issue that requires multistakeholder collaboration and policy consideration is security. The ability to 3D print weapons encourages proliferation rather than control because individuals and non-state actors can easily distribute the digital templates necessary to print the weapons rather than disseminate the weapons themselves. Already, enthusiasts can 3D print guns and, as the technology becomes more sophisticated, they will be able to incorporate complex materials into 3D printed weapons, including biological tissues, cells and chemicals.

Policies for Maturing an Additive Manufacturing Industry

By Phill Dickens, Professor of Manufacturing Technology, University of Nottingham, United Kingdom

The barriers to exploit the technologies of additive manufacturing are many. They are common worldwide and require intentional strategies and policies to be solved. This work has already begun in the United Kingdom.

The Strategy for Additive Manufacturing being developed in the United Kingdom has identified seven barriers that are common worldwide:

Issue	Summary of common perceived barriers
Materials	Understanding properties in different processes/machines/ applications, quality assurance, costs, availability (intellectual property constraints, independent suppliers), use of mixed materials, recyclability, biocompatibility
Design	Need for guides and education programmes on design for AM – better understanding of design for AM constraints, availability of AM-skilled designers, security of design data
Skills and education	Lack of appropriate skills (design, production, materials, testing) preventing adoption, upskilling current workforce vs training the next generation, education of consumers, awareness in schools
Cost, investment and financing	Funding to increase awareness and reduce risk of adoption (testing, scale-up, machine purchase) – especially for small and medium-sized enterprises, understanding of full costs (including post-processing, testing), cost of materials
Standards and regulation	Lack of standards (perceived or actual) – all sectors/sector-specific (especially aero/health/motorsport), for processes/ materials/software/ products/applications

Measurement, inspection and testing	Need for data libraries, standards for tests (general and sector-specific), materials/in-process/final part, tests for higher volumes, non-destructive testing, quality assurance through lock-in c.f. open access to data
IP/protection/secrecy	Balancing need for openness to share knowledge with need for commercial protection to capture value from investments, enforcement of intellectual property rights

The skills and education problem is probably the most urgent and possibly the greatest as, unless it is addressed, no benefit will be derived from overcoming the other barriers. The immediate need is to upskill the existing workforce so exploitation can begin immediately. However, a prerequisite is an awareness and understanding programme for senior management so they can develop a company strategy for exploitation.

Trying to use existing computer-aided drafting systems to design very complex parts often results in large file sizes. This then causes the software and/or hardware to crash or work very slowly. Even if the design is completed, these large files lead to problems in data transfer. To fully exploit 3D printing, designers will need to understand the physics around the product rather than produce a slightly modified new product. This will require very different design tools and new ways of interacting with the software.

Five key ideas

1. 3D printing and additive manufacturing technologies allow for the production of unique parts and products that conventional manufacturing technologies cannot achieve. Advancing over the last 25 years, additive manufacturing is now capable of producing multimaterial products, materials with integrated circuits and organic tissues.
2. 3D printing is impacting almost every industry, from food to health to aerospace, with bespoke products and services. Additive manufacturing technologies enable economically feasible low-volume production, fast prototyping, and the decentralization and distribution of manufacturing. The growth trajectory for the technologies is set to swiftly rise in the next decade.
3. One important economic outcome of more widespread additive manufacturing technologies could be the reshoring of manufacturing to already developed economies, as the technologies replace low-cost labour. The impact could leave developing economies with concerns over their labour strategies and employment rates.
4. These technologies require more consideration around issues such as product liability or ownership because of the distributed nature of their design and production. The distributed nature of sourcing and printing objects is also of concern because production files rely on data, which brings data regulation policies into the equation.
5. As with other Fourth Industrial Revolution technologies, the combination of 3D printing with other technologies, such as advanced materials, IoT, blockchain or biotechnologies, increases the opportunity for innovation, but also increases the need for collaborative multistakeholder discussion about security, safety and policy recommendations.

Special Insert

The Upside and Downside of Drones

Among Fourth Industrial Revolution technologies, drones hold a unique status. Unlike blockchain, quantum computing and geoengineering, drone technology is well beyond the developmental stages. Drones are in use by the military and are commercially available to the public. In addition, they represent a convergence of aerospace, new materials science, robotics and automation technologies. They can carry surveillance cameras, as well as medication, both of which provide aid in search and rescue operations. They can also carry bombs. They can be operated with individual oversight or via automation from the cloud. Such manifold utility demonstrates their flexibility, from innovation for the common good, to advancing extremist agendas. They appear as multipurpose tools of the 21st century, and they feel like neutral technologies, because whether or not they are used in a way that harms others depends on human choices. Nevertheless, like other technologies, they contain social attitudes and choices in their design, structure and purpose, and these influence their use. Their existence is the embodiment of decisions about what we find valuable, what we wish to develop, what such devices should do, and what we are willing to disrupt to realize their promise.

The primary motivation for drone development is economic value. This is true for military, police and municipality uses, as well as for business applications. Drones have lowered the costs for military reconnaissance by replacing manned aircraft that are 10 to 50 times more expensive.[152] They have reduced flight training time and replaced the potential loss of multimillion-dollar aircraft with expendable unmanned vehicles. In commercial aviation, autopilots have long been available, but according to David Shim, Associate Professor

Written in collaboration with David Shim, Associate Professor, Department of Aerospace Engineering, Korea Advanced Institute of Science and Technology (KAIST), Republic of Korea; Andreas Raptopoulos, Chief Executive Officer, Matternet, USA; and Dapo Akande, Professor of Public International Law, Faculty of Law, University of Oxford, United Kingdom.

of Aerospace Engineering at KAIST, helicopter pilots are likely to lose their jobs first because many helicopter services don't handle passengers, meaning liability and loss compensation are lower.[153] Drones, just like robots in factories, have the potential to add to job loss from automation technologies or, at least, to displace pilots with a growing number of ground operators. This may result in the future of local airspace becoming far more crowded. Mid-sized drones will need to be managed by groups of flight monitors working in rotating shifts, though small drones may be too numerous and difficult to track.

Drones represent a new type of cost-cutting employee working among us and performing jobs that once involved real people. They remind us of wider employment issues facing society in the Fourth Industrial Revolution and highlight the uncertainty over the types of job opportunities that will be available to the displaced. Drone pioneers, such as Andreas Raptopoulos, Chief Executive Officer of Matternet, acknowledge that drones will create massive change and require step-by-step protocol development, all of which will need multistakeholder input. For Raptopoulos, the primary requirement when it comes to commercial drones is that they pose no public safety risk.[154] To meet this imperative and prevent accidents, injuries and collisions, municipalities will need to be involved in air traffic monitoring, tracking and emergency response. From a broader view, defence ministries must be involved in developing the drone ecosystem and its regulation, as well as in tracking unmanned aerial vehicles. Cybersecurity and drone disablement are real risks. Hijacked drones could become a hazard or be used nefariously. Such criminal activity demands reliable encryption technology to secure operations. In addition, opponents of small and mid-sized drones have discovered field-jamming methods to disable their navigation systems from as far away as a mile.[155] Such equipment is a welcome addition to security teams looking to manage vulnerable airspace at an airport, but it could also be a nightmare for logistics companies that may see a disruption to deliveries by do-it-yourself protesters.

Increasing urbanization, e-commerce and on-demand services are also drivers of drone development, along with municipal needs for traffic monitoring and management, infrastructure imaging and aerial videography. Drones are arriving in multiple sizes – larger transport types, governed by the rules of the International Civil Aviation

Authority – and the smaller versions often flown by individual operators. While the military uses large, long-range drones operated by trained pilots, some commercial drones could weigh only a few kilograms and have short-to-medium-range limitations. Several challenges must be overcome to realize the benefits of drones, not the least of which is expanding airspace traffic management in controlled and uncontrolled airspace. NASA has been working on an unmanned-aircraft traffic-management system for several years,[156] and major companies such as Google and Amazon are also submitting their positions on the topic.[157] Such regulations are a requirement for technologies that will share airspace with humans and may even transport humans, as in the case of potential passenger drones. Further policy questions arise on issues of privacy, photographic permissions, safety, noise, use of lights, etc. Such hazards must be addressed. Without deep consideration, commercial developers risk losing critical public acceptance.

Thus far, last-mile solutions are the trickiest parts for the variety of drone service possibilities. Managing public perception and regulatory reaction to the technology, drone makers are looking for insertion points at a scale that will allow societal stakeholders to see the value of the unmanned aerial vehicles. Some strategies include restricting drones to single municipalities and emergency response uses, or offering them as a premium service, to give companies, local government and local populations more experience with drones without overwhelming the populace. The long-term vision, however, according to Raptopoulos, would be for drones to become our symbiotic counterparts as machine vision, sensors and communications technologies expand their capabilities. By 2040, cloud robotics and AI could enable swarms of drones that work in tandem. They could communicate and learn from each other, as well as map new terrain, much like autonomous transportation vehicles. Indeed, a world full of drones offers a world full of possibilities. There are clearly many upsides for governments, businesses and consumers, but we must address the cost and impact on ideals and attitudes.

Drones, for instance, don't just change how we deliver cargo; they change how we think about human rights and the regulation of armed conflict. According to Dapo Akande, Professor of Public International Law at the University of Oxford, drones impact the moral argument for the permissibility of states to execute individuals, foreign and domestic. That a technology can blur the lines of the ethics of conflict engagement, whether in a war zone or in a civilian environment, gives us an idea of the technology's agency in decision-making. By lowering the cost of killing, especially on the grounds of defence, drones can normalize the exceptional act of state-sponsored killing. Examples of the latter range from war to police response. This problematizes the established rules of engagement and the attribution of responsibility for actions taken. Currently, operators manage drones to address these difficult issues. Should drones become autonomous weapons with the help of image recognition algorithms that enable them to make decisions to engage targets without human input, the ethical debate will become even more complicated. The examination of the technology alone, however, does not answer these difficult ethical questions. Deciding when to apply normative measures to the acceptable behaviours and uses of drones is a question for society and its values. The challenge of drone ethics highlights a clear space in which society can exert constructive limitations and agency of its own.

The questions we must ask are whether the benefits and the disruptions are being adequately conveyed to various stakeholders and whether companies are thinking beyond the bottom line. Public acceptance is the critical factor for small to mid-sized commercial drones. As drones become more integrated into the social sphere, companies will need to educate the public about their technologies. For them to be successful, an orientation that places the public first must be visible in their design and management and must reflect the perspectives adopted at the organizational level. According to Raptopoulos, "There is a moral responsibility on the part of the creator." Thinking first about those benefiting or suffering from the impact of drones is one way that companies can avoid the downsides and show societal stakeholders that they are listening.

Altering the Human Being

Chapter 11

Biotechnologies

Biotechnologies will change the future, and they will change us. Firms are already engineering bacteria to produce everything from resins to personal care products, and Chinese scientists have used CRISPR to combat cancer.[158] *Mitochondrial replacement therapy, otherwise known as three-parent in vitro fertilization, is facing regulatory decisions in several countries, and scientists are preparing for a gene-drive against malaria by targeting mosquitos in Africa.*[159] *This is just the science present. The future will challenge our understanding of what it means to be human, from both a biological and a social standpoint. Emerging biotechnology agendas promise to improve and augment human lifespans and to enhance physical and mental health. The opportunity for the integration of digital technologies with biological tissues is also growing, and what that portends for the next decades is inspiring a range of emotions, from hope to wonder to fear. Optimists depict a more sustainable world, free from the diseases that we battle today. Pessimists warn of a dystopian future of designer babies and unequal access to the fruits of biotechnology. These opposing views highlight the debate about how to use new biotechnology capabilities and underscore the complex questions posed by each scientific advance.*

The Promethean power of biotechnology

In healthcare and agriculture, biotechnology provides tools and strategies that can redefine our relationship with nature. Advances in digital technologies and new materials over the last 20 years have enabled forward leaps in areas such as the understanding of genomes, genetic engineering, diagnostics and pharmaceutical development. Like fire in ancient Greek mythology, stolen from the gods by Prometheus and given to humans, the power represented by biotechnology is sometimes portrayed as a civilizational leap for humankind. Some worry that biotechnology could antiquate the presumption of human equality on which liberal democracy depends.

Written in collaboration with the World Economic Forum Global Future Council on the Future of Biotechnologies.

Biotechnology differs in three significant ways from other enabling technologies of the Fourth Industrial Revolution. First, it evokes more emotive responses than changes caused by digital technology. In particular, technology that alters biological systems causes unease in many people who see manipulating DNA as courting danger. This reaction manifests differently in different cultures. Europeans, for example, have been reluctant to cultivate genetically modified crops, despite their widespread use in the United States, while stem cell research has been controversial in the United States and Europe, but less so in China. Second, biotechnology is less predictive than digital technologies because it deals with living organisms, which evolved with very complex metabolic, gene regulatory and signalling networks. Changes to any aspect of an organism are difficult to model, and manipulating them may lead to unforeseen outcomes. Third, biotechnological development is capital intensive, generally requires longer time-to-market and presents high risk. It is a field in which millions of dollars might be spent on a hopeful idea that fails.[160]

Nevertheless, money is being spent. In 2015, venture financing for biotechnology reached nearly $12 billion, in addition to more than $50 billion in debt financing and follow-on public offerings.[161] Much of this money flows towards areas such as diagnostics, therapeutics and pharmacogenomics, the study of how genes affect responses to drugs. These rely on the advancing capabilities of digital technology. Relative to the billions invested, few products have entered the healthcare market. One reason is that much of the research in biotechnology remains disaggregated, with some researchers now aiming to promote greater collaboration and transparency to expedite the validation of new discoveries.

Applications for biotechnology in human health and nature

A major area where biotechnology is expected to revolutionize healthcare is precision medicine (PM), whereby therapies are tailored to individuals rather than to a generic patient (Figure 21). PM is being driven by the increase in the availability of comprehensive data sets on an individual's molecular make-up, including genomic, transcriptomic, proteomic, metabolomic and microbiomic profiles. In addition to guiding therapeutic choices, progress in machine learning coupled with big data should also generate practical applications: diagnostic tests can easily produce hundreds of gigabytes of data, from which machine learning should become proficient at extracting the data necessary to identify issues and to predict how individual patients will respond to possible treatments. PM is being used most widely to treat cancer, but successes have also been noted in cystic fibrosis, asthma, monogenic forms of diabetes, autoimmune and cardiovascular disease, and neurodegeneration. However, PM remains largely aspirational, limited by cost and our inability to integrate multiple data sets into a unified picture of patient health. As costs reduce, we are likely to see an exponential increase in the knowledge gleaned from these large biological data sets that can be translated back to clinical practice.

Agriculture is the second major area where biotechnology has enormous potential. To feed the world in the next 50 years, we will need to produce as much food as produced in the last 10,000 years. A classic example is Golden Rice, enriched rice that could eliminate childhood blindness and development defects that lead to the deaths of almost 2 million children every year because of Vitamin A deficiency. Agriculture also is likely to be impacted by dedicated hardware, such as soil and weather sensors, drones and imaging systems, to monitor and predict crop production. Linking such data to the genotype of the crop could enable a crop-management and variety-selection scheme capable of meeting global demands for food quality, quantity and functionality. Such global food security will only be achieved, however, if regulations on genetically modified foods are adapted to reflect the reality that gene editing offers a precise, efficient and safe method of improving crops.

Figure 21: New Paradigm Shift in Treatment

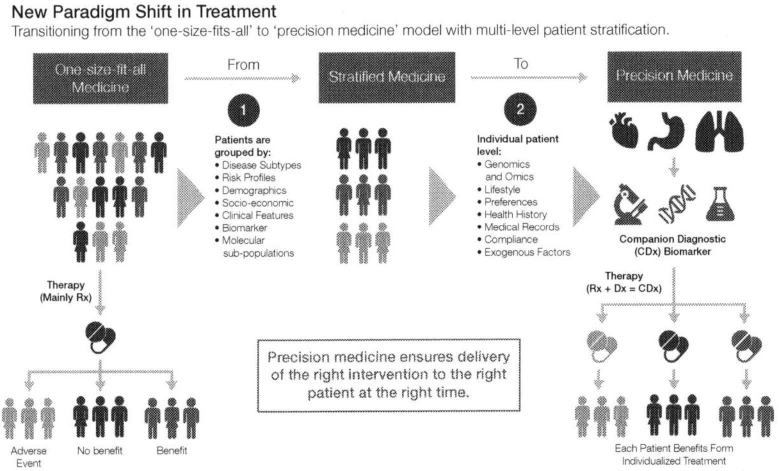

Source: Das (2010)

Yet another area where biotechnological advances are impacting human health is biomaterials, a relevant field given the current historic growth in the ageing population. Biotechnology could help tackle many of the typical challenges of senescence by merging new biomaterials with advanced engineering. One example is osteoporosis, the most common type of bone disease. Biotechnological breakthroughs could enable replacement with bones lab-grown from 3D printed patients' stem cells. This development is closer than it may sound; scientists are actively exploring this avenue of research and entrepreneurs are researching how to translate it into a viable business.

The new wave of biotechnology may also help us reduce our ecological footprint by improving the sustainability of many industries. Large-scale oil refineries may be complemented by biorefineries using renewable feedstocks that exploit catalytic properties of microorganisms. Metabolic engineering, synthetic biology and systems biology are seamlessly being integrated to develop microbial cell factories capable of producing diverse chemicals and materials from renewable non-food biomass.[162] We will continue developing creative ways to harness naturally occurring diversity for the environmentally-friendly bioindustry. For instance, the use of Halomonas, a bacterium that grows under high osmotic pressure, could be used for microbial fermentations using sea water when fresh water is too scarce. Engineering different types of smart cell factories could also empower us to cope with emerging infectious diseases, for example by the accelerated generation of vaccines and therapeutic antibodies or even antidotes for bioterrorist threats. Ordinary citizens may also be able to generate bioproducts in their own backyard. Materials such as bioplastics could be produced in this fashion, thereby democratizing access to products. Finally, contemporary biosciences will do more than help reduce emissions of greenhouse gases; they will also repurpose CO_2 as a feedstock for the biotechnological industry.[163]

Such developments will require techniques beyond traditional lab research, such as predictive quantitative modelling. Biological systems display a level of complexity rarely found in other technologies, creating major challenges for the optimization of biotechnological systems. Changes occurring in one component may cause unforeseen, recursive effects in others. The increasing power of quantitative models to simulate biomolecular networks and cell physiology may allow biotechnicians to link system performance to the components of intracellular machinery. Predictive platforms, coupled with growing computational power and the big data revolution, could provide a dynamic backbone between the conception, prototyping and deployment of engineered biological systems. Ultimately, the convergence between biotechnology and quantitative modelling may underpin the construction of robust and reliable biotechnological solutions within a design-build-test cycle, much like in every other engineering discipline.

The convergence of molecular biology, materials engineering, computational approaches and predictive mathematical modelling is poised to impact our society, industrial landscape and global environment. With such potential power at our fingertips, however, we must carefully consider the consequences of our actions as we move towards this biotechnologically sophisticated future.

Regulating biotechnology

Given the power of biotechnology, many worry that it will be at the root of unexpected societal and environmental problems, especially as we extend the capacity of humanity to intervene in, and assert control over, the biological realm. Effective and legitimate governance regimes developed in accordance with ethical norms provide avenues for society to reap the benefits of biotechnological development, while seeking to mitigate their associated risks.

The governance of biotechnology must be anchored in universal, humanistic values. The future results of biotechnology will be embedded in complex life itself and, as such, unbound by national borders. Regional differences in biotech governance can lead to trade disruptions, and perpetuate social inequality and injustice. Thus, we must develop overarching global governance principles while respecting nations' different historical, economic, social and cultural systems, ethical norms and values. This will require finding common, broadly accepted values and building on existing governance, such as the Universal Declaration of Human Rights and the UN Sustainable Development Goals. It should also reconcile these shared values and guidelines with regional or local preferences, through principles of proportionality, solidarity and justice.

Governance regimes should remain grounded in sound scientific evidence and operate in a transparent and accountable manner. This may entail biotechnological regulations based on the resulting effect of the induced biological change rather than a specific technology. Regulation will have to consider both the means and the ends of biotechnologies in order to be effective.

The governance mechanism should also build public trust by fostering a dialogue among all stakeholders. Over the last two decades, even in higher-income countries, trust in science is under pressure. To advance in a manner positive for society, developments in biotechnological innovation must earn the support and confidence of stakeholders and the public. Hence, we must re-establish a dialogue among all stakeholders to ensure mutual understanding that further builds a culture of trust between regulators, non-governmental organizations, professionals and scientists. The public must also be considered because it must participate in the democratic shaping of biotechnological developments that affect society, individuals and cultures. Such discussion should consider facts, feelings and value commitments, while maintaining a clear-eyed view of the benefits and risks. Only a policy that embraces the result of such discussions will reach the goal of being fair, unbiased, transparent and stable, which will promote flourishing individuals and benefit their communities.

Questions and concerns that require multistakeholder dialogue and collective governance include:

- Building trust among all stakeholders, including the public, when developing and practising biotechnology; this imposes a responsibility that companies and regulators communicate truthfully and effectively

- Defining an ethical framework to guide biotechnological research and use; this requires broad-based discussions about biotechnology's potential impact on such issues as democracy, individuals' opportunities, societal equality and distributive justice, and what limits ought to be imposed

- Establishing agile, flexible and soft regulation on emerging biotechnologies that enables the ratification of technologies once matured and ready for use

- Leading long-term funding governance to ensure that innovation and commercialization benefit all people

- Providing avenues through which communities can parse the use of biotechnological problems and opportunities, as well as determine when and how these technologies should be deployed, and how the benefits should be distributed and the side effects addressed

Biology by Design

By the World Economic Forum Global Future Council on the Future of Biotechnologies

Biotechnology has grown considerably over the last several decades with respect to both complexity and impact. In particular, the ability to introduce not one but many layers of genetic changes (mutations or variants) into cells and organisms has rapidly improved due to advances in DNA sequencing, DNA synthesis and genome editing. Simply stated, the scale of biological engineering and the scope of the challenges these engineered systems seek to address are unprecedented and ever-expanding. This engineering is already taking place in agriculture and non-human animals. Human genome modification is being undertaken experimentally in embryos and in a limited number of gene therapy trials with existing patients. The scope of application is incredibly broad, spanning the environment, agriculture and human health.

Our ability to generate complex engineered biological systems is greatly enhanced by the capacity to make targeted genetic mutations facilitated by computational approaches, that is, to modify biology by deliberate design. Consider the example of the engineering of a microbial cell to produce a chemical compound of interest. Beyond yeast fermentation for beverages and microbial fermentations to produce organic acids and antibiotics, we are becoming adept at training them to behave as chemical factories to produce the compounds we desire. Human insulin to help diabetics can now be produced in essentially unlimited quantities in bacteria or yeasts. With the help of computational approaches to design novel metabolic pathways and to predict the outcome of our tinkering, we are entering an unprecedented age of metabolic engineering and synthetic biology. Not only can we introduce new circuits for synthesis, but we can control their output.

Computational approaches that combine good engineering principles with inherent biological capabilities will transform our ability to produce designer organisms. While the example above describes the engineering of microbial cells for chemical production, analogous approaches can be employed for biological systems as diverse as crops and stem cells. Modern agriculture has developed as a result of breeding and selection for desired phenotypes. Advances in plant genome engineering methods and the availability of genetic parts to modulate plant systems allow for more targeted manipulations, based on an understanding of genotype-phenotype relationships that can facilitate the development of new crop species that are resistant to drought, heat, pestilence and other damaging environmental factors, while providing better nutrition. Similarly, stem cells could be precisely engineered to enable differentiation into organoids that provide an ideal platform for regenerative medicine. Pluripotent stem cells can be transdifferentiated into any kinds of cells representing three germ layers of the body, and thus are the most promising source of regenerative medicine for tissue regeneration, drug screening and disease therapy.

Biological design is incredibly promising. Yet it also gives rise to ethical issues. An overarching ethical issue is to critically interrogate the justifications and motivations for biological design per se. Before engaging in these kinds of processes, it is important to pause and reflect on why they are being proposed or implemented and whether the same goals could be achieved in other ways. In biological design, the benefits are usually justified as twofold: first, the types of applications described above; and second, the benefit to inherent biological knowledge that these kinds of investigations will give rise to. But when considering both ethics and governance in technologies like this, which are characterized by a change in scope (from limited to almost limitless), it is important to think widely and creatively about the possible future scenarios for their application, and to draw out ethical concepts that have both positive and negative value.

As well as considering fundamental justifications for biological design, and thinking creatively and reflecting critically about its future applications, more readily identifiable ethical issues are also relevant. These include the ethical significance of biosafety and biosecurity aspects; the potential for one technology to be used both to benefit and to harm (the "dual use" problem); the just or equitable distribution of benefits of the outcomes of biological design (including benefit sharing); and issues arising in changing the germ line of complex organisms such as humans.

Governance needs to be responsive to both science and ethics and also needs to be wary of "governing because it can be governed" – does a new technology belie governance gaps, or can existing governance also apply to new technologies? In the space of biological design, governance approaches thus far have tended to adopt such a "gap-filling" approach, although more overarching questions remain as to what might be optimal governance mechanisms and how these should be executed in an increasingly global research and commercial arena. No single governance approach has yet been shown to be a standout, and debate continues over issues such as whether governance should be precautionary in scope: only governing to allow a technology to proceed when it is known to be safe.

Five key ideas

1. Biotechnologies differ in three significant ways from the digital technologies of the Fourth Industrial Revolution. They evoke more emotive responses from people, are less predictive because they are organic, and are more capital and regulatory intensive, requiring longer investment horizons. There are also deep cultural stances that affect the acceptability and use of various biotechnologies, and they will have an impact on the permissibility of scientific endeavours.
2. Biotechnologies are set to have an impact on society through their application in precision medicine, agriculture and biomaterial production. The latter would affect the creation of bioproducts for industries such as healthcare and food, but would also affect all the industries for which microbes are being engineered to produce chemicals and custom materials.
3. Many new biotechnologies require heavy computational power, and benefit from the increasing capabilities of machine learning, growing volumes of data and platforms that help with modelling outcomes. The convergence of biotechnologies with digital technologies raises many hopes and concerns about the potential for human enhancement and the promise of biological and digital interoperability.
4. The convergence of molecular biology, materials engineering, computational approaches and predictive mathematical modelling will have an impact on society, industry and the environment. Regulators will need to consider issues that range from scientific freedoms to human rights. The governance of biotechnology could be more usefully anchored in universal, humanistic values, and should operate in a transparent and accountable manner, grounded in sound scientific evidence.
5. Governance concerns for biotechnologies include respecting cultural norms, maintaining ethical standards, mitigating potential biorisks, building trust and dialogue among stakeholders, managing the impact on equality and issues of justice, and establishing flexible and soft regulatory approaches.

Chapter 12

Neurotechnologies

It's 2030 and you're sitting in front of a screen when a pop-up grabs your attention. "Your concentration levels are low," it announces. You realize you've been staring blankly at the screen for the last few minutes. Stifling a yawn, you click a link to analyse the recent readouts from a system monitoring your brainwaves and assessing your real-time mental state. It recommends you sleep, but you still have hours of work to complete. Just one more nootropic pill perhaps, to push through to 03:00? Friends are starting to say that over-reliance on chemical enhancers is harmful, but you are constantly being monitored for signs of Alzheimer's and Parkinson's. No problems yet.

The category "neurotechnologies" describes a wide set of approaches that provide powerful insights into the workings of the human brain, allowing us to extract information, expand our senses, alter behaviours and interact with the world. This may sound like science fiction, but it is not. Neuroscience is slowly leaving the medical and scientific labs to penetrate our daily lives. The field of neurotechnology is maturing rapidly. It represents an opportunity to create entire new systems of value in the Fourth Industrial Revolution, while raising significant risks and governance concerns.

What are neurotechnologies and why do they matter?

Neurotechnologies enable us to better influence consciousness and thought and to understand many activities of the brain. They include decoding what we are thinking in fine levels of detail through new chemicals and interventions that can influence our brains to correct for errors or enhance functionality. They also help us find new ways to communicate and interact with the world, as well as opportunities to dramatically expand our senses.

Contributed by Olivier Oullier, President, Emotiv, USA, and the World Economic Forum Global Future Council on the Future of Neurotechnologies and Brain Science.

The complex human brain is a fascinating domain. A skull has around 1.4 kilograms of cells, including over 80 billion neurons connected in over 100 trillion ways. If each of the 7.4 billion people living on earth knew everyone else, understanding their social relationships would be simplistic compared to understanding the pattern-making potential of the human brain.

For millennia, humans have influenced their behaviour through altering brain chemistry, long before they had proof that the brain was the primary engine of human cognition and experience.[164] Drinking alcohol, chewing coca leaves, smoking tobacco and eating psilocybin mushrooms are examples of how people have influenced their own thought processes or behaviour for religious or recreational reasons.

Such uses have often been controversial. Even benign substances, such as coffee, were banned multiple times when they first emerged.[165] Indeed, from dissection to philosophy, to psychology and brain scans, people throughout history have tried various techniques to understand how the brain works. But now new technologies are enabling great leaps in measuring, analysing, translating and visualizing the chemical and electrical signals that exist in the brain. This will initiate not just a series of economic opportunities and medical breakthroughs but a huge range of ethical and social concerns.

Neurotechnologies matter for three reasons. First, the ability to "read and write to" the brain heralds new industries and systems for value creation, which will have deep social, political and economic impacts. As with biotechnologies (discussed in Chapter 11), the ability to correct deficiencies or add enhancements will be a huge boon for those wealthy enough to buy or sell neurotechnologies and associated services. At the same time, the ability to access a person's innermost thoughts and influence their thinking is a huge concern in a world driven by algorithms and ubiquitous data collection. Could the next trending business model involve someone trading access to their thoughts for the time-saving option of typing a social media post by thought alone?[166]

Second, neurotechnologies are driving improvement in other areas of the Fourth Industrial Revolution, enabling new forms of cognitive computing and improving the design of machine-learning algorithms. The more neurotechnologies tell us about how the brain works, the more useful they are in a feedback loop that shapes the technologies interacting with and/or mimicking the functionality of the brain.

Third, and most fundamentally, our brains are at the core of what makes us human – they enable us to perceive and make sense of the world, to learn, imagine, dream and interact with others. Influencing the brain in more precise ways could change our sense of self, redefine what it means to have experiences and fundamentally alter what constitutes reality. By affecting how we govern ourselves, the system management of human existence, brain science encourages a huge step for humans beyond natural evolution.

How do neurotechnologies work?

As with all the technologies discussed in this book, advancements in brain science have been driven by rapid increases in computing power, the development of smaller, cheaper and more sophisticated sensors, and machine-learning approaches that can discern patterns in huge amounts of unstructured data. The brain works through electrical signals initiated by chemical interactions; these can be measured, desirable signals mimicked and undesirable ones prevented from propagating through the brain, all by influencing either brain chemistry or electrical signalling. Specialized technologies, such as modern microelectrodes, can record the activity of a single neuron, or trigger it as needed. Functional magnetic resonance imaging can reveal how different regions of the brain are active in different circumstances.

Thanks to these capabilities, researchers have made stunning advances in the last decade. Geoffrey Ling, Director of the US Defense Advanced Research Projects Agency Biological Technologies Office from 2014 to 2016, argues that, "In a few years we will look back at the 2008 experiments, where a monkey was able to control a robotic arm with brain signals alone, as a major breakthrough in human history."[167]

Laboratories such as the Aldo Faisal Lab at Imperial College London use eye tracking combined with machine learning as a proxy for brain waves, a technique incredibly precise at detecting movement intentions. Such approaches are reducing the cost of brain–machine interfaces, giving quadriplegics the ability to control wheelchairs or robotic limbs with their minds.[168] Other methods are deepening our understanding of the sources of neurological diseases and mental health conditions, such as schizophrenia, mood disorders and Alzheimer's.

Electroencephalogram devices detect brain waves and, in some cases, emit signals that influence your brain. They have exited the lab to become consumer wearables.[169] Other products promise to influence brains indirectly through sound and light therapy. Encouraging techniques include the use of focused ultrasounds to image and treat tissue noninvasively, and optogenetics, where light is used to trigger genetically modified cells in the brain.

Chemical approaches include a range of substances and nootropic pills developed to enhance brain function in numerous ways. Drugs such as Modafinil and Adderall are commonly used for purposes beyond those for which they were designed, i.e. to promote wakefulness and (it is hoped) to enhance cognition. Such drugs are an extension of the common use of caffeine to raise alertness and promote visual attention.

The increased ability to measure brain activity could greatly improve the testing of drugs designed to treat disease or to enhance brain activity. Currently, more than 65% of drugs developed to treat brain disorders fail during phase III clinical trials. Psychiatrists prescribing drugs for brain disorders have no real possibility to test and compare their efficacy within and between patients.

Nitish Thakor, Director of the Singapore Institute for Neurotechnology at the National University of Singapore, points out that certain neurotechnologies have applications beyond the brain, helping reverse the impacts of damage to spinal cords and nerve endings. Neural modulation (nerve stimulation) can help restore functionality not just to limbs, but also to other vital organs such as the lungs, bladder and heart.[170]

Neurotechnologies may even enable human beings to expand their senses beyond those developed by millions of years of natural evolution. Ling argues that within a few years, humans will be able to see in infrared, record or re-experience memories and dreams, interpret multiple streams of visual information from different devices, and simultaneously control multiple limbs and autonomous objects. These abilities might be closer to reality than we think. Engineer and inventor Elon Musk recently announced that he has invested in a company focused on developing brain–computer interfaces, arguing that he foresees "a closer merger of biological intelligence and digital intelligence".[171]

What could the impact of neurotechnologies be?

Neurotechnologies create opportunities both to improve a range of neurological conditions and physical disabilities, and to drive an industry of human enhancement. Brain disorders afflict tens of millions of people, with an estimated annual economic cost of over $2.5 trillion.[172] This fails to consider the unquantifiable human and social cost of poor mental health. An improved understanding of the brain promises to revolutionize the process of detecting, treating and preventing these disorders. SharpBrains' analysis of more than 10,000 intellectual property filings in neurotechnology suggests that imminent developments could include cochlear implants to restore auditory functions, exoskeletons to help disabled people walk again, and the improved ability to monitor sleeping patterns. Neurotech Reports puts the overall current size of all neurotechnology-related businesses at around $150 billion, with a growth rate nearing 10%.[173]

According to Neal Kassell, Founder and Chairman of the Focused Ultrasound Foundation, technologies on, or just over, the horizon include wearable scanners to image the structure and function of the brain in real time, and ways to regenerate neurons or modulate brain function noninvasively.[174] Such breakthroughs would help to diagnose, treat and rehabilitate people suffering from a variety of neurological disorders, from Alzheimer's and Parkinson's diseases to depression, epilepsy and pain caused by the nervous system.

Neurotechnologies could have a far greater economic impact by enhancing human brains, improving worker productivity. Education and training systems could also see vast improvement by merging a deeper understanding of the brain with personalized learning. And for advanced economies with rapidly ageing populations, neurotechnologies improve the quality of life for older citizens by prolonging their engagement in productive activities.

Governments are aware of the potential competitive advantage of leading the field and are funding major efforts in scientific and medical research. In 2013, for example, the US government launched its ambitious BRAIN project, and the European Commission began its own Human Brain Project. Japan started its Brain/MINDS project in 2014, and in 2017 the Chinese government joined with the China Brain Project.[175] Much of the funding and leading research on neurotechnologies come from military agencies. They frame them within the contexts of defence, and to support returning veterans with issues such as post-traumatic stress disorder (PTSD). The brain is centred at the frontier of warfare and security.

However, compared to other areas of the Fourth Industrial Revolution, such as space technologies, neurotechnologies are moving from the laboratory to the mass market slowly. In October 2016, the World Economic Forum Global Agenda Council on Brain Research published a paper on the digital future of brain health, arguing that the trend in the "consumerization" of healthcare is for patients to take control of their own health and well-being. This dynamic will increasingly play out in the market and through the impact of neurotechnologies but will also raise significant questions about how and which people will benefit.[176]

To achieve these impacts, far greater levels of interdisciplinary collaboration are required. Neurotechnology needs mathematicians, engineers, social scientists, designers and physicists, as well as brain scientists. According to neuroscientist Nancy Ip, Dean of Science and the Morningside Professor of Life Science at Hong Kong University of Science and Technology, "Breaking down silos is the biggest challenge to the field. We need more patience, tolerance and the desire to learn from other disciplines in order to have fruitful collaboration."[177]

The governance and ethics of neurotechnologies

A greater understanding of how the brain functions will raise a wide range of difficult ethical questions.[178] The more widespread the use of brain monitoring devices becomes, the more it will be possible to generate data helpful to understand brain functions. But this development raises significant issues of data privacy and intellectual property. Images of brain scans are now used as artwork to illustrate magazine articles on neuroscience, but such data could soon be as sensitive as medical test results or a patient's DNA.

The justice sector is being challenged to rethink fundamental ideas about personal responsibility, as the link between brain states and behaviour becomes better understood. In many countries, courts are wary about relying on devices that claim to interpret a person's thoughts, such as the lie detector or polygraph. However, as capabilities in this area improve, the temptation for law enforcement agencies and courts to use techniques to determine the likelihood of criminal activity, assess guilt or even possibly retrieve memories directly from people's brains will increase.[179] Even crossing a national border might one day involve a detailed brain scan to assess an individual's security risk.

Meanwhile, the retail industry is using brain monitoring devices in focus groups to understand consumers' decision-making patterns to tailor the consumer experience in physical and online shops. This extends the current trend towards deep data gathering for prediction, since knowing how an individual's mind operates increases the ability of firms to design strategies to influence that individual to act in certain ways. As with all behaviour-influencing technological systems, this is an area of huge concern, not just because of privacy or security issues, but because it grants asymmetric power to those who gather and use the data, while reducing accountability and agency for those being influenced.

Employers will increasingly consider if neurotechnologies can improve the way they assess candidates and train or monitor employees. After controversy about the uses of radio frequency identification tracking and biometric systems in the workplace, employers monitoring employees' brains directly or indirectly could become the next concern. Finally, ethical dilemmas also surround the use of neurotechnologies to improve the function of healthy brains. While some worry about interfering with nature, others raise issues of social and economic inequality; if neurotechnologies that improve brain functions are not affordable to all, a gap will likely form between those able to enhance themselves and those left behind.

In this area as in many others, innovation is currently outpacing regulation and is even outpacing reflection about the potential issues.

Neurotechnologies may appear to be among the most futuristic technologies of the Fourth Industrial Revolution but, along with the futuristic benefits they hold, they are emerging rapidly also with the promise to be highly disruptive. Public discussion about their use in various contexts and for different purposes is urgently needed to ensure they support an inclusive future.

The Systemic Impact of Neurotechnologies

By Olivier Oullier, President, Emotiv, USA

Early in 2017, quadriplegic Rodrigo Hübner Mendes became the first person to drive a Formula 1 car with his mind.

For people in the neurotechnology sector, controlling objects using brain–computer interfaces has become quite common. What is interesting in Hübner Mendes' performance is that the device he used to control the race car – EMOTIV's Epoc neuroheadset – can be ordered online, costs hundred rather than thousands of dollars, and is already used by tens of thousands of people in their daily lives, to enhance their video gaming experience or monitor their sleep. What was recently only science fiction is now mere clicks away from being part of people's daily routines. And this is just the beginning.

It is often said that electricity was not invented to create a better candle. Similarly, neurotechnologies are not incremental improvements of existing technology. They offer unprecedented insights not only on how the brain interacts with the physical and social environments but on new ways to experience life. Neurotechnologies therefore embody the essence of the Fourth Industrial Revolution more than any other sector.

The fact that neurotechnologies are penetrating our lives has raised concerns and caught the attention of public authorities, with interesting lessons for our attempts to govern emerging technologies. In 2011, France became the first country to include a section of law specifically related to governing neurotechnologies, formally recognizing their power to impact everyone's lives. The government's goal was to limit the commercial use of neuroimaging technology while enabling their use in courts. Interestingly, the scientific experts the government consulted in reviewing the law were unanimously against the use of neurotechnologies in court, but were not overly concerned by the commercial uses of brain scanning technology. Nevertheless, the government decided against the experts – an interesting illustration of the regulatory challenges that countries face with regard to the technologies of the Fourth Industrial Revolution.

The pace of innovation and the pace of regulation have always differed – but the rate of change and the scope of impact of the Fourth Industrial Revolution expose this mismatch in ways that call for entirely new governance models.

In addition to governance issues, the process to help neurotechnologies move from the laboratory to the production line as a safe, trusted consumer product constitutes a significant barrier that could prevent the benefits of neurotechnologies from being distributed. Kunal Ghosh, Founder and Chief Executive Officer, Inscopix, USA, and a World Economic Forum Technology Pioneer, argues that a lack of incentives for university-based innovators to iteratively refine and improve ideas means that "many disruptive neurotechnologies languish in the laboratories in which they were invented". Here, the neurotech industry can look at what the private sector in biotechnology, space exploration and the mobile phone industry have achieved in terms of highly successful commercialization approaches and service-driven business models.

Five key ideas

1. Neurotechnologies help us to better understand the brain and how it works, and also to influence consciousness, mood and behaviour. Improving these capabilities could ameliorate diseases and injuries affecting the brain and improve brain functionality. The line between repair and enhancement may be controversial and will require thinking about the impact of how the technologies are used.
2. Neurotechnologies in the Fourth Industrial Revolution will create new areas of value for industries and have important social ramifications. They will also, through feedback loops, help inspire new computational architecture and software as well as fundamentally challenge what we think we know about being human.
3. The ability to better measure brain activity could improve drug testing and help understand consumer decision-making. And advances in electrochemical interaction between digital and biological signals could help spur breakthroughs such as sidestepping spinal cord injuries, providing feeling and functionality to limbs and organs, and aiding the use of prosthetics.
4. Brain and computer interaction doesn't need to break the skin. Objects can be worn that help diagnose disorders and augment behaviours. The opportunity for personalized learning, candidate screening, improving productivity or countering depression will make neurotechnologies attractive to industry players.

5. The complexity of neurotechnologies means that interdisciplinary collaboration is needed for products to be developed and brought to market. The variety of ethical and legal issues connected to neurotechnologies – privacy, intellectual property, accessibility, judicial applications – is cause for prompting multistakeholder discussion about the potential impact of their truly revolutionary capabilities.
4. Brain and computer interaction doesn't need to break the skin. Objects can be worn that help diagnose disorders and augment behaviours. The opportunity for personalized learning, candidate screening, improving productivity or countering depression will make neurotechnologies attractive to industry players.
5. The complexity of neurotechnologies means that interdisciplinary collaboration is needed for products to be developed and brought to market. The variety of ethical and legal issues connected to neurotechnologies – privacy, intellectual property, accessibility, judicial applications – is cause for prompting multistakeholder discussion about the potential impact of their truly revolutionary capabilities.

Chapter 13

Virtual and Augmented Realities

In the realm of science fiction, the dream of traveling back into the past or into the future has long mesmerized people. Time travel is not yet possible, and may never be. But virtual reality (VR) is already here and soon may be a suitable alternative. It can create immersive experiences, such as visiting the battlefields of the Napoleonic Wars, following in the footsteps of Columbus or walking through the Jurassic among brachiosaurus and tyrannosaurus rex. Less immersive than VR, augmented reality (AR) and mixed reality (MR) bring layers of data, information and virtual objects into real environments. These technologies provide incredible opportunities to learn new skills, share experiences with others and create novel forms of art and entertainment.

VR, AR and MR are revolutionizing how we experience, understand and interact with the world around us while opening up the opportunity to experience an infinite number of worlds bounded only by imagination. The result could be more community, collaboration and empathy, and they promise faster ways to work together, develop skills and test ideas. Yet the technology could also be used to manipulate our perspectives of the world and influence our behaviour. Uncritical use could also tempt us to escape from the real world, or at least from parts we do not wish to engage with, rather than seeking to change it for the better.

Altering the real world

VR is a rich, multisensorial, three-dimensional, 360-degree computer-simulated environment in which we can immerse ourselves and with which we can interact. Using enveloping VR headsets, a person experiences realistic images, sounds and other sensations that replicate a known environment or create an imaginary one.

AR and MR are forms of "porous" VR that add digitally-generated layers of sound, video or graphics to the user's physical surroundings. Whereas VR replaces the real world with a simulated one, both

Contributed by Anne Marie Engtoft Larsen, World Economic Forum.

AR and MR enhance the user's perception of reality. AR provides visible information about the real world, such as with the example of Google Glass or the Microsoft HoloLens, increasing the interactivity of physical spaces and objects. MR, in a similar fashion, adds realistic virtual objects and characters into the world, such as with games like Pokemon Go that are so sophisticated that they seamlessly blend in.

VR and AR are not new ideas. Stereoscopic photographs and panoramic paintings were early attempts to immerse humans in a fictional world, followed in the 20th century by film, television and computer gaming. Computer scientist Ivan Sutherland first coined the phrase "virtual reality" in 1968 for his head-mounted display. However, early simulation devices such as the Toshiba Head Dome Projector were unwieldy. They tended to make users nauseous due to lags between user movement and change in visuals. Forty-five years of the digital revolution passed before the hardware became powerful enough and the devices comfortable and accessible enough to be marketable.

The latest developments in VR owe much to the power of crowdsourcing, as well as low-cost, high-definition liquid crystal displays manufactured for smartphones. On 1 September 2012, 20-year-old Palmer Luckey initiated a crowdfunding campaign for a head-mounted display called the Oculus. In a short time, his Kickstarter campaign had raised $2.4 million, almost 1000% of its original target. Two years later, Facebook bought the company for $2 billion with the promise of changing the way we interact via its social media network.[181]

Why did five decades pass from Sutherland's first VR device to Luckey's success? On the supply side, VR and AR build on digital capabilities of the third Industrial Revolution. VR requires the great advances made in computational power to draw and analyse the real world, along with mobile, high-definition imaging, all made possible by developments in cell phones.

Perhaps just as importantly, the digital revolution created the demand. At least two generations have grown up with the idea that what is imagined in science fiction may be possible. They have felt comfortable with computer-generated worlds. When Nintendo released its first video gaming system in 1985, many parents worried about what it was doing to their children's minds; but many of those children went on to design and program computer applications, hardware and networked systems that have become the backbone of the Fourth Industrial Revolution. Video games and simulations are mainstream: militaries, to take one example, use them to train drone pilots to fight in combat zones half a world away.

VR, AR and MR technologies are more than new ways of experiencing digital environments. They represent platforms and systems where value can be created, exchanged and distributed. Offering a completely new channel for perceiving and interacting with the world makes them one of the most transformative technologies of the Fourth Industrial Revolution. However, their immersive nature means that, even more than other digital channels, they blur the line between artificial technology, the external world and the role of human intuition and agency. By changing how we interact with the internet and digital environments, VR and AR pose profound questions about the meaning of how humans experience the world.[182]

VR and AR technology can also create exciting experiences. They enable users to interact with people in other rooms, or even on other continents. A person can realistically simulate being in another country, or even in outer space. It is already possible to simulate other sensations beyond sight and sound. Haptic feedback devices are able to replicate myriad sensations; various forms of resistance give the user a sense of physical impact. This will further enhance emotional responses when using VR and AR. Advances in neurotechnology, nanotechnology and AI could enable VR to be controlled from inside our brains. The prospect of connecting our brains to VR through cortical modems, implants or nanobots is still many years away, but brain–computer interfaces are moving closer to becoming reality. The external devices for experiencing VR, AR and MR will unavoidably evolve a great deal in the coming years and could eventually become antiquated and replaced by internal, embedded "wet" devices.

Interface Is Everything

By Yobie Benjamin, Co-Founder, Avegant, USA

The tools we've relied on for decades to manipulate and interact with computers – the mouse and keyboard – will quickly fade with next-generation technology. Interface will move towards the fidelity of the real world, as simple as the sound of your voice and a blink of your eyes.

AR, VR, virtual retinal displays (VRD), light field display and holographic computing (HC) all represent the next generation of interaction and experience between humans and computers. These technologies are the world's next forward leap, moving away from tired and limited interfaces like the QWERTY keyboard, the mouse and the swipe/pinch of mobile phones. In the future, experiences and interfaces will be integrated with your voice, gestures, physical motion and even your eye movements. Devices such as the Oculus, Avegant Glyph, HTC Vive and the Microsoft HoloLens, as well as Vntana's holographic technology, present exciting near-eye immersive and non-immersive end-user experiences. These technologies can take people to real and virtual environments and provide an interactive perspective only previously imagined. Unfortunately, all the current devices are hobbled by their size, weight, power requirements and setup complexities.

But that was yesterday. These technologies are actually becoming ever more accessible. Goldman Sachs predicts the AR/VR/VRD market will grow to $85 billion by 2025. Twelve million VR/VRD headsets were distributed by the end of 2016 (7 million tethered high-end and 5 million mobile low-end headsets). This number will more than double in 2017 and 2018 (Figure 22).

Figure 22: Number of Active Virtual Reality Users Worldwide, 2014-2018 (in millions)

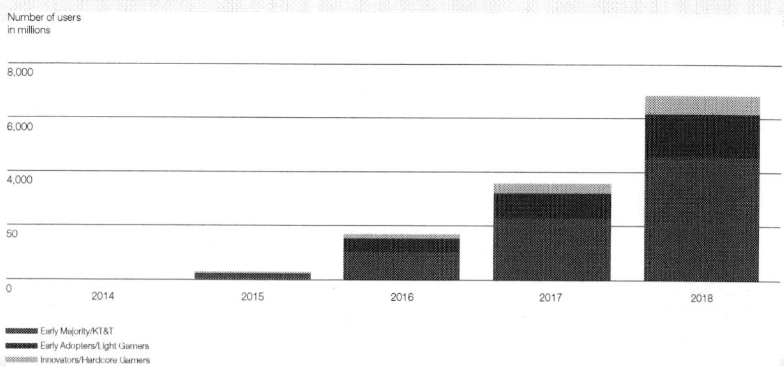

Source: Sebti (2016)

At first, kids – and eventually, adults – will increasingly spend significant amounts of their money and lives inside these VR, AR and MR environments. The Fourth Industrial Revolution is delivering massive technological, corporate, government and social disruption with a speed that history has never seen. Futuristic technologies from Hollywood movies less than 20 years old are already here. For example, 2002's Minority Report and its computer holographic interfaces are now a reality. Star Trek's Geordi La Forge and his head-mounted display, which connected his human intelligence to AI and the universe's entire knowledge base, is reminiscent of current internet and application enabled wearables.

Shippable and usable first-generation products are available for the early adopters. And even more exciting – the speed of technological development is creating faster and cheaper processors, and faster and cheaper hardware that use even less power. These processors and hardware are enabling smaller, lighter and more practical computer–human interface systems. This means lighter head-mounted displays and wearable computers that are fashionable and socially acceptable, like a pair of cool audio headsets or sunglasses. Add natural language processing and AI to these devices and a new future awaits. While we are familiar with Siri, Watson and Alexa and their respective AI engines in mobile and home devices, within the next 12 months, we will see VR, AR, VRD and possibly HC interactions with natural voice triggers.

The groundwork for VR and AR has been laid. We all saw the phenomenon of Pokemon Go as it gave the world a taste of augmented reality in a sort of 2D fashion. Multiply this phenomenon as education takes advantage of these technologies and transforms them into experiential "real-world" education. History teachers will transport their students to the live debates of the Roman senate, and biology teachers will take their entire classes to the centre of a chromosome for some synthetic biology experimentation. Making these abstract spaces real will make education more powerful and immediate to the senses. What we have considered a computer for the last 30 years will change dramatically.

The new computer and its interfaces, which we will become accustomed to, is a far departure from the days of the keyboard-driven 640K IBM PC or the first Apple iPhone. The new computer and its VR, AR paradigm will continue to evolve into smaller, lighter formats and more attractive designs. We may even see the end of the handheld mobile phone. With new interface technologies, we can all become Geordi La Forge and be the helmsmen of our connected worlds. The die is cast. Pokemon Go is here. Smartphone overlays are now. Sales of AR/VR/VRD are increasing, and voice and AI functionality are being embedded in everything mobile. Ultimately, the distinctions between AR and VR will likely disappear; the devices will converge and be multifunctional. Their vast capabilities to blend natural and synthetic vision will cause us to rethink everything from the social norms of human interaction to how private and public spaces are designed and navigated.

Just as the horse-drawn carriage was killed by the Model T, the old interfaces will die sooner than we think.

In the near future, we may face a plethora of possibilities. In education and on-the-job training, for example, AR can be used to aid people learning a skill: remote experts can help local technicians wearing AR devices to accomplish a task they could not have done alone. Massive open online courses, better known as MOOCs, can use VR to enable students from across the world to sit together in virtual classrooms. VR can bring history lessons to life, letting students experience, say, Rosa Parks' ride on a bus in Montgomery, Alabama in 1955.

Likewise, VR can make current affairs more compelling. In 2016, *The New York Times* issued a VR video, *The Fight for Falluja*, allowing the viewer to experience the battle to retake the Syrian city of Falluja from ISIS through the eyes of Iraqi forces. Scopic Virtual Reality Studio's award-winning movie, *Refugees*, places the viewer in the life of a refugee fleeing war-torn Syria towards an unknown future in Europe. VR has applications in live coverage of sports, allowing users to experience being in the crowd at the stadium, and in museums, businesses and virtual shopping.

VR and AR hold great potential for enhancing health and well-being. AR can assist surgeons as they perform operations, for example, by displaying a 3D scan of a tumour to be removed. VR is already used in hospitals to reduce pain medication during surgery. With time, AR combined with sophisticated AI will mimic human sensory work for object recognition. This will enable blind people to navigate and experience the real as well as the virtual world. And experiments with using VR to treat PTSD patients are showing promise in helping with recovery by allowing the patient to re-experience past trauma in a safe environment.

The Future Is Virtual, and Exciting: An Artist's Perspective

By Drue Kataoka, Artist and Technologist, Drue Kataoka Studios, USA

Take a look at the Sistine Chapel, one of the most amazing creations of the human spirit, which single-handedly changed our ancestors' perceptions of what it means to be human. The spirit of the Creator flying in the sky, the powerful, athletic figures in forceful poses, and, of course, the stern warnings of the Last Judgement. Michelangelo's imagination created a whole universe of visuals, messages and emotions that we can still feel today.

Yet, in the not-so-distant future, the Sistine Chapel will look to the Leonardos and Michelangelos of tomorrow just like the cave paintings of Lascaux would have looked to a Renaissance artist – amazing, powerful and yet – a bit two-dimensional.

This will be because of the advent of VR – a new medium for creation, for social interactions and for living life that will change absolutely everything we do, in ways we cannot fully comprehend yet. But let's try to lift the curtain hiding the future, and use our weak, short-sighted and oh-so-human eyes and senses to peek into the coming decades.

VR is the materialization of a dream artists have had since the dawn of history: to play God – to create whole worlds, whole universes, atom by atom, pixel by pixel. They dreamed of building worlds in which one can live, one can socialize, one can play and, yes, one can create. Worlds that are so amazing, so inspiring, that they will unleash a new wave of human creativity and allow us to discover a higher level of human performance. Worlds where everybody is just the blink of an eye – or a thought – away from anybody else, living or dead (of course, if the desire to connect is mutual). Worlds that are not just visual, but tactile, olfactory, aural – creating immersive experiences of almost supernatural proportions.

But will we be lonely?

Some ask whether this Brave New World of VR will be solitary and sad, like a lonely gamer locked away in a basement. Not at all. Facebook is one of the main leaders in VR. The corporation sees VR as the future of communication and social interaction. It sees a world where people will come together, and stay together better than ever before, where distance and borders will disappear. It sees a world where distance or lack of time is a poor excuse not to see a friend, or a relative. This world will be much more capable of direct democracy. The will of the people will be more accurately reflected than ever before, with citizens and voters much more informed and engaged. The future of VR is social, incredibly social. After all, in virtual reality, the family or school reunion, the town hall, and date night don't ever have to end.

A new way of compassionate communicating

Perhaps even more importantly, VR opens new ways of communicating that were previously unimaginable. Instead of saying how we feel, we can fully convey how we feel to a loved one or a co-worker – through immersive 3D visuals and sound, and by engaging every sense. This opens a whole new world of empathy for everybody with an open heart and an open mind, and can create a better, more compassionate society.

We can also easily put ourselves not just in somebody's shoes, but in somebody else's body and experience what they experience. We could become African American or Latina, gay or transsexual, quadriplegic, Hasidic Jew or Orthodox Muslim. Then, we will return back to our original identities better informed and in a way transformed. In a few years, instead of sending an emoticon, we will be able to send a file containing an immersive VR experience, so, through their senses, the recipient can exactly understand how we feel.

Is this the world from Pixar's WALL-E?

Somebody may ask: won't all of this somehow stifle creativity? What will happen to our brains when every image is defined, every sound is specified and every touch is precisely calibrated? Where is the space for imagination here? Won't we all just become the passive, satisfied consumers from Pixar's WALL-E movie? Actually, VR will unleash creativity unlike any previous set of experiences. Creativity is born out of variety. The biggest enemy of creativity is routine. And the variety, the range of experiences in VR will be unparalleled to anything in prior history – not even within an order of magnitude. It is no accident that many of the most creative people in history have travelled more than their contemporaries, visiting faraway lands. With VR, everybody can be a world traveller, reaching the deepest corners of the universe and the human imagination. Also, VR is not a passive experience. Through creative tools, we will be able to shape our environment more than anything which is feasible or affordable in the "real world". Everybody will literally be an artist and will be incentivized to push his or her abilities and imagination to their limits. No, not everybody will be a Michelangelo, but humanity's creative pool will be larger than at any time before.

Is the technology ready for this?

One may look at today's HTC Vive and Oculus Rift or Microsoft HoloLens and struggle to see this coming. However, they are the Apple II's of the coming VR revolution, and looking at them and predicting the future VR devices would be like looking at the Apple II and imagining the super-powerful gaming desktops of today. That's quite a jump, for sure.

This is true. However, the important point is that for the first time, the Vive, Rift and HoloLens present viable mass products, which are also starting to get mass adoption. Yes, they are still expensive, somewhat buggy and at times clunky. But unlike the VR devices of yesteryear, they do not require a full lab of technicians to operate and, most importantly, they work. Those two aspects mark the start of a revolution. Slowly but surely, humanity is getting onto the VR wave of intensifying network effects – gaming studios are starting to create content, Google Tilt Brush and Oculus Medium are opening up creative possibilities and, just like in the early days of personal computing, the early adopters, enthusiasts and tinkerers are working in garages and basements throughout the Americas, Europe, Asia and every other continent. And as is the case with network effects, every technologist, every artist and every user makes the platform of VR more powerful and more useful for everybody else. We are entering the very early stages of exponential growth. Looking at prototypes here in Silicon Valley, it is easy to appreciate how new mass-market VR devices will be smaller, more powerful, faster, more intuitive. Just around the corner, there will also be a next generation of high-end devices that incorporate more of the senses – haptic, olfactory and gustatory. Soon after, those will be incorporated into the more mass-market devices and, further down the road, brain computer interfaces will open up new possibilities. The future for VR is beyond bright – it is stunning. A revolution is starting, hiding in plain sight.

Blurred lines

VR, AR and MR technologies have definite challenges. When Google Glass was released in 2013, it was perceived as violating others' privacy. Its front-facing camera challenged the unwritten social contract that we should ask permission, explicitly or implicitly, before taking a video or picture of someone. It also created awkwardness because asking someone to put down a camera phone is more socially acceptable than to take off their glasses. The success of VR and AR devices will depend on reconciling these social-acceptance norms. This is not, however, a significant issue in immersive VR. In fact, the recent Snapchat AR glasses have addressed some of these issues while becoming a resounding success.

Practical issues also exist, notably comfort, battery life and costs. Current prices are prohibitive, even for the mass market in the developed world, and out of reach for much of the global population. Even if people everywhere had sufficiently powerful and reliable internet access, which is not the case for about half of the world's population, such technology could take years to be fully adopted. The technology is far from being globally empowering and inclusive.

VR also raises privacy concerns. VR devices can learn much about how their users respond to different stimuli by tracking their eye movements and head positions and even monitoring their emotional state. Such information could be used to influence behaviours or even to incriminate and embarrass. VR could become a social challenge: it could increase isolation by putting the users in fully enclosed worlds where they interact with digital avatars instead of physical human beings. The excessive use of VR could distance people from their loved ones and erode community structures.

To address these concerns, a policy framework should be developed that empowers citizens, increases democratization and prevents the technologies from turning into means of manipulation. Stakeholders must ask how the development and deployment of VR, AR and MR can be shaped to foster rather than undermine trust, empathy and collaboration.

Five key ideas

1. Virtual reality (VR), augmented reality (AR) and mixed reality (MR) are all versions of an immersive audio-visual set of technologies that allows people to either place themselves into a virtual environment or add virtual elements to their real environment. These reality-altering digital technologies have been under development for more than 50 years, but the convergence of computing power, mobility and interactive capabilities is now driving advances.
2. The potential to connect VR, AR and MR to other types of technologies that provide sensory feedback, from both virtual and imaginary worlds, could enable tremendous new experiences, but their ethical permissibility could prove challenging, especially if they require surgical interfaces. These technologies will face many of the same concerns previous entertainment platforms confronted, such as the impact on human psychology, socialization and an understanding of agency and responsibility.
3. VR, AR and MR can be considered as another step in the interface evolution, which began with punch cards, transitioned to the keyboard and mouse, and incorporated the touchscreen and voice, and is now moving towards gesture and natural movements.

4. VR, AR and MR have shown promise for increasing empathy and well-being, and helping people with sensory needs. They may provide new avenues for educational media and allow people everywhere to experience other parts of the world and other people's daily surroundings. But there are concerns about their potential effects on a stable sense of reality, as sensory deprivation creates compelling environments for users.
5. VR, AR and MR create distinct challenges related to privacy, social acceptability and accessibility due to cost. The effects of stimuli, sensory deprivation and long exposures to the technology are not yet clear. Treating them as substitutes for current media delivery is too simplistic, as these technologies may have different biological implications.

Special Insert

A Perspective on Arts, Culture and the Fourth Industrial Revolution

In Lynette Wallworth's Emmy-nominated virtual reality film *Collisions*, Nyarri Morgan, an indigenous elder from the Western Australian desert, sits watching a video of J. Robert Oppenheimer, the American theoretical physicist who led the construction of the first atomic bombs. Nyarri's life was shaped in more ways than one by the moment, sometime in the 1950s, when he witnessed a mushroom cloud take shape in front of his eyes. He thought at the time that it was a message from the gods. He learned later that the British government was testing the atomic bomb on his land, and he continued to live for decades through the resulting devastation.

Sixty years after that life-changing encounter, Nyarri is under the desert sky again, a screen and projector rigged to his truck, watching Oppenheimer speak. Oppenheimer talks about the moment of the first ever nuclear test; sullen, he shares the realization, as he quotes Lord Vishnu, that "Now I am become death, the destroyer of worlds." Slowly, Nyarri walks up to the screen. We see the two men in the same shot and, in that moment, we understand how their lives, worlds apart, are intertwined.

In both content and in form, *Collisions*, for which the World Economic Forum acted as executive producer and gave the film its world premiere during the Annual Meeting 2016 in Davos-Klosters, provides a space for reflection on how art and culture are fundamental to understanding our relationship with technology and the trajectory it has taken in the last century. The film uses the latest in virtual reality technology to create an experience meant to trigger dialogue about the unintended consequences of our actions, and in this case our thirst for technological progress. It aims to inspire reflection about

Contributed by Nico Daswani, World Economic Forum, and Andrea Bandelli, Executive Director, Science Gallery International, Ireland.

the desire, or belief, that humans can crack any code, that anything in the universe is merely, in the words of the philosopher Heidegger, a "standing reserve" – an inert set of resources available for the purpose of human exploitation.

The film explores technological hubris, how it is often overlooked and perhaps never truly appreciated in terms of its scope. Like the art of ancient dramas, the virtual reality experience functions to reveal how we constrain the world through our own limited perspectives. The ancient dramas of Greece told us that fighting nature was futile, and that fate was one part prophecy and one part our own doing. Many societies, before this modern era, have understood the world in their own ways, filled with experiences and perceptions as rich and dense and valuable as any technological analysis. Technology in the modern era, however, has helped shape a mindset focused on ordering the world and has bolstered the human project to overcome nature and control fate.

The arts, the original *techné*,[184] provide us with something else. They give us channels to express and to critique our projects before the values and orientations they represent are embedded in technology. In this sense, the role of the arts is not so much to predict the future as it is to provide cognitive and emotional tools to imagine the future and achieve creative breakthroughs. In the Fourth Industrial Revolution, emotional intelligence is especially needed to gain new competency and fluency to become comfortable with the unknown; to remain both hopeful and alert about what comes next; to be creative in how we respond to the complexity of the systems around us; and to be humble enough to know that we cannot understand it all.

Consider for instance the life-size portraits in "Stranger Visions" by Heather Dewey-Hagborg, presented at the World Economic Forum Annual Meeting 2016. To create this work, the artist took the DNA left behind on cigarette butts and chewing gum collected on the street, performed a screening of the genome and attempted to reconstruct the face of the person with that DNA. A work such as this provokes endless conversations about our identity and the widespread availability of genetic screening. While the technology might still be a few years away, its implementation has become tangible in this piece of art.

But what if this isn't only a speculative piece of art; what if the process becomes reality? An initiative in major cities is currently using this technology to identify those who litter from DNA found on the streets, and exposing their portraits for public naming and shaming. This is "The Twilight Zone" of technology in the making, with values and technology running in two different paths, not yet synchronized. Art makes it possible to uncover our emotional response to technology, before we face the consequences of the actual technology.

Through art and culture, we build the capacity to navigate and appreciate what is different from us. We challenge and change our mindset, and can become comfortable with what at first makes us uncomfortable. Through art we see differences not as threats but as new frontiers of human connections, which helps to build empathy – the ability to understand and share the feelings of others. By preparing ourselves for possible futures, we also become more resilient and learn to absorb the shocks of the impossible and think of it as real. We learn to question the foundations of our own world views.

In *Collisions*, we are presented with a sharp challenge to the orientation that assumes technology is for controlling the world. The film reminds us that while a pervasive world view may be taken for granted, that view is not the only one of value. A few weeks after Lynette Wallworth presented *Collisions* to members of the Australian parliament, after more than 50 years of advocacy on the issue, its members decided to include in the federal budget, for the first time, provisions to increase health protections for the people who were affected by the British government's atomic bomb testing in the 1950s. Art here instigated powerful reparations. But what would have happened had Oppenheimer and Nyarri met years before the nuclear testing? Could that encounter have changed the course of history?

It took an artistic virtual reality experience to profoundly immerse people in the emotional space of indigenous peoples. Here, art is employing technology, cautioning against the unreflective pursuit of technological power and submission to a technological mindset. This tangled relationship with technology calls for thoughtful discussion on how we employ it. Technology can certainly be used to destroy both our physical world and our conceptual knowledge of it. But in the hands of inspired, creative and caring people, art and technology can also become means to convey empathy and build bridges between varied world views. In the story of Oppenheimer and Nyarri, two cultures collided – one that valued the world as an object to be controlled and the other that valued it as a sacred space. Exposing where our assumptions and expectations collide is precisely where art reveals myriad worlds of meaning.

Integrating the Environment

Chapter 14

Energy Capture, Storage and Transmission

The first and second Industrial Revolutions were built on energy sector transitions, first to steam and then to electricity. Now, at the beginning of the Fourth Industrial Revolution, the energy sector is on the brink of another historic transition as fossil fuels give way to renewable energy sources. Clean energy technologies and improved storage capabilities are moving from laboratories to factories and markets, and with a broad coalition of countries investing in potential history-changing breakthroughs, such as nuclear fusion, a new energy future could be on the horizon.

The global availability of clean, affordable energy would benefit the environment and particularly the citizens of developing nations, whose electricity supplies are unreliable or non-existent. In addition, sustainable energy technologies could reduce costs to companies and consumers, and reverse the environmental impact of the last century's industrial emissions. To make the transition a success, however, international collaboration, long-term vision and multistakeholder dialogue to unlock the necessary investment in technologies and infrastructure will be required. Missing the mark could derail collective progress towards a potentially revolutionary achievement.

Clean energy, efficient distribution and storage at scale

Many technologies of the Fourth Industrial Revolution appear to be mixed blessings. Along with their hopeful prospects, they can also potentially create inequality, unemployment, social fragmentation and environmental damage. In the energy sector, however, the outlook is more optimistic. With the right investment, new energy technologies could lower prices, reverse the dependence on fossil fuels created by the first Industrial Revolution, and help create a sustainable future for communities rich and poor, urban and rural.

Written in collaboration with the World Economic Forum Global Future Council on the Future of Energy.

Advances in production and distribution since the first Industrial Revolution have given humans access to great stores of energy. The human body can produce a rough average of 100 watts, enough to power an old-fashioned light bulb. Athletes can produce three or four times as much. But the average global citizen now has access to more than 8,000 watts, with per capita rates in some developed economies reaching more than 35,000 watts.[185] The problem is the impact burning fossil fuels to generate this power has on the planet. The US Energy Information Administration estimates that global electricity demand will almost double to 39 trillion kilowatt hours by 2040, most of which will come from developing nations that currently have poor infrastructure.[186]

Figure 23: Investment in Power Capacity, 2008-2016

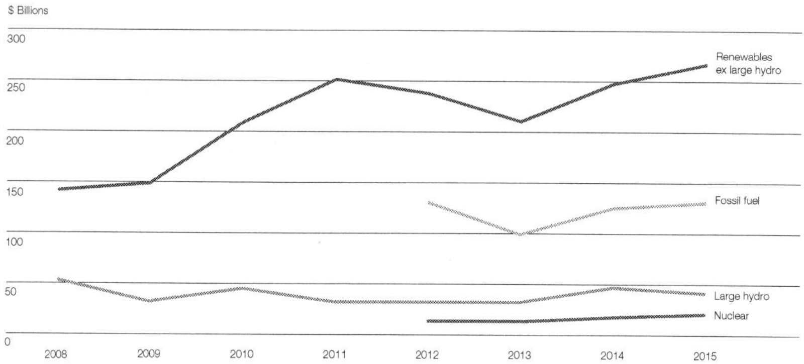

Source: Frankfurt School of Finance & Management (2017), based on figure 25

Concern about climate change, reflected by the UN Sustainable Development Goals, already spurred the deployment of renewable energy technologies, such as solar and wind, to a record $265 billion in 2015 (Figure 23), though the figure dropped to $226 billion in 2016.[187] Investment has also been spurred by dropping wind and solar prices. In 2016, for the first time, renewables accounted for more than 50% of new power production, but still only 10% of the world's electricity overall. To meet our growing energy needs, reduce conventional fuel consumption and slow climate change, the energy industry is under pressure to innovate further.

Optimistic forecasters believe that breakthroughs in energy-storage capabilities may help reach production targets. These technologies, however, need far more investment; thus, keeping a price point in line with the continuing decline of liquid fuel prices is critical. The current rate of $8-9 billion in renewable R&D investment shows a ratio of approximately 1:27 versus other investment spending in 2017.[188] A more ideal figure, according to Cameron Hepburn, Director, Economics of Sustainability, Institute for New Economic Thinking at the Oxford Martin School, would be closer to 1:1.[189] With the right investment, new technologies, such as biobatteries, energy-efficient nanomaterials, modular grid storage, synthetic biological-waste conversion and tidal energy, could make further headway.

Other Fourth Industrial Revolution technologies will also shape developments in energy. AI promises to smarten grids, increasing efficiency and reducing costs.[190] Nanotechnologies, such as carbon nanotubes and nanoporous foams or gels, will increase efficiency and lower energy loss throughout the source-to-usage energy cycle. Automated vehicles can enhance resource efficiency by coordinating them for optimal routes and energy usage, and biotechnology may offer bacterial engineering and the harnessing of photosynthesis for the creation of biofuel cells.[191]

Perhaps the ultimate possibility is nuclear fusion, which – if it works as hoped – will deliver clean, abundant, sustainable and relatively inexpensive energy. The year 2035 is the target by which 35 nations are hoping the technology will reach operational success at France's ITER (International Thermonuclear Experimental Reactor), a facility billed as the most advanced nuclear fusion project ever built.[192] The impact on industries, economies and geopolitics is expected to be immense. With no guarantee that this $18 billion wager on fusion will succeed, however, diversification in energy source development seems prudent. Other approaches gaining momentum include tidal energy and more experimental ideas, such as microwave transmission from orbiting solar arrays.[193]

Whatever the future sources of energy will be, efficient storage must also be a priority. Since solar and wind farms, in particular, fail to generate energy continually, breakthroughs in energy-storage capabilities could enable the use of renewables on a much wider scale. Battery technologies are rapidly advancing, at least in the laboratory, and the next 15-20 years may see further innovations built on nanotechnologies.[194] An order of magnitude increase in battery power relative to volume or weight would vastly increase the value and utility of intermittent energy sources, as well as transform our ability to provide electricity to the 1.2 billion people who currently lack access.

Collaboration is needed to unlock potential

New cooperation incentives on clean energy must be devised to compete with established geopolitical and economic structures that have been built around such industries as oil and gas. These structures are so entrenched that redrawing the lines of fossil-fuel dependence could create major systemic risks. Falling oil prices have already had profound economic and societal impacts in such oil-producing nations as Venezuela, the Russian Federation and Nigeria. A breakthrough in battery technology, for example, could have serious geopolitical implications for regional security because of its impacts on fiscal systems and employment.

These risks must be taken, however, given the threat of climate change. China has begun to invest heavily in lessening its carbon footprint, but this effort will take time. Nevertheless, optimism is increasing globally that, if nations work together, technologies will accelerate a transition towards a zero-carbon economy.

Indeed, the biggest risk around the clean energy transition is that it is happening too slowly. Past energy system transitions combined science, infrastructure and regulatory and product ecosystems; these systems emerged over generations because of lengthy lead times for the deployment of materially intensive technologies. Left to the market's short-term goals, a public-driven transition to clean energy will be slower without the help of governments. A lesson can be learned from the example of Silicon Valley, which has been an important economic driver in the last 20 years: it came into being due to government investment in the 1960s and 1970s.

In addition to investment, diversification is needed to encourage a sustainable future. By the time France's ITER reaches peak power, renewables could achieve 50% of electricity production in Europe.[195] With steady advances in energy storage and nearly 20 years to invest in infrastructure, we will have established a clear path towards sustainability, even if the billions spent on ITER are lost. Other novel approaches in energy production exist, such as the potential for international cooperation and smart grids to integrate markets and deliver lower energy costs through more efficient energy distribution.

We still face the challenges of transitioning to renewable energy technologies, reducing emissions and providing greater access to societies in developing nations. Clean energy production and distribution will be vital in a century that could see the global population reach a staggering 11 billion people.[196]

The Grid of the Future

By David Victor, Professor, University of California, San Diego (UCSD), USA

Essentially every economy has become more electrified as it has modernized. Typically, in the most advanced economies, almost half of the primary energy that powers them is converted to electrons before it is sent cleanly over power lines to final users. As pressure to clean up the energy system mounts, an even greater shift to electric power is expected.

As society depends ever more on electricity, will the power system of the future continue to look like the one that has emerged over the last 100 years? In today's grid, large central power stations and arrays of renewable energy producers, such as wind farms, are connected to users through long distance power lines and complex distribution networks that electric utilities and other operators manage centrally. These grids are the biggest machines on the planet. Will the grid of the future be much more decentralized – where prosumers are both producers of power and consumers?

The rapid technological changes that are emblematic of the Fourth Industrial Revolution are poised to make both these competing visions for the electric grid of the future more viable. On the one hand, massive improvements in the performance of central power stations along with long-distance power lines (China, for example, operates the world's largest network of one-million volt power lines) are making centralized grids more reliable and cost-effective. Even more interesting are a suite of decentralized technologies ideally suited for prosumers. These include small turbines and microgrids well-sized for industrial buildings and campuses, as well as even smaller heat pumps that can provide heating and cooling at extremely high levels of efficiency.

Low-cost sensors along with high-powered computing and big data analytics are making it possible for these many decentralized systems to operate autonomously, giving consumers much more control over exactly what kind of energy services they buy. The cost of battery systems needed to store and smooth power locally is plummeting.

While the winners of this great contest are still unknown, it is plausible that the technologies of decentralization have an edge and that the grid of the future will be much more decentralized than today's system. Although central power stations will still have a role to play, utilities are now deploying technologies that allow more automated and immediate local control with the hope that reliability will be improved – so that if some parts of the grid fail, as periodically happens after ice storms and other events, the local system can automatically reconfigure itself and keep the lights on. Investment in microgrids is soaring as are many other elements of a prosumer revolution. Some regulators are also adopting new rules that are specifically designed to shift investment away from centralized to more local supplies and control systems – for example, New York's Reforming the Energy Vision.

The question of whether this decentralization will be good news for the grid remains very hard to answer. In theory, more sophisticated local control and decentralization will allow users to take advantage of the fact that networks can promote reliability. More control by users can unleash market forces that are weak or non-existent in today's electric power system, which remains a monopoly in many respects and is often controlled by state enterprises or regulated utilities. The ability to micromanage energy supplies could also be a boon to policy-makers who are keen to target subsidies and other benefits just to the neediest users – something that will be key if the goal of providing energy services for all in the world is to be achieved at an acceptable cost.

These benefits have been demonstrated in many different settings, but looking across the whole of the world's grids, they are still largely a working hypothesis. Much could go wrong. Decentralized control, badly managed, could actually make power grids more unstable. So far, the centralized power grid has generally proved quite robust against hacking – despite some incidents, such as the hacking of parts of the Ukrainian grid in late 2015 – but a more decentralized control system could open many more doors for malice. And a truly decentralized grid will still require massive investment – perhaps even more investment than central systems, which will need reliable business models and good governance so that investments are recovered. And while decentralization has favoured cleaner technologies, some of the most cost-effective approaches to decentralization are not emission free.

Most microgrids, for example, rely on efficient natural gas – a clean fuel, but one that will need to be sharply curtailed (or decarbonized) for the world to achieve the goal of zero emissions of warming gases.

It is crucial that customers, utilities and policy-makers stay focused on whether the benefits of decentralization are becoming a reality. Because the technologies are changing quickly, it will be necessary to be able to adjust policy and to strike the right balance of centralized and decentralized power systems.

Figure 24: Changes in GDP and Energy Demand in Selected Countries and Regions, 2000-2014

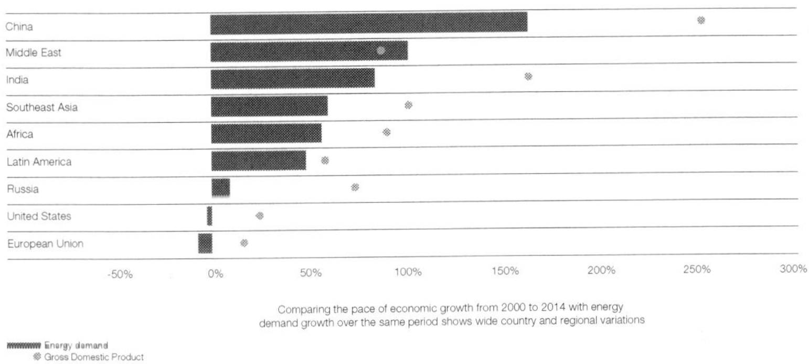

Source. IEA (2016), Figure 1.2

This challenge is especially true when high-growth regions cause much of the global energy demand (Figure 24). A long-term, multistakeholder perspective is needed to inform decisions on building physical infrastructure with challenges including communications, control systems, measurements and maintenance, as well as with the creation of integrated, international energy markets. Long-term thinking may, for example, dictate that we should focus investment on developing completely carbon-free technology rather than encouraging low-carbon infrastructure for the next 20-30 years.

As with other pressing global challenges, stable governments' commitment to multistakeholder agreements is required. Most studies suggest that achieving deep reductions in emissions requires building capital-intensive electricity networks. And history shows that firms and governments are willing to provide massive investments in energy networks only if they are confident in the predictability of policy and regulatory frameworks. This expectation requires agreements, such as investment treaties, arbitration mechanisms and the coordination of national energy policies around international standards, to mitigate cross-border risks.

In the World Economic Forum *Global Risks Report 2017*, emerging energy technologies hold the envious place of being considered the technological area with the least likelihood of negative consequences, while simultaneously holding the second-place position for greatest potential benefits. Squandering this potential would be a catastrophic lapse in collective responsibility.

Five key ideas

1. The Fourth Industrial Revolution could break the world's dependency on fossil fuels and greenhouse gas emitting energy production, which was established in previous industrial revolutions. This is ever more urgent as the world's population is growing, economies are industrializing, the effects of climate change are becoming more acute and the demand for energy globally is expected to double by 2040.
2. The renewable energy transition needs to continue to accelerate and encompass more sectors more quickly. Long-term investments must be made now to reap the benefits in the coming decades, especially in high-growth regions. Renewable energy R&D investment requires a boost in comparison with deployment spending. Coupled with advances in energy-storage technologies, it could be possible to reach targets for energy production to meet demand.
3. New energy technologies are being explored, from tidal energy to nuclear fusion, and advanced materials and nanotechnologies. These could help increase efficiency and lower energy losses. Combined with AI, large-scale system-wide efficiencies could also be improved through smart grids, the dynamic routing of energy or battery-driven transportation.
4. A major switchover to renewable energies places the fossil-fuel industry in jeopardy, along with the security of its longstanding geopolitical structures. Collaboration to deal with the social and political ramifications of a switchover is of the utmost importance.
5. Multistakeholder collaboration and global stability is required if we want governments to be confident and willing to make large long-term investments. Predictable policies and regulatory frameworks can help to engender trust for collaboration.

Chapter 15

Geoengineering

Geoengineering is the idea that humans can deliberately and successfully control the behaviour of the earth's highly complex biosphere. Many scientists, however, see technologies that purport to intervene in this space as immature and insecure at best and existentially threatening at worst, with consequences that are both unforeseeable and unmanageable.

This chapter should not be taken as legitimising geoengineering as a practice. Attempts to meddle on a large scale in the complex systems of the natural world have often ended in disaster, whether it be deliberately introducing new species or deforesting large sections of land. The authors are highly aware of the inability to predict or control the outcomes of so-called trophic cascades.

Nevertheless, the fact that technological interventions are being proposed to offset challenges ranging from air pollution and droughts to global warming suggests a chapter devoted to this topic is required. Proposals include installing giant mirrors in the stratosphere to deflect the sun's rays, chemically seeding the atmosphere to increase rainfall and the deployment of large machines to remove carbon dioxide from the air.

Technology may be able to intervene in these systems, but with our limited understanding of the ramifications, actions of this type may well cause irreparable damage to our world. Geoengineering is hence a controversial issue that demands new governance frameworks and requires reflective examination on the prudence of any action that would affect the shared resource of Earth's atmosphere.

Contributed by Anne Marie Engtoft Larsen, World Economic Forum, in collaboration with Janos Pasztor, Senior Fellow and Executive Director, Carnegie Climate Geoengineering Governance Initiative (C2G2), USA; and Jack Stilgoe, Lecturer in Science and Technology Studies, University College London, United Kingdom.

Can technological intervention directly offset global warming?

Geoengineering is defined as large-scale, deliberate interventions in the earth's natural systems. Some of its promised applications include shifting rainfall patterns, creating artificial sources of sunshine and altering biospheres using biotechnologies. Most discussions about geoengineering, however, focus on counteracting climate change. Geoengineering can also be considered in relation to extraterrestrial activities, such as the human colonization of other planets (in this context called "terraforming"). For instance, this is often brought up in science fiction-esque discussions of altering the composition of Mars' atmosphere to support long-term, human habitation.

Though currently theoretical for the most part, climate geoengineering techniques are proposed reactive measures that are needed to mitigate the greenhouse gases emitted into the biosphere (Figure 25). These reactive measures include carbon sequestration, ocean fertilization, the building of artificial islands and the creation of natural carbon sinks through large-scale tree plantations (Figure 26). More recently, techniques have been proposed to cool the planet. These fall into two categories: techniques to remove carbon dioxide from the atmosphere, thereby addressing a root cause of climate change, and solar-radiation-management techniques to reflect some of the sun's radiation back into space, which could provide a temporary solution to rising temperatures. Some of the required technologies are based on those developed in past centuries, such as enormous mirrors and aerosols, but new approaches are currently being imagined through the combination of Fourth Industrial Revolution technologies, such as nanoparticles and other advanced materials.

Enthusiasts eager for geoengineering argue that it could correct centuries of pollution and environmental degradation caused by the unwanted side effects of the first Industrial Revolution's socio-economic progress. Unconcerned about history repeating itself, they argue that the risks of further side effects are worth the potential benefit of reducing climate risks and buying extra time to address carbon emissions. More circumspect experts counter that current limits of scientific knowledge mean the potential negative side effects are too unpredictable and uncertain to risk. They point to terrifying domino effects that have happened following natural alterations in the earth's radiation balance. For example, the 1815 eruption of Mount Tambora in Indonesia triggered Europe's "year without a summer" in 1816, bringing crop failure, famine and disease.

In either case, geoengineering cannot be realistically viewed as a panacea. To achieve a stable climate, the economic and social systems of the Fourth Industrial Revolution must achieve net zero carbon emissions, i.e. reducing emissions significantly and counteracting any remaining emissions through carbon dioxide removal. Achieving these goals is not possible through a "tech solutionist" perspective, though new technologies and policies will be needed to address them. Thus, some proponents of geoengineering suggest that policy-makers consider a combination of both strategies to avoid the worst effects of climate change.

A global governance framework

Geoengineering could theoretically benefit some regions, while causing damage, drought or floods in others.[197] Such a scenario raises significant issues about how to move forward, how to balance costs against benefits and how to compensate affected populations. Geoengineering proponents highlight the need for a coherent intergovernmental governance framework to guide research and decision-making on any potential deployment. Though a grand vision for global collaboration, only limited elements of such a framework currently exist; the full framework would have to be developed in parallel with the technologies themselves that, without well-functioning intergovernmental collaboration, would raise potential risks to a global commons.

Janos Pasztor, Executive Director, Carnegie Climate Geoengineering Governance Initiative, argues that in the absence of multilateral agreements, there is a possible risk that a small group of countries, a single country, a large company or even a wealthy individual might take unilateral action on climate geoengineering.[198] And those who do not like these actions and their impacts might engage in counter-climate geoengineering, creating a geotechnological arms race.[199] As developing countries have fewer resources to change the climate, this raises the unfortunate possibility that the populations of states severely impacted by climate change will least be able to defend themselves against further ecological disruptions.

Figure 25: Geoengineering as a Direct Intervention into the Climate System

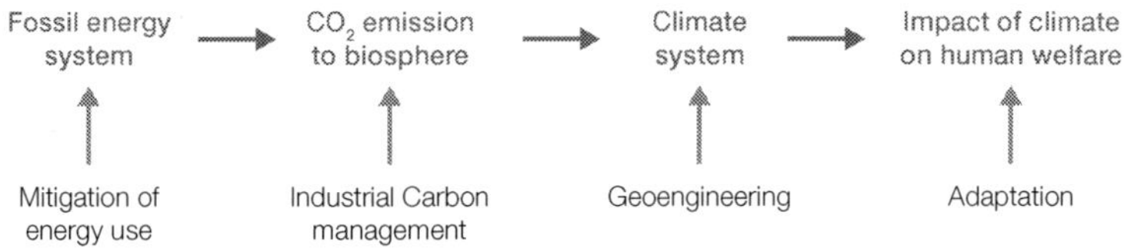

Source: Keith (2002)

The potential for climate geoengineering has long been debated by members of the scientific community, but it is quite a new topic in policy circles. In 2013, it was mentioned in the summary for policy-makers of the fifth report of the Intergovernmental Panel on Climate Change (IPCC).[200] More recently, scientific advisers from the US Global Change Research Program urged Congress to fund federal geoengineering research.[201] In April 2017, Harvard University launched the largest and most comprehensive research programme on geoengineering to date. The $20 million project aims to establish if the technology can simulate the atmospheric cooling effect of a volcanic eruption.[202]

Governance issues arising out of proposed geoengineering techniques range from questions of control and decision-making to ensuring the effective participation of affected societies. Within the current global governance architecture, only the UN General Assembly seems to possess the legitimacy to mandate the development of a governance framework by a suitable professional international authority.[203] We can look to peacekeeping or nuclear proliferation as an analogue to this needed mandate. However, scope exists for the development of other, possibly better approaches involving all relevant stakeholders.

Any multistakeholder governance mechanism would need to address:

- Whether the uncertainties surrounding geoengineering are too great to countenance any deployment
- How to balance the risks and opportunities of geoengineering against those of other climate change mitigation methods

- What kinds of international cooperation, mandates, limits and policy guidance should be required for geoengineering research to move from computational modelling and scenario building in the lab to empirical experimentation in the atmosphere
- How to balance the need to reduce global temperatures with unequal regional and local impacts that would raise cross-border and transgenerational ethical issues and impact both justice and human rights
- How to balance the need for democratic oversight with the need to be resilient to geopolitical changes over the decades, given that geoengineering would need to be deployed with long-term objectives; any decision to deploy geoengineering would need to specify how to govern future decisions to change or stop that deployment (for example, once solar radiation management techniques are started, stopping them would result in a rapid rise in temperatures)

Figure 26: Categorizing Approaches to Climate Geoengineering

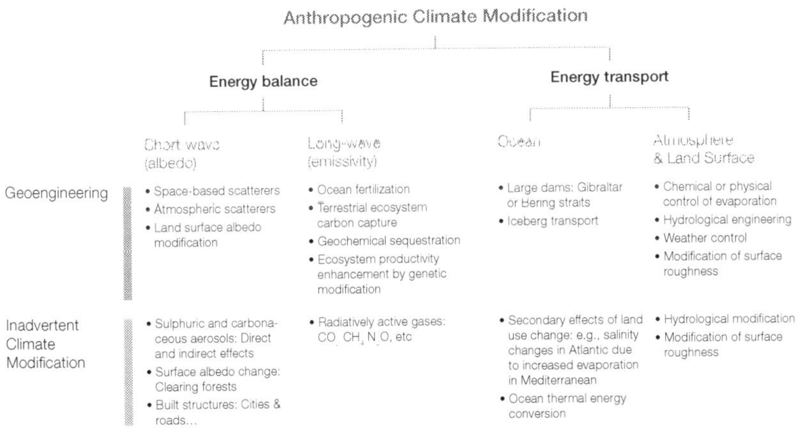

Source: Keith (2002)

The Ethical Dilemmas of Mastering Nature

By Wendell Wallach, Scholar, Interdisciplinary Center for Bioethics, Yale University, USA

The various approaches to engineering the climate pose a web of ethical, environmental, political and economic dilemmas. There are trade-offs and risks. Global climate change can be slowed to the extent that energy needs are met using clean, efficient and renewable sources. Energy needs, sources of energy, global climate change and pressures to geoengineer climate are entangled issues.

Less controversial means to manage the climate – such as recycling, planting forests to absorb carbon from the atmosphere, or painting rooftops white to reflect sunlight back into the atmosphere – must be enacted on a massive scale to mitigate even a fraction of the yearly increase in global warming. Some of the technological approaches, such as seeding the higher atmosphere with sulphate or nanoparticles, are conceivably more dangerous than the problem they are ostensibly meant to solve. Furthermore, advocates for conservation and clean energy are concerned that the illusion of any technological fix to global climate change could undermine the will to embrace necessary but difficult adjustments in behaviour or the political commitment to embrace clean sources of energy.

All strategies to address global climate change require large-scale interventions to have anything more than short-term local effects. Even massive reforestation might not offset the ongoing yearly deforestation in the Amazon and elsewhere. Tall industrial towers that suck carbon out of the atmosphere and sequester it could be built, but will not have quick or appreciably dramatic effect. Implementing this form of carbon dioxide removal on a large scale could be even more expensive than the economic costs of strong measures to reduce the greenhouse gases released into the atmosphere.

Seeding the upper atmosphere with sulphate particles or specially designed nanoparticles year in and year out seems a relatively inexpensive way to reduce the amount of sunlight that reaches the earth. Computer models indicate that this form of solar radiation management could cut the yearly increase in global warming by as much as 50%. It does not solve the problem of global warming, although it will slow down the rate of increase. But might constantly seeding the stratosphere upset climate patterns in a manner that is more destructive than the global warming it is designed to mitigate? We don't know. Without appropriate and rigorous research, it is impossible to determine whether seeding the stratosphere will have unintended consequences. And even small-scale experiments could be insufficient to fully reveal the complex feedback loops between the various layers of the atmosphere. Complex systems can act in unpredictable and occasionally destructive ways.

Given the political sensitivity of geoengineering experiments, scientists have rightly refrained from moving forward without the establishment of an international agreement. But it has been very difficult to forge agreement on an international governance framework to decide which experiments on the atmosphere can be performed. Without effective international oversight, rogue states and actors could elect to initiate their own geoengineering projects to meet near-term needs, without attention to the longer-term consequences of their actions. The simplicity of seeding the atmosphere, for example, suggests that one nation might elect to employ this approach to engineer local climate while disregarding its effect on weather in neighbouring regions. Indeed, as climate becomes increasingly problematic, a nation may feel forced to act independently to meet the needs of its citizens.

Some geophysicists and environmentalists have resisted even testing geoengineering strategies. They express three core issues with allowing research on geoengineering. First, investing in geoengineering will take resources away from environmentally sound approaches, such as conservation measures and developing clean sources of energy. Second, research groups could turn into interest groups that advocate for deploying whatever technologies they develop. Third, geoengineering could signal the "end of nature". Once countries and regions begin to directly tinker with weather patterns, the necessity and continual pressures to manage weather for both local and global needs will be constant.

Given our limited understanding of climate science, attempts at geoengineering could lead to a series of ill conceived and potentially disastrous experiments. While the mastery of nature has been a scientific dream, it has continually turned out to be naïve ambition. Even presuming that managing weather successfully is an attainable goal, negotiating the competing demands from various regions and countries would be daunting.

Five key ideas

1. Geoengineering is large-scale intervention in the earth's natural systems. In most discussions, however, it refers to still theoretical technological interventions aimed at reducing greenhouse gases or altering atmospheric processes to combat climate change.
2. Many scientists argue that interference in atmospheric systems with our current level of scientific knowledge is both dangerous and irresponsible, while proponents of geoengineering see it as a way to correct for centuries of human impact on the environment and atmosphere.
3. The ability to achieve a stable climate, i.e. net zero emissions, requires both reducing emissions and countering the carbon dioxide that is produced. The goal cannot be achieved through a quick technology fix, but technology will need to play a role in achieving it.

4. Any responsible move forward with geoengineering would require a framework for global intergovernmental collaboration. Currently only limited elements of such a framework exist and, without it, the risks to the global commons space are markedly higher.
5. Geoengineering is a new topic in policy circles that has experienced very little funding and little active experimentation. Governance for this set of technologies must consider a wide range of issues, from the authority to deploy the technologies to less risky alternatives to cross-border impact.

Chapter 16

Space Technologies

By 2030, we will likely have witnessed a surge in space-related technologies. Major leaps in aerospace technologies, astronomical observation capabilities, microsatellite development, nanomaterials, 3D printing, robotics and machine vision are promising an unparalleled era of exploration as well as scientific and economic return. Both the developed and developing worlds stand to benefit from what is happening beyond the atmosphere. Researchers and businesses will be the recipients of vast amounts of data that will drive entirely new processes of value creation and exchange. New scientific knowledge will spur innovation and ecological responsiveness, and the lucrative potential of space-based resource utilization and manufacturing are set to redefine the industrial trade routes of the future. All this promise, however, could be jeopardized without international agreements on areas like space traffic management, orbital debris mitigation, space mining and basic enforcement of conduct guidelines in outer space.

The Fourth Industrial Revolution and the final frontier

The Fourth Industrial Revolution will bring the cosmos closer to home. Commercial companies, such as SpaceX and Blue Origin, aim to dramatically reduce spacefaring costs as they boost access to orbit. At the same time, the aerospace company BAE Systems has invested over £20 million in Reaction Engine's SABRE (Synergetic Air-Breathing Rocket Engine) propulsion technology, which will enable aircraft to conduct direct return flights into low earth orbit without needing special landing strips and facilities.[204] NASA aims to send people into deep space and, ultimately, to the moon and/or Mars, and SpaceX has been championing that vision as well. A new class of pioneers is supporting space tourism and asteroid mining, and looking for ways to expand the space sector of the global economy. Add to this the advancements in telescope and satellite capabilities on both the ground and in space, and humans are likely to get a

Written in collaboration with Brian Weeden, Technical Adviser, Secure World Foundation, USA, with contributions from the Global Future Council on Space Technologies.

new perspective on the role space plays in contextualizing everything from innovation to world view.

In the next few decades, space-based resources for manufacturing may become a reality, vindicating early investors in the commercialization of space. In addition, with increased accessibility to space, we can imagine new industries that include space trawling, orbital sanitation and maintenance, and VR platforms for visiting other bodies in the solar system. All of these scenarios have the potential to reduce the burden on terrestrial resource extraction and depletion. Potential success in this area may explain why investment firms spent $1.8 billion in commercial space start-ups in 2015 alone;[205] these investments go far beyond just flying people into space, though space tourism could be a huge draw if it can be made affordable. Furthermore, new and advanced materials are part of the design and manufacture of spacesuits;[206] nanomaterials are being proposed to protect against solar radiation;[207] and many of the new space technologies are aimed at using data to transform our terrestrial lives.

The costs of all but the most cutting-edge, bespoke space technologies are decreasing. Even satellite technology is moving towards the production of smaller and cheaper payloads for deployment. More readily available satellite data will support the monitoring of crops, wildlife, human populations, supply chains and urban development. Satellites themselves will blanket the planet with communications pathways that could help connect the more than 4 billion people still lacking online access. New perspectives are needed on how to manage ourselves and our environments, such as the application of AI and new computing technologies to the exabytes of data that will be generated and that current computers fail to manage well. Concerted effort and good faith among international stakeholders will be required for humanity to optimize the benefits of these technologies.

For example, the opportunity to use global survey data to increase energy and transportation efficiencies could help solve systems-level issues, such as lowering emissions and optimal energy distribution and transmission challenges. Currently, several young innovative companies are using machine-vision algorithms to extract information from satellite imagery data to provide analysis and to generate actionable information about trade, agriculture, infrastructure, and more. Such analytic capabilities could move downstream for stakeholders who need social and ecological insights and applications. Add to this the scientific knowledge generated from investment in exploration through probes, telescopes, deep space missions and potential human space travel, and an entire new era of understanding how humans fit into the global and cosmic setting awaits.

Despite such potential, the World Economic Forum *Global Risks Report 2017* revealed the perception of space technologies to be benign, with fewer benefits in comparison to other technological areas. This can be seen as a surprising result, given the cutting-edge applications and hardware required for satellites, space exploration, aeronautics, earth science and climate modelling, not to mention the research agendas that drive these envelope-stretching projects. Another way of interpreting this result, however, is that the years of multistakeholder cooperation to develop the technologies that orbit our planet and perform feats beyond most people's understanding are considered quite safe, if they are thought about at all.

The trust that people have in deploying technologies in space has been well earned. In addition, space technologies are an amalgamation of computing, advanced materials and energy technologies, all of which ranked high on last year's *Global Risks Report* benefits scale. The push for exploration and the next competitive advantage will bring new possibilities for the global economy as well as for society. The year 2030, though, may be too soon for most of us to start planning about experiencing space. Nevertheless, we might be able to purchase a subscription to drive a real rover or fly a drone on a choice of several moons using VR gear. Space technologies already connect nearly half of the planet's population to each other and soon may connect everyone everywhere.

Driving Innovation from the International Space Station

By Ellen Stofan, Chief Scientist, NASA (2013-2016); Honorary Professor, Hazard Research Centre, University College London (UCL), United Kingdom

Since the inception of the International Space Station (ISS), over 1,900 investigations from various disciplines have been conducted or are still in progress, including human health research. The ISS provides a variety of multipurpose laboratories with unique equipment and tools in which weightlessness research can be conducted. Microgravity has many unique biological effects on humans and how our bodies work, such as altered immune and cardiovascular systems, bone density and muscle loss, and ocular deficiencies. These effects have challenged NASA and international partners to explore ways to mitigate risks; they've also increased our knowledge about the many health challenges we face on earth.

The research being performed on ISS is continuing to change the face of medicine and technology in many different health fields. Ongoing research indicates a class of drugs known as bisphosphonates, eating healthily and having a regular exercise routine can reduce bone loss. Plasma, which is easily studied in microgravity, assists in healing wounds and fighting cancer by boosting tumour inactivation. Current research on the growth of high-quality protein crystals in microgravity can lead to better medical treatment for individuals with Duchenne Muscular Dystrophy. These are just examples of the work that is being done over 200 miles (320 kilometres) above the earth.

Many of the human health investigations conducted on ISS through international partnerships have generated important results and prompted the development of new technology. These life-saving devices have produced extraordinary outcomes worldwide, including – but not limited to – the ultrasound 2 scanner that is currently in use on ISS and in remote areas on earth to provide quick and accurate medical diagnosis for individuals who are injured or sick; the portable device, NIOX MINO, that is used to monitor asthma and prevent future attacks; improved technology to detect early stages of osteoporosis and immune changes; and even technology that wasn't initially designed for human health, like the neuroArm. Doctors are now able to perform brain surgery while patients are inside a magnetic resonance imaging machine by using the neuroArm, designed using the same materials and techniques as the robotic Canadarm, which is used on the ISS for heavy lifting and maintenance.

In addition to the work being performed daily to prepare for a journey to Mars, NASA is collaborating with other government agencies and private companies on finding a cure for cancer by contributing to the US Cancer Moonshot initiative.

Teams are discussing how to engineer the immune system in order to increase our understanding of prevention techniques and to accelerate the detection and treatment stages. In the quest to find ways to protect humans from radiation exposure in space, NASA has developed technology that enables research into alternative treatments for cancer, namely particle beam radiotherapy, which may provide the appropriate dose of radiation to be deposited to tumour cells with less damage to the surrounding healthy cells. This field is not a new territory for the agency – NASA's research on microcapsule development on the ISS advanced the cancer treatment process and resulted in new technology for producing unique microballoons that contain drugs to be released over a 12- to 14-day period.

We have made great strides in understanding the human body on earth and in a microgravity environment, all from our experience in low earth orbit; however, there's still more work to be done. Humans face even more health challenges for longer and farther space travel, and we must continue joining forces to combat these challenges. As we push boundaries, new ideas and partnerships can be developed, allowing for more research and the production of space technology that is beneficial to all of humanity.

Lowering barriers to entry and raising the bar for success

Human societies have benefited tremendously from space technologies. Satellites provide services used every day for synchronizing global financial networks, monitoring the earth's climate, sustainably managing natural resources, providing education and critical services to remote communities, as well as early warnings of natural disasters. Yet the space sector, like many others, is on the cusp of a massive change driven by technological development. With this change, the promise for even more societal benefits exists, but only if the potential challenges facing the sector can be addressed.

Space is often seen as being at the cutting edge of technological development, but the reality is more complex. The massive amounts of government investment in the early part of the space age in the 1950s and 1960s did generate a huge amount of new science and innovation. The spin-off technologies planted the seeds of future industries, such as microchips and software engineering. However, the high cost of space launches and the harshness of the space environment drove an increasing emphasis on reliability and capability, which limited innovation and kept barriers to entry high.

Today, the space sector is experiencing a huge degree of innovation, but it is largely being driven by "spin-in" benefits from other sectors. For example, the microchip and software industries that the space age helped spawn have matured and are now feeding back into the space industry in two important ways. The first spin-in benefit is the technology. The manufacturing infrastructure that supports smartphones, laptops and other computing devices is being leveraged to develop a new generation of smarter, faster and cheaper space components and satellites. Cloud computing is commoditizing the processing and storage of information, the primary output of most satellites. Newer technologies, such as 3D printing, advanced robotics and AI, are also dismantling barriers to what we thought was the limit for satellite manufacturing and capabilities. For example, the company Made in Space has demonstrated the ability to 3D print tools on the ISS, and NovaWurks is developing modular satellite components that can self-assemble or reconfigure themselves on-orbit.

The other spin-in benefit is materializing through financing and workforce. The tech world is awash with venture capitalists looking for the next big investment opportunity and with skilled young engineers seeking new challenges. Many of the investors and engineers grew up dreaming about space, either by watching real-life astronauts or by immersing themselves in science fiction. These purpose-driven professionals are discovering newfound excitement in contributing to space. For example, Planet is one of several start-up space companies based in Silicon Valley that was founded by former NASA engineers; it is leveraging software and hardware engineering talent from the broader IT world.

Figure 27: New Spaceflight Companies by Destination

	Company	Vehicle(s) or Spacecraft	Services
Space Access	Blue Origin	New Shepard, Biconic Spacecraft	Suborbital and orbital launch services including human spaceflight
	Masten Space Systems	Xaero, Xogdor	Suborbital launches of small payloads
	Virgin Galactic	SpaceShipTwo, LauncherOne	Suborbital launches of small payloads, suborbital human spaceflight, and air-launched nanosatellite launches
	XCOR Aerospace	Lynx	Suborbital launches of small payloads, suborbital human spaceflight, and nanosatellite launches
	Orbital Sciences Corporation	Pegasus, Tauris, Antares, Cygnus	Orbital launches of satellites and ISS cargo
	SpaceX	Falcon 9, Falcon Heavy, Dragon	Orbital launches of satellites and ISS cargo, with orbital human spaceflight planned by 2017
	Stratolaunch Systems	Stratolauncher	Air-launched orbital launch services
	United Launch Alliance	Atlas V, Delta IV	Orbital launch services
Remote Sensing	Planet Labs	Dove, Flock 1	Frequent imaging of the Earth and open access to acquired data via website
	Skybox Imaging	SkySat	Frequent imaging and HD video of the Earth, data analysis, and open access to acquired data via website
LEO Human Spaceflight	Bigelow Aerospace	BA 330	Inflatable habitats for use in orbit or on the Moon
	Boeing	CST-100	Crewed LEO transportation
	Sierra Nevada Corporation	Dream Chaser	Crewed LEO transportation
	Space Adventures	Soyuz	Crewed LEO and lunar expeditions
Beyond LEO	B612 Foundation	Sentinel	Detection and characterization of potentially hazardous asteroids
	Inspiration Mars Foundation	Inspiration Mars	Crewed Mars flyby expedition
	Moon Express	Moon Express	Prospecting and mining lunar resources
	Planetary Resources	Arkyd 100, Arkyd 200, Arkyd 300	Prospecting and mining asteroid resources

Source: NASA (2014)

The result of this influx of technology, capital and people is a profound degree of change and innovation in the space sector. The traditional space applications are being made even more productive, i.e. remote sensing, communications and precision navigation and timing. The cost to design, manufacture, launch and operate satellites is decreasing, along with the ability to store, process and organize the data they produce. Simultaneously, new space activities are emerging, including cheaper ways to launch satellites, plans to manufacture them and other goods in space, maintenance and refuelling of space-based assets to extend their services and capabilities, and even the mining of asteroids for water and valuable minerals, all of which are now within the realm of possibility (Figure 27).

But changes in the space sector are complicating existing challenges and introducing new ones. The dramatic lowering of barriers to entry encourages countries and private companies to engage in space activities, and the technological influx is enabling orders of magnitude increases in the number of satellites launched. Today, more than 70 countries have owned or operated a satellite in orbit; the most recent are Iraq, Uruguay, Turkmenistan and Laos. Plans exist for roughly 12,000 new commercial satellites to be launched over the next decade to provide broadband internet and other services. The resulting congestion in heavily-used parts of the earth's orbit is increasing, creating challenges for tracking and managing space traffic, and detecting and preventing potential collisions on-orbit. The radio frequency range of the electromagnetic spectrum is also becoming more congested, as both space and terrestrial services face insatiable demands for more bandwidth. And the growing reliance on space for military and national security applications increases the chance that future conflicts on earth might extend into space, potentially jeopardizing the ability to use space in the future.

These challenges are not insurmountable, and efforts are already under way to address them. States are engaged in bilateral and multilateral discussions on some of the pressing security challenges and in the development of transparency and confidence-building measures to mitigate mistrust. States are also working with the private sector to develop best practices for ensuring the long-term sustainability of space, including limiting the creation of space debris, improving space situational awareness and avoiding collisions on-orbit. But more effort is needed by the global community to ensure that the space sector can realize the potential benefits it can offer to humanity in the foreseeable future.

The development of technologies in space needs leadership and innovative governance in the following areas:

- The creation of more mechanisms for private business input into the international regulatory framework. Currently, no mechanism exists to formally capture the ideas of private business within the Committee on the Peaceful Uses of Outer Space process, created in 1959 to oversee all legal frameworks related to space activity. An analogous structure to the B20, the group of corporate leaders representing the G20 business community is needed to gather all the new business actors entering the space arena. Sharing information, creating new opportunities and collaborating on challenges would be clear objectives of such input.

- Attention to alignment between national and international regulation with respect to space mining and other privately funded activities. With more private money being invested, governments need to ensure that businesses act in accordance with national laws that abide by international regulation. Addressing regulatory issues sooner rather than later will allow for good-faith actions from new market entries.

- A new space-traffic management system. With the increasing number of actors in the space domain, a more robust system is needed to manage objects, operational and not, in earth orbits. With the proliferation of commercial satellites, a collective approach towards orbital protocols and guidelines is critical for the sector's success.

- Enforcement of space-debris mitigation. While broad guidelines stipulate the need to sustainably manage functioning and defunct satellites and spent rocket bodies, no formal enforcement mechanism exists that ensures all actors protect and maintain safe earth orbits. At the velocity rates of orbiting material, these protocols are needed to ensure the safety of investments and people's lives.

- The possible lack in smaller countries of the necessary mechanisms to control the space-related activity happening from their territory. This could lead to unforeseen conflicts as new state and non-state actors enter the space domain. Clear mechanisms are needed for all nations to follow the established guidelines of behaviour in space.

Five key ideas

1. Space-based and space-related technologies are at an inflection point. The world is seeing a surge in deployment as private company development and renewed government investment push the frontier of space exploration and commercialization. Engineers and investors looking for a challenge find space to be a profound opportunity, as well as one that generates excitement attached to a vision of a future they can help create.
2. Years of multistakeholder cooperation among engineers, regulators and investors are building the trust that deploying technologies in space is relatively safe. Continued cooperation is needed to tackle looming roadblocks, such as proliferating space debris, uncoordinated space traffic and the lack of universal conduct guidelines for space.
3. Space has been a successful generator of spin-off industries, such as microchips and software engineering. In an important feedback loop, space is also a recipient of spin-in benefits, such as the technologies developed from the spin-off industries. Mobile computing, batteries, 3D printing and AI will all help increase efficiencies and help new space technologies to flourish.
4. New challenges in the final frontier include managing the number of new players in the industry and in orbit, reducing congestion as more satellites and companies put resources in space, sharing radio frequency spectrum and bandwidth, and defining the rules and procedures for potential space-resource harnessing.
5. Multistakeholder alignment and agreement is needed to foster trust in public-private partnerships, to ensure space is used for the common good and not to heighten geopolitical conflict, to help build accessible avenues for the global community including smaller nations, and to develop guidelines for behaviour in space.

Conclusion

What You Can Do to Shape the Fourth Industrial Revolution

The framing of the Fourth Industrial Revolution presented in this book – exploring the dynamics, values, stakeholders and technologies of a transforming world – creates the opportunity for a broad cross section of leaders and citizens to think more deeply about the relationship between technology and society, understanding the ways in which our collective actions (and inactions) create the future.

However, as much as the Fourth Industrial Revolution demands a shift in mindsets, it is not enough to merely appreciate the speed of change, scale of disruption and types of new responsibilities implied by the development and adoption of emerging technologies. Action and leadership are required from all organizations, sectors and individuals in the form of "systems leadership", involving new approaches to technology, governance and values.

For governments, the most urgent action involves investments in more agile governance approaches and strategies that empower communities and deeply engage business and civil society. For businesses, the priority should be to understand the opportunities of Fourth Industrial Revolution technologies and launching experiments to develop or adopt new ways of working that are sensitive to their impact on employees, customers and communities. For individuals, the priority should be to be part of local, national and global conversations around the topics raised in this book, as well as taking every opportunity to directly learn about and experience the new technologies themselves.

Being alive at a time of huge technological change comes with a responsibility to act. The more mature technologies and technical architecture become, the more uses and habits are established by default, and the harder it is to bring systems into the kind of equilibrium that truly serves the widest possible cross-section societies, nations and industries. The speed and scale of the Fourth Industrial Revolution mean the world cannot afford delay – we must work hard, together, to establish the norms, standards, regulations and business practices that will serve all humanity in a future filled with the mature capabilities of AI, genetic engineering and autonomous vehicles, and a virtual world every bit as difficult to master as the real one.

The numerous risks and pressures facing economies and societies that are referenced every day in the media – rising inequality, increasing political polarization, falling trust levels and critical environmental fragilities – provide both impetus for and barriers to the kind of multistakeholder collaboration and leadership required to make these decisions. As this book suggests, such a range of challenges cannot be met by any one corporation, sector, nation or even continent alone. Solving them will require collective leadership – collaborative and inspired leadership – to address the systemic changes and to succeed in delivering a better future for the planet and its societies.

The complex, transformative and distributed nature of the Fourth Industrial Revolution demands a new type of leadership – an approach we call "systems leadership".

Systems leadership is about cultivating a shared vision for change – working together with all stakeholders of global society – and then acting on it to change how the system delivers its benefits, and to whom. Systems leadership is neither a call for top-down control, nor for subtle influence by powerful groups, but rather a paradigm that empowers all citizens and organization to innovate, invest and deliver value in a context of mutual accountability and collaboration. Ultimately, it's a set of interconnected activities that have the goal of shifting the structures of our social and economic systems to succeed in an area where previous industrial revolutions have failed – to deliver sustainable benefits to all citizens, including for future generations.

In the context of the Fourth Industrial Revolution, systems leadership can be broken down into three areas of focus: technology leadership, governance leadership and values leadership. Systems leadership requires action from all stakeholders, including individuals, business executives, social influencers and policy-makers.

In a context where collaborative problem-solving is essential, we all share the responsibility to become systems leaders. However, as described at the end of this chapter, governments, businesses and individuals also have specific roles to play.

Technology leadership

Being a technology leader or even a fast follower in any sector requires making decisions about the proportion of capital allocated to technology investments, navigating the choices of technology pathways and platforms, and adapting organizational structures, skills needs and relationships across the value chain – all in the name of creating greater value for stakeholders. As the world experienced in the three previous industrial revolutions, the vast majority of these benefits will flow from businesses adopting and leveraging new technologies to create value in the form of higher-quality and lower-cost goods and services.

The world's most innovative companies, governments and civil society organizations are combining new technologies in new products, services and processes that are reshaping existing ways of delivering value – as in the example of Singapore's myResponder app that uses geolocation to save lives and support paramedic response by alerting volunteers within 400 meters of a cardiac arrest, or Adidas' partnership with Carbon, employing rapid 3D printing techniques to mass-produce light and durable midsoles for athletic footwear.[208] But how can those organizations that are not already at the innovation frontier grasp the opportunities of emerging technologies?

First, the fact that all Fourth Industrial Revolution technologies rely and build on digital systems means ensuring that, as much as possible, organizations are investing in digital communication and collaboration tools, data management and cybersecurity. It is often said today that "data is the new oil".[209] This is not a bad analogy – it is a significant and often untapped asset. It must also be refined to be useful in most applications. Its use, however, requires significant investment in both strategic decision-making and technical infrastructure that can help categorize, store, distribute and analyse diverse (and sometimes overwhelmingly large) flows of data.

And, just like oil, a leak of data can be catastrophic. In fact, the combination of new computing approaches, AI and an expanding set of use cases for personal data is accelerating cyber-risks at an alarming rate. As with oil, there are important reasons to protect data, but to make the most of this resource, we must find ways to treat data as a collective asset to be used for the common good, rather than a privatized resource that is fully transferred and exploited by a few powerful organizations.

Second, as the Singaporean and Adidas examples indicate, being a technology leader means adopting collaborative innovation strategies. The process of learning, refining and specializing within organizations means that in-house R&D models are extremely good at delivering incremental innovation within a specific product category to existing customers. However, research by Clayton Christensen and others suggests that these models are far less effective at creating and adapting to disruptive products within entirely new markets – exactly the industry landscape foreshadowed by the technologies of the Fourth Industrial Revolution. Technology leadership in the Fourth Industrial Revolution will require working with a range of external partners, which could range from young, dynamic and entrepreneurial firms, academic institutions or organizations in entirely different sectors that offer radically different perspectives, approaches or market access.

Third, making the most of new technologies requires new skills and mindsets from executives and employees alike. The World Economic Forum *Future of Jobs* report from 2016 indicates that 35% of skills will change across industries as new technologies, business models and markets develop. McKinsey Global Institute research suggests that, while only 5% of occupations are fully automatable based on currently available technologies, close to 60% of current jobs have at least 30% of tasks that can be performed by computers today.[210]

Figure 28: Change in Demand for Core Work-related Skills, 2015-2020, All Industries

Share of Jobs Requiring Skills Family as Part of Their Core Skill Set, %

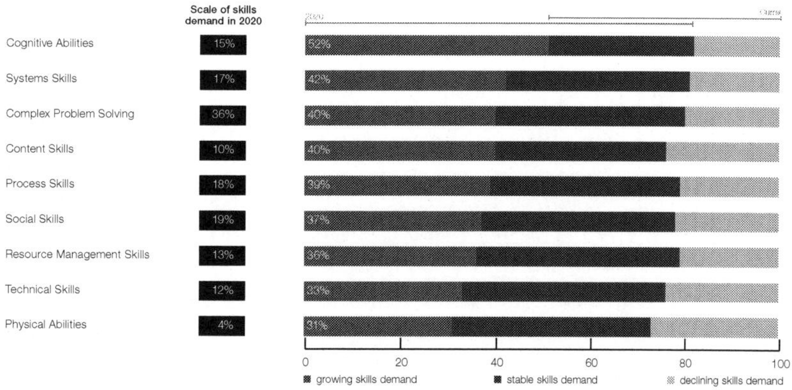

Source: Future of Jobs Survey, World Economic Forum

New research by economic consulting firm AlphaBeta shows that the impact of technology on skills to date has not been widespread unemployment, but rather increases in the amount of time that workers spend on creative, interpersonal and information synthesis tasks. They estimate that, in the case of Australia, more than two hours of a typical workweek have shifted from routing physical and administrative tasks to activities that are more enjoyable and that create greater value for firms.[211]

The skills that are expected to be most in demand as a result of these shifts are displayed in Figure 28. It shows that creative and interpersonal skills are rising in importance – meaning that organizations should be investing in recruitment and training programmes that emphasize problem-solving, management skills and creative skills to thrive in the Fourth Industrial Revolution.

Governance leadership

While the benefits of new technologies are delivered primarily through the channel of the private sector, the quality and distribution of those benefits are intimately tied to how the technologies are governed. Governance, however, is not just government: the formal structures we have for creating laws and regulations. Governance includes the development and use of standards, the emergence of social norms that can constrain or endorse use, private incentive schemes, certification and oversight by professional bodies, industry agreements and the policies that organizations apply voluntarily or by contract in their relationships with competitors, suppliers, partners and customers.

One of the characteristics of the Fourth Industrial Revolution, and perhaps the 21st century as a whole, is that the pace of change is increasing at an uncomfortable rate for many national institutions. The increasing pace of technological change has been especially challenging for policy-makers and governments.

The ongoing and potential disruptions of the Fourth Industrial Revolution require leadership on governance from two different perspectives.

The first requires leaders to rethink "what we govern, and why". Debates around technology governance in previous industrial revolutions have tended to focus on the role of the public sector in ensuring that innovations are safe for human health or the environment. This remains a critical priority for the technologies of the Fourth Industrial Revolution – but as the chapters above have outlined, emerging technologies raise new sets of concerns from labour-market impacts to protecting human rights.

Eight cross-cutting governance questions are particularly important to ensure the benefits and risks of the Fourth Industrial Revolution are well managed:

- What mechanisms can ensure that the Fourth Industrial Revolution reduces, rather than exacerbates, income and wealth inequality within countries?
- How can emerging and developing economies employ new technologies and systems to rapidly advance their human and economic development and reduce inequality across countries?
- What new policies, approaches and social protection systems are required to manage the disruptions to labour markets heralded by the Fourth Industrial Revolution?
- In what ways should skills development, employment models and technological systems be (re)designed to ensure that human labour and creativity are augmented, rather than replaced?

- Given the power granted by Fourth Industrial Revolution technologies to individuals and groups, how should societies avoid creating trade-offs between individual freedom and collective prosperity?
- What norms, standards or regulations might be required to ensure that democratic participation and citizen agency are preserved in light of the predictive and influencing power of emerging technologies?
- How do the dynamics and disruptions of the Fourth Industrial Revolution impact different genders, cultures and communities with less voice, and what new roles and opportunities might be required?
- How can societies ensure that a sense of common purpose, meaning, spirituality and human connection remain core sources of value?

The second perspective is to move beyond the "what" of governance and to rethink the "how". Standards, both at the industry and cross-industry levels, are particularly powerful governance mechanisms, which have been essential in the second and third Industrial Revolutions. Developing the technical standards for the Fourth Industrial Revolution is already under way – in 2016 the International Organization for Standardization (ISO) released standard 15066:2016, focused on safety requirements for collaborative industrial robot systems.[212] ISO is also currently developing four standards around unmanned aircraft systems and the civilian use of drones.[213] In fact, since 1946, more than 160 national standards organizations have come together within the ISO to publish approximately 22,000 global standards covering almost all aspects of technology and manufacturing and many service activities.

Communities of professionals are essential for establishing the right standards – especially standards that reflect a consensus of values and stakeholder priorities. The IEEE, for example, draws on 423,000 members to build consensus among organizations and deliver safety, reliability and interoperability in a range of electrical and digital systems. Their guidelines for AI show that they are thinking through the broad impact of technologies and not just focusing on the technical requirements or compliance. This sensitivity to context may come from IEEE's history that dates to the very beginning of the second Industrial Revolution, to 1884 when electricity became a major influence in society via the telegraph, the telephone and electric power.

Developing standards is an essential part of technology governance, but the scope, impact and speed of change of the Fourth Industrial Revolution require even more than the current approaches to developing technical standards or government regulations. Governance leadership in the Fourth Industrial Revolution means exploring new, more agile, adaptive and anticipatory governance approaches.

This goal is at the heart of the World Economic Forum Center for the Fourth Industrial Revolution in San Francisco, which opened in March 2017. The Center is designed as a new space for global cooperation, dedicated to developing principles and frameworks that accelerate the application of science and technology in the global public interest. These frameworks will be tested through piloting and rapid iteration in collaboration with public, private and civil society partners, and will initially cover nine critical areas for governance, as shown in Figure 30. The ultimate purpose of the Center is to catalyse a network of similar institutions and activities in all regions around the world to provide national, multistakeholder, co-ownership of the issues presented by new technologies. In addition, through the Global Future Councils, particularly the Council on Technology, Values and Policy, the Center is exploring a variety of innovative approaches to agile governance.

Figure 30: Center for the Fourth Industrial Revolution Projects

Center Project	Related World Economic Forum System Initiative
Accelerating Innovation in Production for Small and Medium Enterprises	Future of Production
Artificial Intelligence and Machine Learning	*Cross-Center project*
Blockchain – Distributed Ledger Technology	*Cross-Center project*
Autonomous Vehicles	Future of Mobility
Civilian use of Drones	Future of Mobility
Digital Trade and Cross Border Data Flows	Future of International Trade and Investment and Future of Digital Economy and Society
New Vision for the Oceans	Future of Environment and Natural Resource Security
Internet of Things (IoT) and Connected Devices	Future of Digital Economy and Society
Precision Medicine	Future of Health and Healthcare

Source: World Economic Forum

While governments naturally will play a critical role in defining more agile governance structures for society, leading technology governance in the Fourth Industrial Revolution is not something that can or should be the sole domain of governments – rather it is a multistakeholder challenge that concerns every sector, industry and organization. Organizations that contribute to the creation of more effective and sustainable approaches to technology governance can therefore have an outsized, and significantly positive, impact in shaping the future.

Values leadership

Systems leadership is more than investing in better technology leadership and new models of governance. To generate the momentum and illuminate the importance of working together, leaders also need to address the Fourth Industrial Revolution from a values-based perspective. Societal values provide the motivation and sustaining power to work with technologies and to optimize the benefits rather than maximize the return for singular stakeholders.

The discussion of values can be complicated, but the existence of different perspectives, incentives and cultural contexts does not mean a lack of common ground. No matter our agendas, the importance of preserving the planet for future generations, the value of human life, the international principles of human rights, and a sincere concern for global commons issues can serve as starting points for recognizing that the true ends of technological development are ultimately and always the planet and its people. To put it simply, the way forward in the Fourth Industrial Revolution is through a renaissance that is human-centred.

In Chapter 1, we defined human-centred as empowering individuals and communities, providing them with meaning and the agency to shape the world. Practically, this means attending to the impact of technology on our broader environmental and social systems, and ensuring that emerging technologies support the Sustainable Development Goals as well as economic institutions and mechanisms that fairly distribute material well-being. Being human-centred also requires protecting and enhancing the rights of citizens within and across countries, particularly those with the least amount of power and status. Finally, while digital technologies are increasingly determining our behaviour and fragmenting our experience, driving a human-centred agenda means enhancing the ability of individuals to construct meaning in their lives on a daily basis. To be human-centred, emerging technologies must actively contribute to more harmonious and meaningful interaction among individuals.

Values leadership is therefore active, rather than reactive – values should be cultivated as a positive feature of technological systems, as opposed to being considered a "bug", or mere afterthought.

There is no reason that societies must be purely reactive to the changes in technological capabilities. Societies have the power to decide what kind of future they want and which technologies serve their purpose. Formulating a values-based approach to technology means recognizing the political nature of technologies, putting societal values forward as priorities, and thinking deeply about how an organization contributes to the values that become part of the technologies we produce and use to mediate social and economic exchange. It requires considering how our own values and perspectives as individuals are shaped and affected by technologies as we make important technology-related decisions. And finally, a values-based approach relies on the input of others, even those who don't usually have a voice but who are affected, to determine how we want to influence technological development.

Leaders have the greatest opportunity to change how businesses and communities engage with technologies. The ability to step back from the economic pressures that incentivize a great deal of technological development and consider the systemic impact of technologies, and what kind of future they point towards, matters in the long run. The start-up culture and, indeed, larger corporate cultures look to their leaders for how to act when it comes to difficult decisions, especially values-based decisions. Strong commitment to societal values can ripple through an organization, provide purpose for employees who want to contribute positively to society through their work, and have an impact on the organization's reputation both from within and without.

Strategies for stakeholders: What should governments do?

Everyone has the responsibility to contribute to systems leadership. But the varied roles of stakeholders create different opportunities for governments, businesses and individuals to invest in specific strategies.

Strategy 1: Adopt agile governance approaches

The most urgent task facing governments is to open the space for new approaches to technology governance. As described in the Forum White Paper "Agile Governance: Reimagining Policy-making in the Fourth Industrial Revolution",[214] the pace of technological development and a number of characteristics of technologies render previous policy-making cycles and processes inadequate, including their speed of diffusion, the way they cross jurisdictional, regulation and disciplinary borders, and their increasingly political nature in terms of how they embed and display human values and bias. The idea of reforming governance models to cope with new technologies is not new, but the urgency of doing so is far greater in light of the power of today's emerging technologies.

Agile governance is an essential strategy to adapt how policies are generated, deliberated, enacted and enforced to create better governance outcomes in the Fourth Industrial Revolution. Inspired by the Agile Manifesto[215] and a report by the World Economic Forum Global Agenda Council on the Future of Software and Society,[216] the concept of agile governance seeks to match the nimbleness, fluidity, flexibility and adaptiveness of the technologies themselves and the private-sector actors adopting them.

Governments must work hard to overcome a number of risks or even contradictions in seeking to become more agile. After all, public-sector policy-making is often intentionally deliberative and inclusive, attributes that seem to work against the desire for speedier processes and outcomes. Indeed, many situations exist where the most appropriate action is to take time to pause and deliberate widely in order to produce the best outcome. As the White Paper states, the unique responsibilities placed on governments mean that agile governance should not sacrifice rigour, effectiveness and representativeness for speed alone.[217]

However, a critical reason for governments to urgently adopt agile approaches to governance is the fact that agility allows for the creation of new processes that are *more* inclusive and human-centred, involving a greater number and diversity of stakeholders, and allowing for rapid iteration to more effectively meet the needs of the governed.

Agile governance can also support more sustainable policies in the long term, enabling the constant monitoring and more frequent "upgrading" of policies, as well as supporting the enforcement of policies, sharing the workload with the private sector and civil society to maintain relevant checks and balances.

But what does agile governance actually look like? Models of governance adapted for the Fourth Industrial Revolution that governments should explore, catalyse or pilot include:[218]

- Creating policy labs – protected spaces within government with an explicit mandate to experiment with new methods of policy development by using agile principles, such as the UK Cabinet Office's Policy Lab[219]
- Encouraging collaborations between governments and businesses to create "developtory sandboxes" and "experimental testbeds" to develop regulations using iterative, cross sectoral and flexible approaches, as discussed by Geoff Mulgan[220]
- Supporting crowdsourcing policy and regulatory content to create more inclusive and participatory rule-making processes, as in the example of CrowdLaw, a platform designed to enable the public to propose legislation, draft bills, monitor implementation and supply data to support new laws or amending existing ones[221]
- Promoting the development of ecosystems of private regulators, competing in markets to deliver quality governance in line with overarching social goals, as proposed by Gillian Hadfield in *Rules for a Flat World* [222]
- Developing, popularizing and requiring the adoption of principles of innovation to guide researchers, entrepreneurs and commercial organizations receiving public funding, from the idea of Responsible Innovation[223] developed by Richard Owen and others, to the Principles for Sustainable Innovation proposed by Hilary Sutcliffe[224]

- Promoting the integration of public engagement, scenario-based foresight approaches and social science and humanistic scholarship into science and research efforts, as proposed by David H. Guston's Anticipatory Governance model[225]
- Supporting the role of global coordinating bodies to provide oversight, spur public debate and evaluate the ethical, legal, social and economic impacts of emerging technologies, as proposed by Gary Marchant and Wendell Wallach in the form of Governance Coordination Committees,[226] or a possible International Convention for the Evaluation of New Technologies, as proposed by Jim Thomas[227]
- Fostering new approaches to technology assessment that combine far greater public deliberation and participation, with acknowledgement and reflection of the values, incentives and politics influencing decision-making in both research and commercialization, as proposed by Rodemeyer, Sarewitz and Wilsdon[228]
- Incorporating the principles espoused by the World Economic Forum Global Agenda Council on the Future of Software and Society (2014-2016) in "A Call for Agile Governance Principles", which are meant to "improve efficiency, public services and public welfare, better equipping government agencies to respond to change"[229]

Strategy 2: Work across boundaries

The second strategy that governments must urgently pursue is an essential complement to the pursuit of agile governance – investing in working in new ways across traditional sectoral, institutional and geographical boundaries.

Neither the deployment nor the impact of the technologies described in Section 2 is limited to any one domain or jurisdiction. As discussed extensively in *The Fourth Industrial Revolution,* this means that the existence of disciplinary and institutional boundaries – whether between research areas, ministries or organizational departments – can reduce, rather than enhance the efficiency and effectiveness of response by governments.

Silos can be broken. Take for example Singapore's Civil Service College, which helps equip government agencies and staff with opportunities for learning and collaborating across the public service, governed by a board that includes the permanent secretaries of four different ministries, the Prime Minister's office and local academic partners.[230]

Breaking down silos does not mean creating a free-for-all atmosphere, particularly when it comes to sharing data. There are good reasons for protecting data sources and carefully considering the appropriate level of connectivity, particularly where the possibility of human rights being undermined exists. The opportunity is therefore to find new models of balancing the potential for unauthorized or unethical use of a new technology with the benefits that can't be realized without multistakeholder collaboration. Here, medical data is a good example – significant life-saving opportunities are available through sharing large sets of genomic data across different health providers and research organizations. Yet the potential for abuse of genetic information is also high, meaning that, in most jurisdictions, strict controls around patient consent and medical data sharing remain.

One new model of cross-sector collaboration seeks to overcome these limits in the humanitarian space by proposing public-private data-sharing agreements that "break-glass-in-case-of-emergency". These come into play only under pre-agreed emergency circumstances (such as a pandemic) and can help reduce delays and improve the coordination of first responders, temporarily allowing data sharing that would be illegal under normal circumstances.[231]

Strategies for stakeholders: What should businesses do?

Strategy 1: Learn by doing and invest in people

The most important strategy for business leaders is to experiment. The Fourth Industrial Revolution is still in its early stages, and the potential of new technologies is far from fully understood. However, as discussed in Chapter 2, we can anticipate some of the revolution's dynamics, including the fact that disruption more and more often emanates from the periphery of industries and organizations. Businesses need a minimum viable appreciation of new technologies to see the bigger picture and opportunities that may lie at the periphery. Businesses must lean in and be curious, take time to learn about progress in different fields and be willing to trial new technologies. Only by directly experimenting with technologies can organizations see for themselves what they can do.

Businesses should not be daunted by technologies such as AI, new materials, biotechnologies and IoT applications: experimenting can be easier than it might appear, even for a company that is small or in its early stages. In one example of creatively applying new technologies to a novel situation, Japanese farmer Makoto Koike used machine learning application TensorFlow to help his family's business sort cucumbers.[232]

Experimenting brings perspective, revealing not only what technologies can do but also what they cannot: some technological solutions are widely hyped but may not be worth greater investment. Experimenting can provide some idea of when and at what scale the technology is appropriate.

To make the most of experimenting with new technologies, companies must value those who hold institutional knowledge and can leverage it for new ventures, and invest in developing the skills of their existing employees. This includes not only their technological skills but also ensuring that the company's culture is collaborative, willing to take risks and tolerant of failures. Companies that embrace an entrepreneurial mindset can generate valuable assets as employees build domain knowledge on the edge of the innovation space and identify opportunities for spin-out companies to drive growth.

Strategy 2: Adopt and engage in new governance approaches

Businesses must closely examine the ways in which their internal leadership and external collaboration link to the use of new technologies and shape how they are conceived, sourced, developed, deployed, integrated and maintained. From creating new organizational structures to embracing new policies or novel business practices, governance approaches adopted by individual firms can shape norms and influence corporate culture and behaviour across entire industries, up and down the value chain.

Beyond their own organizational structures, businesses must be willing to engage in concerted, intentional action to nurture new norms around managing and developing technologies, such as the kind of multistakeholder governance efforts described above. Working within an organization to develop a strong sense of purpose, ethical codes of conduct and a wider appreciation of the impact of technologies can be powerful and transformative. Changing internal structures, collaborating with other stakeholders and moulding mindsets and behaviours are effective ways to align motivations and incentives with wider sets of goals.

As part of this process, businesses must adopt adequate strategies to respond to new risks, embedding them in their governance repertoires. In particular, many companies are not well equipped to handle cyber-risks emerging from the rapid growth of AI, IoT, blockchain and other new computing and digital technologies. Repeated stories of data breaches, bitcoin heists and IoT vulnerabilities demonstrate that as interconnected digital technologies proliferate, so will the ways in which they can be exploited. Businesses must put together robust cyber-risk strategies to protect assets, develop competencies and build trust among their stakeholders and customers.

Strategy 3: Develop and implement technologies with opportunities in mind

Finally, and fundamentally, businesses must reframe how they think about technological development. Going far beyond R&D and product development, they must try to envision the future in which these technologies, either as resource or product, play a role – and think critically about how their organizational cultures could impact others through the process of development, acquisition or deployment of these technologies.

As this book has repeatedly demonstrated, many Fourth Industrial Revolution technologies will have impacts that are wide-ranging and still susceptible to being shaped. The impact of automation, for example, will depend greatly on how and to what purpose robotic systems are developed. The environmental impacts of many technologies will depend on which stakeholders are included in their design, how materials are sourced and what types of voluntary agreements are reached about how to maintain, recycle or dispose of waste.

Businesses must put in place processes to deliberate on these broader, nonlinear impacts. They must make efforts to understand how organizational processes and incentives value particular opportunities over others can open up perspectives that help firms to empower and augment their staff, customers and local communities. Achieving this requires zooming out to scan the horizon for potential conflicts and negative consequences and being realistic about the prospect of new technologies to impact the firm, consumers and broader society. For example, an IoT firm might consider scenarios for how the availability of sensor data within a city might negatively impact various communities.

Adopting this strategy will enable businesses to go a long way towards building trust with consumers and regulators. Indeed, building relationships with regulators from an early phase, with a wider scope of understanding about how emerging technologies may disrupt the status quo, could help shape the regulatory environment. Reaching out across stakeholder groups for solution building when negative consequences are identified can help to create the inclusive and sustainable future we all desire.

Strategies for stakeholders: What should individuals do?

Strategy 1: Explore, experiment and envision

Individuals, like businesses, need to be willing to familiarize themselves with new technologies. Sometimes this is necessary to prevent negative consequences to themselves and others: much cyber-risk, for example, comes down to individuals who have not exercised the option to use security measures such as strong passwords or two-layer authentication. In other cases, the "democratization" of emerging technologies – as discussed in Chapter 2 – presents opportunities for individuals to play a role in shaping how these technologies develop, even if they are not executives or engineers. Today, there are numerous opportunities for individuals to learn through direct experience with new technologies from spending time in a local fablab[233] and 3D printing a design of one's own making, to participating in a community-based biohacking workshop.[234]

Making sure to learn about what is happening behind the interface and service delivery aspects of digital technologies is crucial for individuals to build and share experiences that can be fed back to businesses and policy-makers representing community stakeholder perspectives, desires and values. Building the necessary skills to use many of the emerging technologies discussed in Section 2 is easier than many people may imagine. For example, the non-profit fast.ai offers a seven-week deep learning course, which is accessible to anyone with basic programming experience, enabling the use of the latest machine learning tools by non-experts in their application of choice.

Exploring and experimenting with technologies also means thinking about the kind of future we want to create, and we must all remember that the future belongs to the upcoming generations. Envisioning how technologies and communities fit together in the future matters deeply, and one way of understanding the potential purposes and uses of new technologies is listening to and being mentored by young people. Any future worth building should include insights from those who will ultimately be most affected and live most closely with technologies emerging today.

Strategy 2: Be political

Individuals are, ultimately, the people who will live in the future that technologies help to create. When individuals develop their own aspirational vision of the future, they can respond politically to how technologies are being developed and adopted – deciding whether to take a position and voice their feelings. Sharing perspectives about how technologies impact individual lives and communities is important because technologies are products of the interests of select groups of people, who may not be familiar with all the social perspectives that are relevant or may not be aware of what the wider effects of a technology might be. Such feedback is critical for society to collectively push for the most desirable uses of Fourth Industrial Revolution technologies and to let businesses and regulators know what issues are most concerning.

Individuals can make their voices heard not only as consumers and voters but also through civil society organizations and social movements, which are also being transformed in the Fourth industrial Revolution. These are important conduits for expressing social desires and aspirations, protecting the rights of individuals and lending support to areas of social need where business plans cannot help and where social interests and governmental interests require mediation. Civil society organizations help ensure that people whose voices might otherwise be overlooked or marginalized are appreciated by those who have more direct decision-making power – helping entrepreneurs, companies, investors and engineers to better understand how the technologies they are developing will impact society as a whole.

Conclusion

During the last 50 years, we have become increasingly aware of the mutually transformative relationship between our societies and the technologies they produce. The first two industrial revolutions and two world wars showed us that technologies are far more than just a set of machinery, tools or systems linked to production and consumption. Technologies are powerful actors that shape social perspectives and our values. They require our attention precisely because we build our economies, societies and world views through them. They shape how we interpret the world, how we see others around us and the possibilities we see for our future.

The issues we are facing at the beginning of the Fourth Industrial Revolution, such as the impact of automation, the ethical implications of AI and the social ramifications of genetic engineering, have been a part of social consciousness since at least the 1960s, when nuclear, genetic and space technologies moved past their infancy and computers began to replace their human counterparts. Short-term expectations exceeded the capabilities of the time but, thanks to the maturity of digital capabilities through the third Industrial Revolution, they have recently emerged as realities that are fast becoming part of daily life for increasing proportions of the global population.

Luckily, academic research and foresight practice have developed analytical tools and helpful sociological perspectives over the last 50 years to better understand how technologies and societies shape and influence each other. Indeed, sensitivity to how technologies instigate widespread social transformation and how values are embedded in the technologies we create has helped us discern the signals of the oncoming disruption and informed much of this book.

Acting appropriately in this complex space requires a new perspective on technology that appreciates the many facets of technological change and seeks to apply the insights from this perspective at the personal and organizational levels.

This is impossible to achieve if we continue to view emerging technologies as "mere tools" that are simply at hand for human use with predictable and controllable consequences. Nor can we fully empower ourselves or others if we give into the complexity and treat technologies as exogenous, deterministic forces outside of our control.

Rather, all stakeholders must internalize the fact that the outcomes of technological advancement are tied to our choices at each level of development and implementation – whether as an individual citizen, a business executive, a social activist, a large investor or a powerful policy-maker. Just as our consumer choices impact the future of companies and the products available to us, so too our collective technological choices impact the structure of the economy and society.

Technologies will inevitably play a part in finding solutions to many of the challenges we face today, but they are also contributors to these challenges and the source of new ones. Just as no one group can tackle the challenges alone, neither can we surmount these issues solely through the use of technologies. Instead, we have to take a broader view of our collective priorities and work on strengthening the areas where we come together and create positive changes by collaborating, building trust and offering goodwill. The challenges of the Fourth Industrial Revolution can only be tackled through cooperation and transparency.

If we can muster our courage and act in the service of the common good, there is significant hope that we can continue an upward trajectory of human well-being and development. Past industrial revolutions have been a significant source of progress and enrichment, though it is up to us to solve for the negative externalities, such as environmental damage and growing inequality. Involving all relevant stakeholder groups will help us overcome the core challenges ahead – distributing the benefits of technological disruptions, containing the inevitable externalities and ensuring that emerging technologies empower, rather than determine, all of us as human beings.

Finding solutions for the governance challenges of the Fourth Industrial Revolution will require governments, businesses and individuals to make the right strategic decisions about how to develop and deploy new technologies. But this will also require taking a stance on societal values and getting better at creating mechanisms for collaborative action. Individuals and organizations will need to connect with and take into account the perspectives of multiple stakeholders, and multinational corporations and nation states will have to become more effective at building formal and informal international agreements. These are not easy obligations to fulfil, and we can expect setbacks. But we cannot turn away from the responsibility.

The scale, complexity and urgency of the challenges facing the world today call for leadership and action that are both responsive and responsible. With the right experimentation in the spirit of systems leadership by values-driven individuals across all sectors, we have the chance to shape a future where the most powerful technologies contribute to more inclusive, fair and prosperous communities.

Acknowledgements

This book is a product of multistakeholder engagement and collaboration. It builds on 18 months of research, interviews, workshops, briefings and summits engaging thousands of experts, senior executives and policy-makers, as well as in-depth interviews and correspondence with over 240 leading thinkers.

The World Economic Forum Global Future Councils and Expert Network contributed extensively to the chapters featured in Section 2, submitting multiple drafts and myriad useful, detailed comments regarding technologies that are both highly complicated and constantly in flux.

As such, it is impossible individually to name everyone who has meaningfully influenced the content in this book. Nevertheless, deep gratitude is owed to all the members of the Forum's Global Future Councils (GFCs), particularly those councils focused on Fourth Industrial Revolution technologies. A significant proportion of experts acknowledged directly in the text and in the endnotes are members of GFCs. The contributors to all chapters are listed below, and the full lists of councils and their members can be found at: https://www.weforum.org/communities/global-future-councils

We would like particularly to thank all the experts who generously gave their time to participate in interviews, informal discussions or exchanges via email, phone and in person throughout the preparation of this book. These include:

Asmaa Abu Mezied, Small Enterprise Center
Asheesh Advani, JA Worldwide
Dapo Akande, University of Oxford
Anne-Marie Allgrove, Partner, Baker & McKenzie
Dmitri Alperovitch, Crowdstrike
Michael Altendorf, Adtelligence
Kees Arts, Protix
Alán Aspuru-Guzik, Harvard University
Navdeep Singh Bains, Minister of Innovation, Science and Economic Development of Canada
Banny Banerjee, Stanford University
Brian Behlendorf, Hyperledger
Emily Bell, Columbia University

Marc R. Benioff, Salesforce.com
Yobie Benjamin, Avegant
Niklas Bergman, Intergalactic
Sangeeta Bhatia, MIT
Burkhard Blechschmidt, Cognizant
Adam Bly, Spotify
Iris Bohnet, Harvard University
danah boyd, Microsoft Research
Edward Boyden, MIT
Kirk Bresniker, Hewlett Packard Enterprise
Winnie Byanyima, Oxfam
John Carrington, Stem
Cong Cao, University of Nottingham
Alvin Carpio, The Fourth Group
Justine Cassell, Carnegie Mellon University
Sang Kyun Cha, Seoul National University Derrick Cham, Strategy Group, Government of Singapore
Joshua Chan, Smart Nation and Digital Government Office, Government of Singapore
Andrew Charlton, AlphaBeta
Fadi Chehadé, Chehadé Inc.
Devan Chenoy, Confederation of Indian Industry (CII)
Hannah Chia, Strategy Group, Government of Singapore
Carol Chong, Singapore Economic Development Board
Jae-Yong Choung, Korea Advanced Institute of Science and Technology
Ernesto Ciorra, Enel
Alan Cohn, Georgetown University
Stephen Cotton, International Transport Workers' Federation
Aron Cramer, Business for Social Responsibility (BSR)
James Crawford, Orbital Insight
Molly Crockett, University of Oxford
Pang Tee Kin Damien, Monetary Authority of Singapore
Paul Daugherty, Accenture
Eric David, Organovo
Charlie Day, Office of Innovation and Science Australia
Angus Deaton, Princeton University
Phill Dickens, University of Nottingham
Zhang Dongxiao, Peking University
P. Murali Doraiswamy, Duke University
David Eaves, Harvard Kennedy School
Imad Elhajj, American University of Beirut
Sherif Elsayed-Ali, Amnesty International
Helmy Eltoukhy, Guardant Health
Ezekiel Emanuel, University of Pennsylvania
Victoria A. Espinel, BSA – The Software Alliance
Aldo Faisal, Imperial College London
Al Falcione, Salesforce.com

Nita Farahany, Duke University
Dan Farber, Salesforce.com
Christopher Field, Stanford University
Brian Forde, MIT
Primavera De Filippi, Berkman Center for Internet & Society, Harvard University
Luciano Floridi, University of Oxford
Tracy Fullerton, University of Southern California
Pascale Fung, Hong Kong University of Science and Technology
Andrew Fursman, 1QBit
Mary Galeti, Shiplake Partners
Brian Gallagher, United Way
Dileep George, Vicarious
Kunal Ghosh, Inscopix
Bob Goodson, Quid
Christoph Graber, University of Zurich
Henry T. Greely, Stanford University
Wang Guoyu, Fudan University
Sanjay Gupta, LinkedCap
Seth Gurgel, PILnet
Gillian Hadfield, University of Southern California
Wang Haoyi, CAS Institute of Zoology
Demis Hassabis, Google DeepMind
Ricardo Hausmann, Harvard University
John Havens, Institute of Electrical and Electronics Engineers (IEEE)
Yan He, Zhejiang University
Imogen Heap, Entrepreneur and recording artist
John Hegel, Deloitte
Cameron Hepburn, University of Oxford
Angie Hobbs, University of Sheffield
Timothy Hwang, FiscalNote
Jane Hynes, Salesforce.com
Nancy Ip, Hong Kong University of Science and Technology
David Ireland, ThinkPlace
Paul Jacobs, Qualcomm
Amy Myers Jaffe, University of California
Davis Ratika Jain, Confederation of Indian Industry (CII)
Sheila Jasanoff, Harvard Kennedy School
Ajay Jasra, Indigo
Chi Hyung Jeon, Korea Advanced Institute of Science and Technology
Feng Jianfeng, Fudan University
Yan Jianhua, Zhejiang University
Sunjoy Joshi, Observer Research Foundation (ORF)
Calestous Juma, Harvard Kennedy School
Anja Kaspersen, International Committee of the Red Cross (ICRC)
Stephane Kasriel, Upwork
Neal Kassell, Focused Ultrasound Foundation

Drue Kataoka, Drue Kataoka Studios
Leanne Kemp, Everledger
So-Young Kim, Korea Advanced Institute of Science and Technology (KAIST)
Erica Kochi, UNICEF
David Krakauer, Santa Fe Institute
Ramayya Krishnan, Carnegie Mellon
Jennifer Kuzma, North Carolina State University
Jeanette Kwek, Strategy Group, Government of Singapore
Dong-Soo Kwon, Korea Advanced Institute of Science and Technology
Peter Lacy, Accenture
Corinna E. Lathan, AnthroTronix
Jim Leape, Stanford University
Jong-Kwan Lee, Sung Kyun Kwan University
Jae Kyu Lee, Korea Advanced Institute of Science and Technology Sang Yup Lee, Korea Advanced Institute of Science and Technology Steve Leonard, SG Innovate
Geoffrey Ling, Uniformed Services University of the Health Sciences
Xu LiPing, Zhejiang University
Simon Longstaff, The Ethics Centre
Stuart McClure, Cylance
William McDonough, McDonough Innovation
Cheri McGuire, Standard Chartered Bank
Chris McKenna, University of Oxford
Katherine Mach, Stanford University
Raffi Mardirosan, Ouster
Hugh Martin, Verizon
Bernard Meyersen, IBM Corporation
Cristian Mendoza, The Pontifical University of the Holy Cross Florence Mok, Monetary Authority of Singapore
Ben Moore, University of Zurich
Simon Mulcahey, Salesforce.com
Geoff Mulgan, NESTA
Sam Muller, HiiL
Venkatesh Narayanamurti, Harvard Kennedy School
Patrick Nee, Universal Bio Mining
Timothy J. Noonan, International Trade Union Confederation (ITUC)
Beth Simone Noveck, New York University
Jeremy O'Brien, University of Bristol
Tim O'Reilly, O'Reilly Media
Ruth Okediji, Harvard Law School
Ian Oppermann, Government of New South Wales, Australia
Michael Osborne, University of Oxford
Olivier Oullier, Emotiv
Tony Pan, Modern Electron
Janos Pasztor, Carnegie Climate Geoengineering Governance Initiative (C2G2)

Safak Pavey, Turkish Grand National Assembly
Lee Chor Pharn, Strategy Group, Government of Singapore
Christopher Pissarides, London School of Economics
Michael Platt, Yale University
Jared Poon, Strategy Group, Government of Singapore
Michael Posner, New York University
Jia Qing, SG Innovate
Limin Qiu, Zhejiang University
Huang Qunxing, Zhejiang University
Iayd Rahwan, MIT Media Lab
Mandeep Rai, Creative Visions Global
Rafael Ramirez, University of Oxford
Andreas Raptopoulos, Matternet
Matthieu Ricard, Karuna-Shechen
Dani Rodrik, Harvard Kennedy School
Jennifer Rupp, Swiss Federal Institute of Technology (ETH)
Wong Ruqin, Smart Nation and Digital Government Office, Government of Singapore
Stuart Russell, University of California, Berkeley
Heerad Sabeti, Fourth Sector Networks
Daniel Sachs, Proventus
Eric Salobir, Vatican Media Committee
Samir Saran, Observer Research Foundation (ORF)
Marc Saxer, Friedrich-Ebert-Stiftung
Chay Pui San, Smart Nation and Digital Government Office, Government of Singapore
Satyen Sangani, Alation
Owen Schaeffer, National University of Singapore
Nico Sell, Wikr
Anand Shah, Accenture
Lam Wee Shann, Land Transport Authority, Singapore
Huang Shaofei, Land Transport Authority, Singapore
Pranjal Sharma, Economic Analyst and Writer
David Shim, Korea Advanced Institute of Science and Technology
Wang Shouyan, Fudan University
Karanvir Singh, Visionum
Peter Smith, Blockchain
David Sng, SG Innovate
Dennis J. Snower, The Kiel Institute for the World Economy
Richard Soley, Object Management Group
Mildred Z. Solomon, The Hastings Center
Jack Stilgoe, University College London
Natalie Stingelin, Imperial College London
Carsten Stöcker, RWE
Ellen Stofan, University College London
Mustafa Suleyman, Google DeepMind

Arun Sundararajan, New York University
Hilary Sutcliffe, SocietyInside
Mariarosaria Taddeo, University of Oxford
Nina Tandon, Epibone
Don Tapscott, The Tapscott Group
Omar Tayeb, Blippr
Nitish Thakor, National University of Singapore
Andrew Thompson, Proteus Digital Health
Charis Thompson, University of California, Berkeley
Peter Tufano, University of Oxford
Onur Türk, Turkish Airlines
Richard Tyson, frog design inc
Christian Umbach, XapiX.io
Effy Vayena, University of Zurich
Rama Vedashree, Data Security Council of India (DSCI)
Marc Ventresca, University of Oxford
Kirill Veselkov, Imperial College London
David Victor, University of California, San Diego
Farida Vis, The University of Sheffield
Melanie Walker, World Bank
Wendell Wallach, Yale University
Stewart Wallis, Independent Thinker, Speaker and Advocate for a New Economic System
Poon King Wang, Lee Kuan Yew Centre for Innovative Cities
Ankur Warikoo, nearbuy.com
Brian Weeden, Secure World Foundation
Li Wei, CAS Institute of Zoology
Li Weidong, Shanghai Jiao Tong University
Andrew White, University of Oxford
Topher White, Rainforest Connection
Will.i.am, Entrepreneur and recording artist
Jeffrey Wong, EY
Lauren Woodman, Nethope
Ngaire Woods, University of Oxford
Junli Wu, Singapore Economic Development Board
Alex Wyatt, August Robotics
Lin Xu, Shanghai Jiao Tong University
Xue Lan, Tsinghua University
Brian Yeoh, Monetary Authority of Singapore
Jane Zavalishina, Yandex Money
Chenghang Zheng, Zhejiang University
Giuseppe Zocco, Index Ventures

Almost 100 colleagues from across the World Economic Forum's offices in Geneva, New York, San Francisco, Beijing and Tokyo also contributed significant amounts of their time, expertise and experience to this book.

Special thanks are due to those who gave generously in terms of strategic advice and technical assistance or who took the time to review drafts, develop material and engage their networks to strengthen the book. Thomas Philbeck helped structure the book, worked closely with contributors, and supplied nuanced perspectives on how technologies impact society and influence systemic change. Anne Marie Engtoft Larsen devoted innumerable hours to researching ideas, working with contributors, and supplying her own expertise on the topic of innovation and economic development, all of which were integral and invaluable parts of the final work. Mel Rogers provided deep insights, structural advice and spiritual counselling, without which this book would not have been possible. Katrin Eggenberger acted as the book's "internal publisher" and was a remarkable, steadfast and indefatigable supporter throughout its development. Other essential contributors and supporters who deserve special thanks include Kimberley Botwright, Aengus Collins, Scott David, David Gleicher, Berit Gleixner, Rigas Hadzilacos, Audrey Helstroffer, Jeremy Jurgens, Cheryl Martin, Stephan Mergenthaler, Fulvia Montresor, Derek O'Halloran, Richard Samans, Sha Song, Murat Sönmez, Jahda Swanborough and Mandy Ying.

We'd like to also recognize the managers of the Fourth Industrial Revolution Global Future Councils for their efforts in convening relevant discussions within their communities and networks: Nanayaa Appenteng, Vanessa Candeias, Daniel Dobrygowski, Daniel Gomez Gaviria, Manju George, Fernando Gomez, Amira Gouaibi, Rigas Hadzilacos, Nikolai Khlystov, Marina Krommenacker, Jiaojiao Li, Jesse McWaters, Lisa Ventura and Karen Wong.

Other Forum staff who contributed meaningfully to online discussions, knowledge sharing and support include David Aikman, Wadia Ait Hamza, Chidiogo Akunyili, Silja Baller, Paul Beecher, Andrey Berdichevskiy, Arnaud Bernaert, Stefano Bertolo, Katherine Brown, Sebastian Buckup, Oliver Cann, Gemma Corrigan, Sandrine Raher, Shimer Dao, Lisa Dreier, Margareta Drzeniek, John Dutton, Jaci Eisenberg, Nima Elmi, Emily Farnworth, Susanne Grassmeier, Mehran Gul, Michael Hanley, William Hoffman, Marie Sophie Müller, Jenny Soffel, Kiriko Honda, Ravi Kaneriya, Mihoko Kashiwakura, Danil Kerimi, Akanksha Khatri, Andrej Kirn, Zvika Krieger, Wolfgang Lehmacher, Till Leopold, Helena Leurent, Mariah Levin, Elyse Lipman, Peter Lyons, Silvia Magnoni, Katherine Milligan, John Moavenzadeh, Adrian Monck, Valerie Peyre, Goy Phumtim, Katherine Randel, Vesselina Stefanova Ratcheva, Philip Shetler-Jones, Mark Spelman, Tanah Sullivan, Kai Keller, Christoph von Toggenburg, Terri Toyota, Peter Vanham, Jean-Luc Vez, Silvia Von Gunten, Dominic Waughray, Bruce Weinelt, Barbara Wetsig-Lynam, Alex Wong, Andrea Wong, Kira Youdina and Saadia Zahidi.

Contributors

Chapter 3: Embedding Values in Technologies
Stewart Wallis, Independent Thinker, Speaker and Advocate for a New Economic System, United Kingdom
World Economic Forum Global Agenda Council on Values (2012-2014)
World Economic Forum Young Scientists Community
Thomas Philbeck, Head of Science and Technology Studies, World Economic Forum

Special Insert: A Human Rights-based Framework
Hilary Sutcliffe, Director, SocietyInside, United Kingdom
Anne-Marie Allgrove, Partner, Baker & McKenzie, Australia

Chapter 4: Empowering All Stakeholders
Anne Marie Engtoft Larsen, Knowledge Lead, Fourth Industrial Revolution, World Economic Forum

Chapter 5: New Computing Technologies
Justine Cassell, Associate Dean, Technology Strategy and Impact, Carnegie Mellon University, USA
Jeremy O'Brien, Director, The Centre for Quantum Photonics (CQP), University of Bristol, United Kingdom
Jennifer Rupp, Assistant Professor, Swiss Federal Institute of Technology (ETH), Switzerland
Kirk Bresniker, Chief Architect, Hewlett Packard Labs, Hewlett Packard Enterprise, USA
World Economic Forum Global Future Council on the Future of Computing

Chapter 6: Blockchain and Distributed Ledger Technologies
Jesse McWaters, Project Lead, Disruptive Innovation in Financial Services, World Economic Forum
Carsten Stöcker, Machine Economy Innovation Evangelist and Lighthouse Lead, innogy SE, Germany
Burkhard Blechschmidt, Head, CIO Advisory, Cognizant, Germany

Chapter 7: The Internet of Things
Derek O'Halloran, Co-Head, Digital Economy and Society, World Economic Forum
Richard Soley, Chairman and Chief Executive Officer, Object Management Group, USA

Special Insert: Highlight on Data Ethics
Luciano Floridi, Professor of Philosophy and Ethics of Information, University of Oxford, United Kingdom
Mariarosaria Taddeo, Researcher, University of Oxford, United Kingdom

Special Insert: Cyber Risks
Jean-Luc Vez, Head, Global Cyber Center, World Economic Forum
Ushang Damachi, Project Lead, Global Crime and Public Security, World Economic Forum
Nicholas Davis, Head of Society and Innovation, World Economic Forum

Chapter 8: Artificial Intelligence and Robotics
Stuart Russell, Professor of Computer Science, University of California, Berkeley, USA
World Economic Forum Global Future Council on the Future of Artificial Intelligence and Robotics.

Chapter 9: Advanced Materials
Alán Aspuru-Guzik, Professor, Department of Chemistry and Chemical Biology, Harvard University, USA
Bernard Meyerson, Chief Innovation Officer, IBM Corporation, USA

Chapter 10: Additive Manufacturing and Multidimensional Printing
Phill Dickens, Professor of Manufacturing Technology, University of Nottingham, United Kingdom

Special Insert: The Upside and Downside of Drones
David Shim, Associate Professor, Department of Aerospace Engineering, (KAIST), Republic of Korea
Andreas Raptopoulos, Chief Executive Officer, Matternet, USA
Dapo Akande, Professor of Public International Law, Faculty of Law, University of Oxford, United Kingdom.
Thomas Philbeck, Head of Science and Technology Studies, World Economic Forum

Chapter 11: Biotechnologies
World Economic Forum Global Future Council on the Future of Biotechnologies

Chapter 12: Neurotechnologies
Olivier Oullier, President, Emotiv, USA
World Economic Forum Global Future Council on the Future of Neurotechnologies and Brain Science

Chapter 13: Virtual and Augmented Realities
Anne Marie Engtoft Larsen, Knowledge Lead, Fourth Industrial Revolution, World Economic Forum
Yobie Benjamin, Co-Founder, Avegant, USA
Drue Kataoka, Artist and Technologist, Drue Kataoka Studios, USA

Special Insert: A Perspective on Arts & Culture
Nico Daswani, Head of Arts and Culture, World Economic Forum Andrea Bandelli, Executive Director, Science Gallery International, Ireland

Chapter 14: Energy Capture, Storage and Transmission
World Economic Forum Global Future Council on the Future of Energy
David Victor, Professor, University of California, San Diego (UCSD), USA

Chapter 15: Geoengineering
Anne Marie Engtoft Larsen, Knowledge Lead, Fourth Industrial Revolution, World Economic Forum
Wendell Wallach, Scholar, Interdisciplinary Center for Bioethics, Yale University, USA
Janos Pasztor, Senior Fellow and Executive Director, Carnegie Climate Geoengineering Governance Initiative (C2G2), USA
Jack Stilgoe, Lecturer in Science and Technology Studies, University College London, United Kingdom.

Chapter 16: Space Technologies
Brian Weeden, Technical Adviser, Secure World Foundation, USA
Ellen Stofan, Chief Scientist, NASA (2013-2016); Honorary Professor, Hazard Research Centre, University College London (UCL), United Kingdom
World Economic Forum Global Future Council on the Future of Space Technologies

Editing
Fabienne Stassen, EditOr Proof, Geneva, Switzerland
Curtis Carbonell
Andrew Wright

Design and layout
Kamal Kimaoui, Head of Production and Design,
World Economic Forum

References

Introduction
Schwab, K. 2016. The Fourth Industrial Revolution. Geneva: World Economic Forum

Chapter 1: Framing the Fourth Industrial Revolution

Centers for Disease Control and Prevention. 2016. "Mortality in the United States, 2015". National Center for Health Statistics Data Brief No. 267.
Crafts, N. F. R. 1987. "Long-term unemployment in Britain in the 1930s". *The Economic History Review*, 40: 418-432.
Gordon, R. 2016. *The Rise and Fall of American Growth*. Princeton: Princeton University Press.
McCloskey, D. 2016. *Bourgeois Equality*. Chicago: University of Chicago Press.
Smil, V. 2005. *Creating the Twentieth Century: Technical Innovations of 1867-1914 and Their Lasting Impact*. New York: Oxford University Press.
UNDP. 2017. About Human Development. Available at: http://hdr.undp.org/en/humandev. [Accessed 1 May 2017].
The World Bank Data Bank. 2017. "Poverty headcount ratio at $1.90 a day (2011 PPP) (% of population)". Available at: http://data.worldbank.org/indicator/SI.POV.DDAY. [Accessed 1 June 2017].

Chapter 2: Connecting the Dots

Autor, D., F. Levy and R. Murnane. 2003. "The Skill Content of Recent Technological Change: An Empirical Exploration". *The Quarterly Journal of Economics* 118(4): 1279-1334.
Berger, T. and C. B. Frey. 2015. "Industrial Renewal in the 21st Century: Evidence from US Cities", Regional Studies. Available at: http://www.oxfordmartin.ox.ac.uk/downloads/academic/regional_studies_industrial_renewal.pdf.
BlackRock Investment Institute. 2014. "Interpreting Innovation: Impact on Productivity, Inflation & Investing". Available at: https://www.blackrock.com/corporate/en-us/literature/whitepaper/bii-interpreting-innovation-us-version.pdf.
CB Insights. 2017. "The Race For AI: Google, Twitter, Intel, Apple In A Rush To Grab Artificial Intelligence Startups", Research Briefs. Available at: https://www.cbinsights.com/blog/top-acquirers-ai-startups-ma-timeline/.
Katz, L. and A. Krueger. 2016. "The Rise and Nature of Alternative Work Arrangements in the United States, 1995-2015". Princeton University and NBER Working Paper 603. Princeton University. Available at: http://dataspace.princeton.edu/jspui/bitstream/88435/dsp01zs25xb933/3/603.pdf.

New Atlas. 2015. "Amazon to begin testing new delivery drones in the US". N. Lavars, New Atlas, 13 April 2015. Available at: http://newatlas.com/amazon-new-delivery-drones-us-faa-approval/36957/.
The New York Times. 2017. "Is it time to break up Google?" J. Taplin, *The New York Times*, 22 April 2017. Available at: https://www.nytimes.com/2017/04/22/opinion/sunday/is-it-time-to-break-up-google.html?mcubz=1&_r=0.
OECD (Organisation for Economic Co-operation and Development). 2016. "Big Data: Bringing Competition Policy to the Digital Era", Background note, 29-30 November 2016. Available at: https://one.oecd.org/document/DAF/COMP(2016)14/en/pdf.
San Francisco Examiner. 2017. "San Francisco talks robot tax". J. Sabatini, San Francisco Examiner, 14 March 2017. Available at: http://www.sfexaminer.com/san-francisco-talks-robot-tax/.
World Economic Forum. 2017a. *The Inclusive Growth and Development Report 2017.* Insight Report. Geneva: World Economic Forum. Available at: http://www3.weforum.org/docs/WEF_Forum_IncGrwth_2017.pdf.
World Economic Forum. 2017b. "Realizing Human Potential in the Fourth Industrial Revolution: An Agenda for Leaders to Shape the Future of Education, Gender and Work", White Paper. Geneva: World Economic Forum. Available at: http://www3.weforum.org/docs/WEF_EGW_Whitepaper.pdf.

Chapter 3: Embedding Values in Technologies

The Boston Globe. 2016. "The gig economy is coming. You probably won't like it." B. Ambrosino, *The Boston Globe*, 20 April 2016. Available at: https://www.bostonglobe.com/magazine/2016/04/20/the-gig-economy-coming-you-probably-won-like/i2F6Yicao9OQVL4dbX6QGI/story.html.
Brynjolfsson, E. and A. McAfee. 2014. *The Second Machine Age.* New York and London: W.W. Norton & Company.
Cath, C. and L. Floridi. 2017. "The Design of the Internet's Architecture by the Internet Engineering Task Force (IETF) and Human Rights". *Science and Engineering, Ethics*, 23(2): 449-468.
Devaraj, S. and M. J. Hicks. 2017. "The Myth and the Reality of Manufacturing in America", June 2015 and April 2017, Ball State University. Available at: http://conexus.cberdata.org/files/MfgReality.pdf.
EPSRC (Engineering and Physical Sciences Research Council). 2017. "Principles of robotics". The Engineering and Physical Sciences Research Council. Available at: https://www.epsrc.ac.uk/research/ourportfolio/themes/engineering/activities/principlesofrobotics/. [Accessed 1 May 2017].
EU General Data Protection Regulation. 2017. "An overview of the main changes under GDPR and how they differ from the previous directive". Available at: http://www.eugdpr.org/key-changes.html. [Accessed 1 June 2017].
Florida Ice and Farm Company (FIFCO). 2015. *Living Our Purpose.* 2015 Integrated Report. Available at: https://www.fifco.com/files/documents/1715515fb6ab1e74f29d3da4aefa30c7b36a05.pdf.
IEEE (Institute of Electrical and Electronics Engineers). 2017. The IEEE Global Initiative for Ethical Considerations in Artificial Intelligence and Autonomous Systems "Executive Summary". Available at: https://standards.ieee.org/develop/indconn/ec/ead_executive_summary.pdf.

Keeley, B. 2015. *Income Inequality: The Gap between Rich and Poor.* OECD Publishing. Paris: OECD Publishing.
Latour, B. and S. Woolgar. 1979. *Laboratory Life: The Construction of Scientific Facts.* Princeton: Princeton University Press.
Mitcham, C. 1994. "Engineering design research and social responsibility". In K. S. Shrader-Frechette (Ed.) *Ethics of Scientific Research.* Lanham: Rowman & Littlefield.
Nuffield Council on Bioethics. 2014. "Emerging biotechnologies, Introduction: A guide for the reader". Available at: http://nuffieldbioethics.org/wp-content/uploads/2014/07/Emerging_biotechnologies_Introduction.pdf.
Oppenheimer, J. R. 2017. "Speech to the Association of Los Alamos Scientists". Los Alamos, New Mexico, 2 November 1945. Available at: http://www.atomicarchive.com/Docs/ManhattanProject/OppyFarewell.shtml. [Accessed 1 June 2017].
Pretz, K. 2017. "What's Being Done to Improve Ethics Education at Engineering Schools". The Institute, 18 May 2017. Available at: http://theinstitute.ieee.org/members/students/whats-being-done-to-improve-ethics-education-at-engineering- schools.
Rankin, J. 2015. "Germany's planned nuclear switch-off drives energy innovation". *The Guardian,* 2 November 2015. Available at: https://www.theguardian.com/environment/2015/nov/02/germanys-planned-nuclear-switch-off-drives-energy-innovation.
Schwab, K. 2016. *The Fourth Industrial Revolution.* Geneva: World Economic Forum.
World Economic Forum. 2013. "A New Social Covenant". Global Agenda Council on Values, White Paper. Geneva: World Economic Forum. Available at: http://www3.weforum.org/docs/WEF_GAC_Values_2013.pdf.
World Economic Forum. 2017. *The Global Risks Report 2017.* Insight Report. Geneva: World Economic Forum.

Special Insert *A Human Rights-based Framework*

Chapter 4: Empowering All Stakeholders

Bloomberg. 2016. "Wind and Solar Are Crushing Fossil Fuels". T. Randall, Bloomberg, 6 April 2016. Available at: https://www. bloomberg.com/news/articles/2016-04-06/wind-and-solar-are-crushing-fossil-fuels.
The Boston Consulting Group. 2016. Self-Driving Vehicles, Robo-Taxis, and the Urban Mobility Revolution. Boston: BCG. Available at: http://www.automotivebusiness.com.br/abinteligencia/pdf/BCG_SelfDriving.pdf.
Catalyst. 2016. "Women In Science, Technology, Engineering, And Mathematics (STEM)". Catalyst, 9 December 2016. Available at: http://www.catalyst.org/knowledge/women-science-technology-engineering-and-mathematics-stem.
Ceballos, G. et al. 2015. "Accelerated modern human-induced species losses: Entering the sixth mass extinction". *Science Advances* 1(5), e1400253. Available at: http://advances.sciencemag.org/content/1/5/e1400253.
Deloitte. 2016. "Women in IT jobs: it is about education, but also about more than just education". Technology, Media & Telecommunications Predictions. Deloitte. Available at: https://www2.deloitte.com/ global/en/pages/technology-media-and-telecommunications/articles/tmt-pred16-tech-women-in-it-jobs.html.

Dietz, S. et al. 2016. "'Climate value at risk' of global financial assets". *Nature Climate Change* 6: 676-679. Available at: http://www.nature.com/nclimate/journal/vaop/ncurrent/full/nclimate2972.html.

Enbakom, H.W., D.H Feyssa and S. Takele. 2017. "Impacts of deforestation on the livelihood of smallholder farmers in Arba Minch Zuria Woreda, Southern Ethiopia", *African Journal of Agricultural Research* 12(15): 1293-1305, 13 April 2017.

Fortune. 2017. "Robots Are Replacing Humans at All These Wall Street Firms". L. Shen, *Fortune*, 30 March 2017. Available at: http://fortune.com/2017/03/30/blackrock-robots-layoffs-artificial-intelligence-ai-hedge-fund/.

Global Challenges Foundation. 2017. "Earthstatement: The result of the Global Challenges Foundation and Earth League joining forces". Global Challenges Foundation. Available at: https://www.globalchallenges.org/en/our-work/earth-statement-2015.

Hausmann, R., C. Hidalgo et al. 2011. *The Atlas of Economic Complexity: Mapping Paths to Prosperity*, first edition. Available at: http://atlas.cid.harvard.edu/media/atlas/pdf/HarvardMIT_AtlasOfEconomicComplexity_Part_I.pdf.

Intergovernmental Panel on Climate Change (IPCC). 2014. *Climate Change 2014: Synthesis Report. Contribution of Working Groups I, II and III to the Fifth Assessment Report of the Intergovernmental Panel on Climate Change* [Core Writing Team, R.K. Pachauri and L.A. Meyer (eds.)]. Geneva: IPCC.

Juma, C. 2017. "Leapfrogging Progress: The Misplaced Promise of Africa's Mobile Revolution". *The Breakthrough* 7. Summer 2017. Available at: https://thebreakthrough.org/index.php/journal/issue-7/leapfrogging-progress.

Milanovic, B. 2016. *Global Inequality: A New Approach for the Age of Globalization*. Cambridge: Harvard University Press.

MIT Technology Review. 2017. "As Goldman Embraces Automation, Even the Masters of the Universe Are Threatened". N. Byrnes, *MIT Technology Review*, 7 February 2017. Available at: https://www.technologyreview.com/s/603431/as-goldman- embraces-automation-even-the-masters-of-the-universe-are-threatened/.

Newshub. 2016. "How drones are helping combat deforestation". S. Howe, Newshub, 22 September 2016. Available at: http://www.newshub.co.nz/home/world/2016/09/how-drones-are-helping-combat-deforestation.html.

Oxford Internet Institute. 2011. "The Distribution of all Wikipedia Articles". Taken from Graham, M., S. A. Hale and M. Stephens (2011), *Geographies of the World's Knowledge*. London: Convoco! Edition. Available at: http://geography.oii.ox.ac.uk/?page=the-distribution-of-all-wikipedia-articles.

Oxford Internet Institute. 2017. "The Location of Academic Knowledge". Taken from Graham, M., S. A. Hale and M. Stephens (2011), *Geographies of the World's Knowledge*. London: Convoco! Edition. Available at: http://geography.oii.ox.ac.uk/?page=the-location-of-academic-knowledge.

Philbeck, Imme. 2017. "Connecting the Unconnected: Working together to achieve Connect 2020 Agenda Targets". International Telecommunication Union (ITU). A background paper to the special session of the Broadband Commission and the World Economic Forum at Davos Annual Meeting 2017. Available at: http://broadbandcommission.org/Documents/ITU_discussion-paper_Davos2017.pdf.

Population Reference Bureau. 2017. "Human Population: Urbanization: Largest Urban Agglomerations, 1975, 2000, 2025". Available at: http://www.prb.org/Publications/Lesson-Plans/HumanPopulation/Urbanization.aspx.

Rockström, J. et al. 2009. "Planetary Boundaries: Exploring the Safe Operating Space for Humanity". *Ecology and Society* 14(2) art. 32. Available at: https://www.ecologyandsociety.org/vol14/iss2/art32/.
Schwab, K. 2016. *The Fourth Industrial Revolution.* Geneva: World Economic Forum.
Steffen et al. 2015. "Sustainability. Planetary Boundaries: guiding human development on a changing planet". *Science* 347(6223), 1259855. Available at: https://www.ncbi.nlm.nih.gov/pubmed/25592418.
Tay, B.T.C. et al. 2013. "When Stereotypes Meet Robots: The Effect of Gender Stereotypes on People's Acceptance of a Security Robot". In *Engineering Psychology and Cognitive Ergonomics. Understanding Human Cognition,* D. Harris, ed., EPCE 2013. Lecture Notes in Computer Science, Vol. 8019. Springer, Berlin, Heidelberg.
University of Sussex. 2008. *Technology Leapfrogging: A Review of the Evidence, A report for DFID.* Sussex Energy Group. Available at: https://www.sussex.ac.uk/webteam/gateway/file.php?name=dfid-leapfrogging-reportweb.pdf&site=264.
UNESCO (United Nations Educational, Scientific and Cultural Organization). 2015. "Women in Science: The gender gap in science". Fact Sheet No. 34. UNESCO Institute for Statistics. Available at: http://uis.unesco.org/sites/default/files/documents/fs34-women-in-science-2015-en.pdf.
UNESCO (United Nations Educational, Scientific and Cultural Organization). 2016. "Leaving no one behind: How far on the way to universal primary and secondary education?" Policy paper 27/Fact Sheet No. 37. UNESCO Institute for Statistics. Available at: http://unesdoc.unesco.org/images/0024/002452/245238E.pdf.
UNESCO (United Nations Educational, Scientific and Cultural Organization). 2017. "Global Investments in R&D". Fact Sheet No. 42, FS/2017/SCI/42. UNESCO Institute for Statistics. Available at: http://unesdoc.unesco.org/images/0024/002477/247772e.pdf.
United Nations, Department of Economic and Social Affairs, Population Division. 2015. "World Population Prospects: The 2015 Revision, Key findings & advance tables". Working Paper No. ESA/P/WP.241. Available at: https://esa.un.org/unpd/wpp/publications/files/key_findings_wpp_2015.pdf.
WIPO (World Intellectual Property Organization). 2017. WIPO IP Statistics Data Center. Available at: https://www3.wipo.int/ipstats/index.htm. [Accessed 1 June 2017].
The World Bank Data Bank. 2017. "Poverty headcount ratio at $1.90 a day (2011 PPP) (% of population)". Available at: http://data.worldbank.org/indicator/SI.POV.DDAY. [Accessed 1 June 2017].
World Bank and Institute for Health Metrics and Evaluation. 2016. *The Cost of Air Pollution: Strengthening the Economic Case for Action.* Washington, DC: World Bank. License: Creative Commons Attribution CC BY 3.0 IGO. Available at: http://documents.worldbank.org/curated/en/781521473177013155/pdf/108141-REVISED-Cost-of- PollutionWebCORRECTEDfile.pdf.
World Economic Forum. 2016. *The Global Gender Gap Report 2016.* Insight Report. Geneva: World Economic Forum.
World Economic Forum. 2016a. *The New Plastics Economy: Rethinking the future of plastics.* Industry Agenda. Geneva: World Economic Forum. Available at: http://www3.weforum.org/docs/WEF_The_New_Plastics_Economy.pdf.
World Resources Institute. 2014. "The History of Carbon Dioxide Emissions". J. Friedrich and T. Damassa, WRI, 21 May 2014. Available at: http://www.wri.org/blog/2014/05/history-carbon-dioxide-emissions#fn:1.

Yale Environment 360. 2016. "How Satellites and Big Data Can Help to Save the Oceans". Yale School of Forestry & Environmental Studies. Available at: http://e360.yale.edu/features/how_satellites_and_big_data_can_help_to_save_the_oceans.

Chapter 5: New Computing Technologies

Cameron, D. and T. Mowatt. 2012. "Writing the Book in DNA". Wyss Institute, 16 August 2012. Available at: https://wyss. harvard.edu/writing-the-book-in-dna/.

Cockshott, P., L. Mackenzie and G. Michaelson. 2010. "Non-classical computing: feasible versus infeasible". Paper presented at ACM-BCS Visions of Computer Science 2010: International Academic Research Conference, University of Edinburgh, 14-16 April 2010.

Cortada, J. W. 1993. *The Computer in the United States: From laboratory to market, 1930-1960*. M.E. Sharpe.

Denning, P. J. and T. G. Lewis. 2016. "Exponential Laws of Computing Growth". *Communications of the ACM* 60(1): 54-65. Available at: http://dl.acm.org/citation.cfm?doid=3028256.2976758.

Ezrachi, A. and M. Stucke. 2017. "Law Profs to Antitrust Enforcers: To Rein in Super-Platforms, Look Upstream". The Authors Guild. 12 April 2017. Available at: https://www.authorsguild.org/industry-advocacy/law-profs-antitrust-enforcers- rein-super-platforms-look-upstream/.

Frost Gorder, P. 2016. "Computers in your clothes? A milestone for wearable electronics", The Ohio State University, 13 April 2016. Available at: https://news.osu.edu/news/2016/04/13/computers-in-your-clothes-a-milestone-for-wearable-electronics/.

IEEE (Institute of Electrical and Electronics Engineers). 2016. "International Roadmap for Devices and Systems". 2016 Edition. White Paper. IEEE. Available at: http://irds.ieee.org/images/files/pdf/2016_MM.pdf.

ITRS (International Technology Roadmap for Semiconductors) 2.0. 2015. *International Technology Roadmap for Semiconductors 2.0*. 2015 Edition, Executive Report. ITRS. Available at: https://www.semiconductors.org/clientuploads/Research_Technology/ITRS/2015/0_2015%20ITRS%202.0%20Executive%20Report%20(1).pdf.

Knight, H. 2015. "Researchers develop basic computing elements for bacteria". MIT News, 9 July 2015. Available at: http:// news.mit.edu/2015/basic-computing-for-bacteria-0709.

Lapedus, M. 2016. "10nm Versus 7nm". Semiconductor Engineering, 25 April 2016. Available at: http://semiengineering. com/10nm-versus-7nm/.

Poushter, J. 2016. "2. Smartphone ownership rates skyrocket in many emerging economies, but digital divide remains". Pew Research Center. Global Attitudes & Trends. 22 February 2016. Available at: http://www.pewglobal.org/2016/02/22/smartphone-ownership-rates-skyrocket-in-many-emerging-economies-but-digital-divide-remains/.

Raspberry Pi Foundation. 2016. *Annual Review 2016*. Available at: https://www.raspberrypi.org/files/about/ RaspberryPiFoundationReview2016.pdf.

Schwab, K. 2016. *The Fourth Industrial Revolution*. Geneva: World Economic Forum.

Solon, O. 2017. "Facebook has 60 people working on how to read your mind."

The Guardian, 19 April 2017. Available at: https://www.theguardian.com/technology/2017/apr/19/facebook-mind-reading-technology-f8.

Weiser, M. 1991. "The Computer for the 21st Century". *Scientific American* 265(3): 94-104. Available at: https://www.ics. uci.edu/~corps/phaseii/Weiser-Computer21stCentury-SciAm.pdf.

World Economic Forum and INSEAD. 2015. *The Global Information Technology Report 2015: ICTs for Inclusive Growth.* Insight Report. Geneva: World Economic Forum. Available at: http://www3.weforum.org/docs/WEF_Global_IT_Report_2015.pdf.

Yang, S. 2016. "Smallest. Transistor. Ever". Berkeley Lab, 6 October 2016; updated 17 October 2016. Available at: http:// newscenter.lbl.gov/2016/10/06/smallest-transistor-1-nm-gate/.

Chapter 6: Blockchain and Distributed Ledger Technologies

Bitcoin Fees. 2017. "Predicting Bitcoin Fees For Transactions". Available at: https://bitcoinfees.21.co/. [Accessed 2 November 2017].

Greenberg, A. 2016. "Silk Road Prosecutors Argue Ross Ulbricht Doesn't Deserve A New Trial". Wired, 18 June 2016. Available at: https://www.wired.com/2016/06/silk-road-prosecutors-argue-ross-ulbricht-doesnt-deserve-new-trial/.

OECD (Organisation for Economic Co-operation and Development) and EUIPO (European Union Intellectual Property Office). 2016. *Trade in Counterfeit and Pirated Goods: Mapping the Economic Impact.* OECD Publishing. Paris: OECD Publishing. Available at: http://dx.doi.org/10.1787/9789264252653-en.

Ruppert, A. 2016. "Mapping the decentralized world of tomorrow", Medium.com, 1 June 2016. Available at: https:// medium.com/birds-view/mapping-the-decentralized-world-of-tomorrow-5bf36b973203.

Tapscott, D. and A. Tapscott. 2016. Blockchain Revolution. New York: Portfolio Penguin

World Economic Forum. 2016. "The Internet of Things and connected devices: making the world smarter". Geneva: World Economic Forum. Available at: http://reports.weforum.org/digital-transformation/the internet of things and connected-devices-making-the-world-smarter/.

Chapter 7: The Internet of Things

Brown, J. 2016. "The 5 biggest hacks of 2016 and the organizations they crippled", Industry Dive, 8 December 2016. Available at: http://www.ciodive.com/news/the-5-biggest-hacks-of-2016-and-the-organizations-they-crippled/431916/.

Columbus, L. 2016. "Roundup Of Internet Of Things Forecasts And Market Estimates, 2016". *Forbes*, 27 November 2016. Available at: https://www.forbes.com/sites/louiscolumbus/2016/11/27/roundup-of-internet-of-things-forecasts-and-market- estimates-2016/#290b6abb292d.

McKinsey Global Institute. 2015. "The Internet of Things: Mapping the value beyond the hype". McKinsey & Company. Available at: file:///C:/Users/admin/Downloads/The-Internet-of-things-Mapping-the-value-beyond-the-hype.pdf.
McKinsey Global Institute. 2015a. "Unlocking the potential of the Internet of Things". McKinsey & Company. Available at: http://www.mckinsey.com/business-functions/digital-mckinsey/our-insights/the-internet-of-things-the-value-of-digitizing- the-physical-world.
Perrow. C. 1984. *Normal Accidents: Living with High-Risk Technologies*. Basic Books.
World Economic Forum. 2015. *Industrial Internet of Things: Unleashing the Potential of Connected Products and Services*. Industry Agenda. Geneva: World Economic Forum.
World Economic Forum and Accenture. 2016. "The Internet of Things and connected devices: making the world smarter". Geneva: World Economic Forum. Available at: http://reports.weforum.org/digital-transformation/the-internet-of-things-and-connected-devices-making-the-world-smarter/.

Special Insert: Cyber Risks

eMarketer. 2017. "Internet Users and Penetration Worldwide", Available at: http://www.emarketer.com/Chart/Internet-Users-Penetration-Worldwide-2016-2021-billions-of-population-change/206259
Greenberg, Andy. 2015. "Hackers Remotely Kill a Jeep on the Highway – With Me in It", Wired, July 2015. Available at: https://www.wired.com/2015/07/hackers-remotely-kill-jeep-highway/
KrebsonSecurity. 2014. "Target Hackers Broke in Via HVAC Company". Available at: https://krebsonsecurity.com/2014/02/target-hackers-broke-in-via-hvac-company/
Miniwatts Marketing. 2017. "Internet World Stats", Available at: http://www.internetworldstats.com/stats.htm
Nuix (2017), "Most Hackers Can Access Systems and Steal Valuable Data Within 24 Hours: Nuix Black Report", website accessed on 23 November 2017 https://www.nuix.com/media-releases/most-hackers-can-access-systems-and-steal-valuable-data-within-24-hours-nuix-black

NYSE Governance Services. 2015. Cybersecurity in the Boardroom. New York: NYSE. Available at: https://www.nyse.com/publicdocs/VERACODE_Survey_Report.pdf
OECD. 2012. Cybersecurity Policy Making at a Turning Point, Paris: OECD. Available at: https://www.oecd.org/sti/ieconomy/cybersecurity%20policy%20making.pdf
Reinsel, D, Gantz, J and Rydning, J. 2017. Data Age 2025, IDC Available at: https://www.seagate.com/files/www-content/our-story/trends/files/Seagate-WP-DataAge2025-March-2017.pdf
Westby, J R and Power, R. 2008. Governance of Enterprise Security Survey: CyLab 2008 Report, Pttisburgh: Carnegie Mellon CyLab. Available at: https://portal.cylab.cmu.edu/portal/files/pdfs/governance-survey2008.pdf
World Economic Forum. 2012. Partnering for Cyber Resilience. Geneva: World Economic Forum. Available at: http://www3.weforum.org/docs/WEF_IT_PartneringCyberResilience_Guidelines_2012.pdf

World Economic Forum. 2017. Advancing Cyber Resilience: Principles and Tools for Boards. Geneva: World Economic Forum. Available at: http://www3.weforum.org/docs/IP/2017/Adv_Cyber_Resilience_Principles-Tools.pdf

Chapter 8: Artificial Intelligence and Robotics

Agence France-Presse. 2016. "Convoy of self-driving trucks completes first European cross-border trip". *The Guardian*, 7 April 2016. Available at: https://www.theguardian.com/technology/2016/apr/07/convoy-self-driving-trucks-completes-first-european-cross-border-trip.

AI International. 2017. "Universities with AI Programs". Available at: http://www.aiinternational.org/universities.html

Baraniuk, C., "The cyborg chess players that can't be beaten". BBC, 4 December 2015. Available at: http://www.bbc.com/future/story/20151201-the-cyborg-chess-players-that-cant-be-beaten.

CB Insights. 2017. "The Race For AI: Google, Twitter, Intel, Apple In A Rush To Grab Artificial Intelligence Startups". CB Insights, 21 July 2017. Available at: https://www.cbinsights.com/blog/top-acquirers-ai-startups-ma-timeline/.

Cohen, M. et al. 2016. *Off-, On- or Reshoring: Benchmarking of Current Manufacturing Location Decisions: Insights from the Global Supply Chain Benchmark Study 2015*. The Global Supply Chain Benchmark Consortium 2016. Available at: http://pulsar.wharton.upenn.edu/fd/resources/20160321GSCBSFinalReport.pdf.

Conner-Simons, A. 2016. "Robot helps nurses schedule tasks on labor floor". MIT News, 13 July 2016. Available at: http:// news.mit.edu/2016/robot-helps-nurses-schedule-tasks-on-labor-floor-0713.

DeepMind Ethics & Society homepage. 2017. Available at: https://deepmind.com/applied/deepmind-ethics-society/.

EPSRC (Engineering and Physical Sciences Research Council). 2017. "Principles of Robotics: Regulating robots in the real world". Available at: https://www.epsrc.ac.uk/research/ourportfolio/themes/engineering/activities/principlesofrobotics/.

Frey, C. and M. Osborne. 2013. "The Future of Employment: How Susceptible Are Jobs to Computerisation?" Oxford Martin School Working Paper, 17 September 2013. Available at: http://www.oxfordmartin.ox.ac.uk/downloads/academic/The_Future_of_Employment.pdf.

Hadfield-Menell, D., A. Dragan, P. Abbeel and S. Russell. 2017. "Cooperative Inverse Reinforcement Learning". *Advances in Neural Information Processing Systems* 25. MIT Press.

Hardesty, L. 2013. "Surprisingly simple scheme for self-assembling robots". MIT News, 4 October 2013. Available at: http://news.mit.edu/2013/simple-scheme-for-self-assembling-robots-1004.

LaGrandeur, K. and J. Hughes (Eds). 2017. *Surviving the Machine Age: Intelligent Technology and the Transformation of Human Work*. Palgrave Macmillan. Available at: http://www.springer.com/la/book/9783319511641.

McKinsey & Company. 2017. *A future that works: Automation, employment, and productivity*. McKinsey Global Institute. Available at: file:///C:/Users/admin/Downloads/MGI-A-future-that-works-Full-report%20(1).pdf.

Metz, C. 2016. "The Rise of the Artificially Intelligent Hedge Fund". Wired, 25 January 2016. Available at: https://www. wired.com/2016/01/the-rise-of-the-artificially-intelligent-hedge-fund/.

Murphy, M. 2016. "Prepping a robot for its journey to Mars". MIT News, 18 October 2016. Available at: http://news.mit. edu/2016/sarah-hensley-valkyrie-humanoid-robot-1018.
OECD (Organisation for Economic Co-operation and Development). 2016. "Automation and Independent Work in a Digital Economy". Policy Brief on the Future of Work. Available at: http://www.oecd.org/employment/Policy%20 brief%20-%20 Automation%20and%20Independent%20Work%20in%20a%20 Digital%20Economy.pdf.
Partnership on AI. 2017. "Partnership on AI to benefit people and society". Available at: https://www.partnershiponai.org/#s-partners.
Petersen, R. 2016. "The driverless truck is coming, and it's going to automate millions of jobs". TechCrunch, 25 April 2016. Available at: https://techcrunch.com/2016/04/25/the-driverless-truck-is-coming-and-its-going-to-automate-millions-of- jobs/.
Pittman, K. 2016. "The Automotive Sector Buys Half of All Industrial Robots". Engineering.com, 24 March 2016. Available at: http://www.engineering.com/AdvancedManufacturing/ArticleID/11761/The-Automotive-Sector-Buys-Half-of-All- -Industrial-Robots.aspx.
Sample, I. and A. Hern. 2014. "Scientists dispute whether computer 'Eugene Goostman' passed Turing test". *The Guardian*, 9 June 2014. Available at: https://www.theguardian.com/technology/2014/jun/09/scientists-disagree-over-whether-turing-test-has-been-passed.
Thielman, S. 2016. "Use of police robot to kill Dallas shooting suspect believed to be first in US history", *The Guardian*, 8 July 2016. Available at: https://www.theguardian.com/technology/2016/jul/08/police-bomb-robot-explosive-killed-suspect- dallas.
Turing, A. M. 1951. "Can Digital Computers Think?" Lecture broadcast on BBC Third Programme, 15 May 1951; typescript at turingarchive.org.
Vanian, J. 2016. "The Multi-Billion Dollar Robotics Market Is About to Boom". *Fortune*, 24 February 2016. Available at: http://fortune.com/2016/02/24/robotics-market-multi-billion-boom/.
Wakefield, J. 2016. "Self-drive delivery van can be 'built in four hours'". BBC, 4 November 2016. Available at: http://www. bbc.com/news/technology-37871391.
Wakefield, J. 2016b. "Foxconn replaces '60,000 factory workers with robots'". BBC, 25 May 2016. Available at: http://www.bbc.com/news/technology-36376966.
World Economic Forum. 2016. *The Future of Jobs: Employment, Skills and Workforce Strategy for the Fourth Industrial Revolution.* Global Challenge Insight Report. Geneva: World Economic Forum.

Chapter 9: Advanced Materials

United States National Nanotechnology Initiative. 2017. "NNI Supplement to the President's 2016 Budget". Nano.gov. official website. Available at: http://www.nano.gov/node/1326.
World Economic Forum. 2017. "Chemistry and Advanced Materials: at the heart of the Fourth Industrial Revolution". World Economic Forum, Agenda.

World Economic Forum. 2017a. "Digital Transformation Initiative: Chemistry and Advanced Materials Industry". White paper. Geneva: World Economic Forum in collaboration with Accenture. Available at: http://reports.weforum.org/digital-transformation/wp-content/blogs.dir/94/mp/files/pages/files/dti-chemistry-and-advanced-materials-industry-white-paper.pdf.

Chapter 10: Additive Manufacturing and Multidimensional Printing

Dickens, P. and T. Minshall. 2016. *UK National Strategy for Additive Manufacturing: Comparison of international approaches to public support for additive manufacturing/3D printing*. Technical Report.

Gartner. 2014. "Gartner Survey Reveals That High Acquisition and Start-Up Costs Are Delaying Investment in 3D Printers". Gartner Press Release, 9 December 2014. Available at: http://www.gartner.com/newsroom/id/2940117.

Gartner. 2016. "Gartner Says Worldwide Shipments of 3D Printers to Grow 108 Percent in 2016". Gartner Press Release, 13 October 2016. Available at: http://www.gartner.com/newsroom/id/3476317.

Parker, C. 2013. "3-D printing creates murky product liability issues, Stanford scholar says". Stanford University. Stanford Report, 12 December 2013. Available at: http://news.stanford.edu/news/2013/december/3d-legal-issues-121213.html.

PwC. 2016. *3D Printing comes of age in US industrial manufacturing*. Available at: https://www.pwc.com/us/en/industrial- products/publications/assets/pwc-next-manufacturing-3d-printing-comes-of-age.pdf.

Rehnberg, M. and S. Ponte. 2016. "3D Printing and Global Value Chains: How a new technology may restructure global production". Global Production Networks Centre Faculty of Arts & Social Sciences. GPN Working Paper Series, GPN2016-010. Available at: http://gpn.nus.edu.sg/file/Stefano%20Ponte_GPN2016_010.pdf.

de Wargny, M. 2016. "Top 10 Future 3D Printing Materials (that exist in the present!)". Sculpteo, 28 September 2016. Available at: https://www.sculpteo.com/blog/2016/09/28/top-10-future-3d-printing-materials-that-exist-in-the-present/.

Wohlers Associates. 2014. *Wohlers Report 2014. 3D Printing and Additive Manufacturing State of the Industry*. Annual Worldwide Progress Report. Wohlers Associates.

Wohlers Associates. 2016. *Wohlers Report 2016. 3D Printing and Additive Manufacturing State of the Industry*. Annual Worldwide Progress Report. Wohlers Associates.

Special Insert: The Upside and Downside of Drones

Amazon Prime Air. 2015. "Determining Safe Access with a Best-Equipped, Best-Served Model for Small Unmanned Aircraft Systems". NASA Unmanned Aircraft System Traffic Management (UTM). Available at: https://utm.arc.nasa.gov/docs/Amazon_Determining%20Safe%20Access%20with%20a%20Best-Equipped,%20Best-Served%20Model%20for%20sUAS[2].pdf.

Kopardekar, P. et al. 2016. "Unmanned Aircraft System Traffic Management (UTM) Concept of Operations". Presented at the 16th AIAA Aviation Technology, Integration, and Operations Conference, 13-17 June 2016, Washington DC. Available at: https://utm.arc.nasa.gov/docs/Kopardekar_2016-3292_ATIO. pdf.

NASA Traffic Unmanned Management. 2015. "Google UAS Airspace System Overview". NASA Traffic Unmanned Management. Available at: https://utm.arc.nasa.gov/docs/GoogleUASAirspaceSystemOverview5pager[1].pdf.
Overly, S. 2016. "Watch this 'gun' take down a flying drone". *The Washington Post*, 29 November 2016. Available at: https://www.washingtonpost.com/news/innovations/wp/2016/11/29/watch-this-gun-can-take-down-a-flying-drone/?utm_term=.c27bfe46b456.
Thompson, M. 2013. "Costly Flight Hours" *Time* Magazine. 2 April 2013. Available at: http://nation.time.com/2013/04/02/ costly-flight-hours/.

Chapter 11: Biotechnologies

Cyranoski, D. 2016. "CRISPR gene-editing tested in a person for the first time". *Nature*, 15 November 2016. Available at: http://www.nature.com/news/crispr-gene-editing-tested-in-a-person-for-the-first-time-1.20988.
Das, R. 2010. "Drug Industry Bets Big On Precision Medicine: Five Trends Shaping Care Delivery". *Forbes*, 8 March 2017. Available at: https://www.forbes.com/sites/reenitadas/2017/03/08/drug-development-industry-bets-big-on-precision- medicine-5-top-trends-shaping-future-care-delivery/2/#62c2746a7b33.
EY. 2016. *Beyond borders 2016: Biotech financing*. Available at: http://www.ey.com/Publication/vwLUAssets/ey-beyond- borders-2016-biotech-financing/$FILE/ey-beyond-borders-2016-biotech-financing.pdf.
Lee, S. Y. and H. U. Kim. 2015. "Systems strategies for developing industrial microbial strains". *Nature Biotechnology* 33(10): 1061-1072.
Peplow, M. 2015. "Industrial biotechs turn greenhouse gas into feedstock opportunity". *Nature Biotechnology* 33: 1123-1125.
Reilly, M. 2017. "In Africa, Scientists Are Preparing to Use Gene Drives to End Malaria." *MIT Technology Review*, 14 March 2017. Available at: https://www.technologyreview.com/s/603858/in-africa-scientists-are-preparing-to-use-gene-drives-to-end-malaria/.

Chapter 12: Neurotechnologies

Constine, J. 2017. "Facebook is building brain-computer interfaces for typing and skin-hearing". TechCrunch, 19 April 2017. Available at: https://techcrunch.com/2017/04/19/facebook-brain-interface/.
Emmerich, N. 2015. "The ethical implications of neuroscience". World Economic Forum, Agenda. 20 May 2015. Available at: https://www.weforum.org/agenda/2015/05/the-ethical-implications-of-neuroscience/.
European Commission. 2016. "Understanding the human brain, a global challenge ahead", 1 December 2016. Available at: https://ec.europa.eu/digital-single-market/en/news/understanding-human-brain-global-challenge-ahead.
Ghosh, K. 2015. "SpaceX for the Brain: Neuroscience Needs Business to Lead (Op-Ed)". Live Science, 9 September 2015. Available at: http://www.livescience.com/52129-neuroscience-needs-business-to-take-the-lead.html.
Grillner, S. et al. 2016. "Worldwide initiatives to advance brain research". *Nature Neuroscience* 19(9): 1118-1122. Available at: https://www.nature.com/neuro/journal/v19/n9/full/nn.4371.html.
Imperial College London. 2017. "Brain & Behaviour Lab". Available at: http://www.faisallab.com/.

Jones, R. 2016. "The future of brain and machine is intertwined, and it's already here". The Conversation, 3 October 2016. Available at: https://theconversation.com/the-future-of-brain-and-machine-is-intertwined-and-its-already-here-65280.
Juma, C. 2016. *Innovation and Its Enemies: Why People Resist New Technologies*. New York: Oxford University Press.
Neurotech. 2016. *The Market for Neurotechnology: 2016-2020. A Market Research Report from Neurotech Reports*. Available at: http://www.neurotechreports.com/pages/execsum.html.
Oullier, O. 2012. "Clear up this fuzzy thinking on brain scans". *Nature* 483(7387) 29 February 2012. Available at: http://www. nature.com/news/clear-up-this-fuzzy-thinking-on-brain-scans-1.10127.
Statt, N. 2017. "Elon Musk launches Neuralink, a venture to merge the human brain with AI". The Verge, 27 March 2017. Available at: http://www.theverge.com/2017/3/27/15077864/elon-musk-neuralink-brain-computer-interface-ai-cyborgs.
World Economic Forum. 2016. "The Digital Future of Brain Health". Global Agenda White Paper: Global Agenda Council on Brain Research. Geneva: World Economic Forum. Available at: https://www.weforum.org/whitepapers/the-digital-future-of- -brain-health.

Chapter 13: Virtual and Augmented Realities

Chafkin, M. 2015. "Why Facebook's $2 Billion Bet on Oculus Rift Might One Day Connect Everyone on Earth", *Vanity Fair*, October 2015. Available at: http://www.vanityfair.com/news/2015/09/oculus-rift-mark-zuckerberg-cover-story-palmer- -luckey.
Goldman Sachs. 2016. *Profiles in Innovation: Virtual & Augmented Reality*. The Goldman Sachs Group, 13 January 2016. Available at: http://www.goldmansachs.com/our-thinking/pages/technology-driving-innovation-folder/virtual-and- -augmented-reality/report.pdf.
Sebti, B. 2016. "Virtual reality can 'transport' audiences to poor countries. But can it persuade them to give more aid?" World Economic Forum, Agenda. 31 August 2016. Available at: https://www.weforum.org/agenda/2016/08/virtual reality- -can-transport-audiences-to-poor-countries-but-can-it-persuade-them-to-give-more-aid.
Zuckerberg, M. 2015. "Mark Zuckerberg and Oculus's Michael Abrash on Why Virtual Reality Is the Next Big Thing", Zuckerberg *Vanity Fair* interview, YouTube, 8 October 2015. Available at: https://www.youtube.com/watch?v=VQaCv52DSnY.

Chapter 14: Energy Capture, Storage and Transmission

Bloomberg. 2016. "Wind and Solar Are Crushing Fossil Fuels". T. Randall, Bloomberg. 6 April 2016. Available at: https://www. bloomberg.com/news/articles/2016-04-06/wind-and-solar-are-crushing-fossil-fuels.
European Commission. 2017. "Renewables: Europe on track to reach its 20% target by 2020". Fact Sheet, 1 February 2017. Available at: http://europa.eu/rapid/press-release_MEMO-17-163_en.htm.

Frankfurt School of Finance & Management. 2017. *Global Trends in Renewable Energy Investment 2017*. Frankfurt School-UNEP Collaborating Centre/Bloomberg New Energy Finance. Available at: http://fs-unep-centre.org/sites/default/files/publications/globaltrendsinrenewableenergyinvestment2017.pdf.
IEA (International Energy Agency). 2016. *World Energy Outlook 2016*. Chapter 1: Introduction and scope. Paris: OECD/IEA. Available at: https://www.iea.org/media/publications/weo/WEO2016Chapter1.pdf.
Kanellos, M. 2013. "Energy's Next Big Market: Transmission Technology". *Forbes*, 30 August 2013. Available at: https:// www.forbes.com/sites/michaelkanellos/2013/08/30/energys-next-big-market-transmission-technology/#71d13b9e31c4.
Parry, D. 2016. "NRL Space-Based Solar Power Concept Wins Secretary of Defense Innovative Challenge," U.S. Naval Research Laboratory, 11 March 2016. Available at: https://www.nrl.navy.mil/media/news-releases/2016/NRL-Space--Based-Solar-Power-Concept-Wins-Secretary-of-Defense-Innovative-Challenge.
Tucker, E. 2014. "Researchers Developing Supercomputer to Tackle Grid Challenges". Renewable Energy World, 7 July 2014. Available at: http://www.renewableenergyworld.com/articles/2014/07/researchers-developing-supercomputer-to- -tackle-grid-challenges.html.
United Nations, Department of Economic and Social Affairs, Population Division. 2015. "World Population Prospects: The 2015 Revision, Key findings & advance tables". Working Paper No. ESA/P/WP.241. Available at: https://esa.un.org/ unpd/wpp/publications/files/key_findings_wpp_2015.pdf.
University of Texas at Austin. 2017. "Lithium-Ion Battery Inventor Introduces New Technology for Fast-Charging, Noncombustible Batteries". UT News Press Release, 28 February 2017. Available at: https://news.utexas.edu/2017/02/28/goodenough-introduces-new-battery-technology.
Woolford, J. 2015. "Artificial Photosynthesis for Energy Takes a Step Forward". *Scientific American*, ChemistryWorld, 6 February 2015. Available at: https://www.scientificamerican.com/article/artificial-photosynthesis-for-energy-takes-a-step--forward/.
World Bank. 2017. "Electric power consumption (kWh per capita), 1960-2014". Available at: http://data.worldbank.org/ indicator/EG.USE.ELEC.KH.PC.

Chapter 15: Geoengineering

Condliffe, J. 2017. "Geoengineering Gets Green Light from Federal Scientists". *MIT Technology Review*, Sustainable Energy, 11 January 2017. Available at: https://www.technologyreview.com/s/603349/geoengineering-gets-green-light- -from-federal-scientists/.
IPCC (Intergovernmental Panel on Climate Change). 2013. *Climate Change 2013: The Physical Science Basis. Contribution of Working Group I to the Fifth Assessment Report of the Intergovernmental Panel on Climate Change* [Stocker, T.F., D. Qin, G.-K. Plattner, M. Tignor, S.K. Allen, J. Boschung, A. Nauels, Y. Xia, V. Bex and P.M. Midgley (eds)]. Cambridge, UK and New York, USA: Cambridge University Press.
Keith, D. 2002. "Geoengineering the Climate: History and Prospect". R. G. Watts (ed.) *Innovative Energy Strategies for CO_2 Stabilization*. Cambridge: Cambridge University Press. Available at: https://www.yumpu.com/en/document/view/50122050/geoengineering-the-climate-history-and-prospectpdf-david-keith.

Neslen, A. 2017. "US scientists launch world's biggest solar geoengineering study". *The Guardian*, 24 March 2017. Available at: https://www.theguardian.com/environment/2017/mar/24/us-scientists-launch-worlds-biggest-solar--geoengineering-study.
Pasztor, J. 2017. "Toward governance frameworks for climate geoengineering." Global Challenges Foundation. Available at: https://globalchallenges.org/en/our-work/quarterly-reports/global-cooperation-in-dangerous-times/toward-governance- -frameworks-for-climate-geoengineering.
Stilgoe, J. 2016. "Geoengineering as Collective Experimentation". *Science and Engineering Ethics* 22(3): 851-869. Available at: https://link.springer.com/article/10.1007/s11948-015-9646-0.

Chapter 16: Space Technologies

BAE Systems. 2015. "BAE Systems and Reaction Engines to develop a ground breaking new aerospace engine". BAE Newsroom, 2 November 2015. Available at: http://www.baesystems.com/en/bae-systems-and-reaction-engines-to- -develop-a-ground-breaking-new-aerospace-engine.
de Selding, P. B. 2015. "BAE Takes Stake in British Air-breathing Rocket Venture". SpaceNews, 2 November 2015. Available at: http://spacenews.com/bae-takes-stake-in-british-air-breathing-rocket-venture/.
Dillow, C. 2016. "VCs Invested More in Space Startups Last Year Than in the Previous 15 Years Combined". *Fortune*, 22 February 2016. Available at: http://fortune.com/2016/02/22/vcs-invested-more-in-space-startups-last-year/.
NASA (National Aeronautics and Space Administration). 2014. *Emerging Space: The Evolving Landscape of 21st Century American Spaceflight.* NASA Office of the Chief Technologist. Available at: https://www.nasa.gov/sites/default/files/files/Emerging_Space_Report.pdf.
Siccloff, S. 2017. "New Spacesuit Unveiled for Starliner Astronauts". NASA, 25 January 2017. Available at: https://www. nasa.gov/feature/new-spacesuit-unveiled for starliner-astronauts
Thibeault, S. et al. 2015. "Nanomaterials for radiation shielding". *MRS Bulletin* 40(10): 836-841.

Conclusion: Systems Leadership for a Better Future

AlphaBeta. 2017. *The Automation Advantage.* AlphaBeta news. 8 August 2017. Available at: http://www.alphabeta.com/the-automation-advantage/.
Carbon 3D. 2017. "The Perfect Fit: Carbon + adidas Collaborate to Upend Athletic Footwear". 7 April 2017. Available at: http://www. carbon3d.com/stories/adidas/. [Accessed 1 June 2017].
Guston, D. 2008. "Innovation policy: not just a jumbo shrimp". *Nature* 454(7207): 940-941.
Hadfield, G. 2016. *Rules for a Flat World.* New York: Oxford University Press.
International Organization for Standardization. 2017. "ISO/TS 15066:2016, Robots and robotic devices – Collaborative robots". Available at: https://www.iso.org/standard/62996.html. [Accessed 3 November 2017].

International Organization for Standardization. 2017a. "ISO/TC 20/SC 16, Unmanned aircraft systems". Available at: https://www.iso.org/committee/5336224/x/catalogue/p/0/u/1/w/0/d/0. [Accessed 3 November 2017].
Marchant, G. and W. Wallach. 2015. "Coordinating Technology Governance". *Issues in Science and Technology* XXXI(4).
Maynard, A. 2016. "A further reading list on the Fourth Industrial Revolution". World Economic Forum, Agenda. 22 January 2016. Available at: https://www.weforum.org/agenda/2016/01/mastering-the-social-side-of-the-fourth-industrial-revolution-an- -essential-reading-list/.
McKinsey Global Institute. 2017. *Harnessing Automation for a Future that Works.* Available at: http://www.mckinsey.com/ global-themes/digital-disruption/harnessing-automation-for-a-future-that-works.
Mulgan, G, 2017. "Anticipatory Regulation: 10 ways governments can better keep up with fast-changing industries". 11 September 2017. Available at: http://www.nesta.org.uk/blog/anticipatory-regulation-how-can-regulators-keep-fast-changing--industries#sthash.N9LV5jdB.dpuf.
Owen, R., P. Macnaghten and J. Stilgoe. 2012. "Responsible Research and Innovation: From Science in Society to Science for Society, with Society". *Science and Public Policy* 39(6): 751-760.
Rodemeyer, M., D. Sarewitz and J. Wilsdon. 2005. *The Future of Technology Assessment.* Woodrow Wilson International Center for Scholars, Science and Technology Innovation Program. Available at: https://www.wilsoncenter.org/sites/default/files/techassessment.pdf.
Sutcliffe, H. 2015. "Why I've ditched the 'Responsible Innovation' moniker to form 'Principles for Sustainable Innovation'." Matterforall blog, 13 February 2015. Available at: http://societyinside.com/why-ive-ditched-responsible-innovation-moniker-form-principles-sustainable-innovation.
Thomas, J. 2009. "21st Century Tech Governance? What would Ned Ludd do?" 2020 Science, 18 December 2009. Available at: https://2020science.org/category/technology-innovation-in-the-21st-century/.
Vanian, J. 2016. "Why Data Is The New Oil". *Fortune*, 11 July 2016. Available at: http://fortune.com/2016/07/11/data-oil- -brainstorm-tech/.
World Economic Forum. 2016. *The Future of Jobs: Employment, Skills and Workforce Strategy for the Fourth Industrial Revolution.* Global Challenge Insight Report. Geneva: World Economic Forum.
World Economic Forum Global Agenda Council on the Future of Software and Society. 2016. "A Call for Agile Governance Principles". Geneva: World Economic Forum. Available at: http://www3.weforum.org/docs/IP/2016/ICT/Agile_Governance_Summary.pdf.
World Economic Forum. 2018. "Agile Governance: Reimagining Policy-making in the Fourth Industrial Revolution". Geneva: World Economic Forum
World Economic Forum. 2017. "How the Fourth Industrial Revolution can help us prepare for the next natural disaster". World Economic Forum, Agenda
The New Yorker. 2017. "D.I.Y. Artificial Intelligence Comes to a Japanese Family Farm" A. Zeeberg, The New Yorker, 10 August 2017. Available at: https://www.newyorker.com/tech/elements/diy-artificial-intelligence-comes-to-a-japanese-family-farm

Endnotes

1 Some sectors grew spectacularly over this period; Crafts estimates that the production of cotton textiles grew at 9.7% per year between 1780 and 1801, slowing to 5.6% per year from 1801 to 1831. Iron production grew at rates of 5.1 % and 4.6% per year over the same periods (Crafts 1987).

2 Vaclav Smil calls it possibly the most impactful invention in history (Smil 2005).

3 McCloskey 2016

4 The United Nations Development Programme defines "human development" as "giving people more freedom and opportunities to live lives they value. In effect this means developing people's abilities and giving them a chance to use them. Three foundations for human development are to live a healthy and creative life, to be knowledgeable, and to have access to resources needed for a decent standard of living. Many other aspects are important too, especially in helping to create the right conditions for human development, such as environmental sustainability or equality between men and women." (UNDP 2017)

5 Gordon 2016

6 McCloskey 2016

7 Centers for Disease Control and Prevention 2016

8 World Bank 2017

9 The New York Times 2017

10 OECD 2016

11 Berger and Frey 2015

12 Katz and Krueger 2016

13 World Economic Forum 2017b

14 The San Francisco Examiner 2017

15 World Economic Forum 2017a

16 New Atlas 2015

17 Schwab 2016

18 Devaraj and Hicks 2017

19 World Economic Forum 2017

20 Brynjolfsson and McAfee 2014

21 The Boston Globe 2016

22 Keeley 2015

23 Rankin 2015

24 IEEE 2017

25 Nuffield Council on Bioethics 2014

26 IEEE 2017

27 World Economic Forum 2013

[28] EU GDPR 2017

[29] This strategy has been suggested in many forms but, in this case, the conceptual model for consideration is that of duty *plus respicere* outlined by Mitcham (1994).

[30] Oppenheimer [2 November 1945] 2017

[31] The trolley problem is a problem of choice used in ethics courses to introduce the complexity of variables that go into moral decision-making. In the problem, a trolley travels towards a person or group of people and the student must make or abstain from making life and death choices by choosing whether or not to divert the trolley along one of two tracks. The outcome in any case is bad for someone, and the student must wrestle with the "why" of the choice and try to find justification for his/her action.

[32] Pretz 2017

[33] Florida Ice and Farm Company 2015

[34] For example, Latour and Woolgar 1979

[35] EPSRC 2017

[36] Cath and Floridi 2017

[37] Schwab 2016, p. 107

[38] The Boston Consulting Group 2016

[39] Philbeck 2017

[40] Ibid.

[41] American writer and political activist Susan Sontag

[42] Milanovic 2016

[43] Hausmann, Hidalgo et al. 2011

[44] University of Sussex 2008

[45] Interview with Calestous Juma 2017

[46] UNESCO 2016

[47] High gender disparities exist with more young women than young men out of school in the Caucasus and Central Asia, Northern Africa, Southern Asia, Sub-Saharan Africa and Western Asia (UNESCO 2016)

[48] Oxford Internet Institute, "The Location of Academic Knowledge" 2017

[49] UNESCO 2017

[50] Ceballos et al. 2015

[51] Population Reference Bureau 2017

[52] World Bank and Institute for Health Metrics and Evaluation 2016

[53] World Economic Forum 2016a

[54] World Resources Institute 2014

[55] Global Challenges Foundation 2017

[56] Steffen et al. 2015

[57] United Nations, Department of Economic and Social Affairs, Population Division 2015

[58] Deforestation also threatens the livelihoods of forest communities and smallholder farmers, and depletes biodiversity (Enbakom, Feyssa and Takele 2017)

[59] Newshub 2016

[60] Yale Environment 360 2016

[61] Bloomberg 2016

[62] MIT Technology Review 2017

[63] Fortune 2017

[64] World Economic Forum 2016

[65] Catalyst 2016; UNESCO 2015

[66] Deloitte 2016

67 Philbeck 2017
68 Tay et al. 2013
69 "2. Smartphone ownership rates skyrocket in many emerging economies, but digital divide remains" (Poushter 2016)

70 The average household in an advanced economy today has more computers than the entire world did in 1950. According to James Cortada, Kenneth Flamm counted the number of digital computers worldwide in 1950 and found five, two in the United States and three in Great Britain. NPD Group, the market research company, conservatively estimates that, including mobile devices, the average American household had 5.7 digital computers in 2013. Today, in 2017, with the rapid adoption of smartphones and the introduction of microprocessors into a wide variety of household devices from televisions to washing machines, it is likely that this number has more than doubled. See Cortada (1993) and Cockshott, Mackenzie and Michaelson (2010)
71 World Economic Forum and INSEAD 2015
72 ITRS 2.0 2015
73 Yang 2016
74 Denning and Lewis 2016
75 Lapedus 2016
76 IEEE 2016
77 Most notably, with the introduction of the Intel 4004 in 1970, followed by the 8008 in 1974.
78 ReRam memory in particular can be used as a part of deep-learning algorithm, replacing the need for large neural networks to be written and recalled from[a][b] memory and promising advances that go beyond binary computing.
79 For problems with large numbers or more than a handful of variables, today's best classical computers would require more time than the universe has existed to date to find the answer. Quantum computers can draw on the probabilistic nature of superposition to simulate multiple states at the same time, thereby providing a shortcut to the best, or close to the best, answer to a problem that is currently unsolvable by digital computers.
80 Absolute zero is the lowest temperature theoretically possible, equivalent to -273.15°C.
81 Peter Shor, Professor of Mathematics at MIT, devised Shor's algorithm – a quantum algorithm for factoring exponentially faster than the best currently-known algorithm running on a classical computer.
82 Weiser 1991
83 See, for example, Frost Gorder 2016
84 Solon 2017
85 Knight 2015
86 Church stored 70 billion copies of a single book within commercial DNA microchips at a density of 5.5 petabits per cubic millimetre. See Cameron and Mowatt (2012)
87 As discussed in Schwab (2016)
88 Spin-Transfer-Torque Magnetic Random Access Memory is an innovative memory technology that uses electron spin instead of charged transistors to store information. It can resist high radiation, operate in extreme temperature conditions and be made tamper resistant, making it suitable for space, industry control and other applications in severe environments. Both Airbus and BMW have used it.

89 Raspberry Pi Foundation 2016

90 Ezrachi and Stucke 2017

91 Blockchain refers to distributed ledgers and smart contracts secured by cryptography as well as a variety of further decentralized and encrypted internet technologies.

92 Tapscott 2016, p. 24

93 It is easy to assume that transaction costs are close to zero on a distributed ledger because there is no need for a centralized intermediary. In reality, transaction costs depend on the way in which the blockchain is verified and can be far higher than a centralized utility. On 11 June 2017, the fastest and cheapest transaction cost on the bitcoin totalled $2.61 for the median transaction size of merely 226 bytes. At this level of transaction expense, bitcoin is not suitable for microtransactions (Bitcoin Fees 2017)

94 World Economic Forum interview with Brian Behlendorf, by telephone, 26 May 2017

95 An alternative model is "proof-of-stake", a model which the Ethereum blockchain hopes to adopt in the future. Proof-of-stake doesn't rely on miners expending large amounts of energy to add information securely to the chain. Instead, it distributes the creation of a block probabilistically across "validators", while building in penalties for anyone that tries to cheat or forge blocks.

96 It is worth noting that the immutability of distributed ledgers does mean that criminal use of them can provide authorities with additional ways of monitoring and gathering evidence for prosecution of illicit activities. The FBI case against Ross Ulbricht (who received a life sentence for maintaining the Silk Road website for sellers and buyers of illegal products and services), was aided by public blockchain records of $18 million in bitcoin transactions that were traced to his laptop (Greenberg 2016)

97 World Economic Forum interview with Catherine Mulligan, by phone, 9 June 2017

98 OECD and EUIPO 2016

99 Ruppert 2016

100 World Economic Forum interview with Peter Smith in London on 27 September 2016

101 A fat-finger error is a keyboard input mistake due to clumsy or inaccurate typing resulting from one finger striking the wrong key or two keys simultaneously. The input error also includes placing financial market orders to buy or sell at the wrong price or for the wrong stock.

102 Columbus 2016

103 McKinsey Global Institute 2015

104 World Economic Forum and Accenture 2016

105 World Economic Forum 2015, p. 8

106 McKinsey Global Institute 2015a

107 Described in Perrow (1984)

108 World Economic Forum 2015

109 Brown 2016

110 Westby and Richard 2008

111 NYSE Governance Services 2015

112 OECD 2012

113 World Economic Forum 2017

114 Miniwatts Marketing 2017

115 eMarketer 2017

116 Reinsel, Gantz and Rydning 2017
117 World Economic Forum 2012
118 Greenberg 2015
119 KrebsonSecurity 2014
120 Nuix 2017
121 Ibid.
122 Thielman 2016
123 Sample and Hern 2014
124 Petersen 2016
125 AI International 2017
126 Metz 2016
127 Partnership on AI 2017
128 DeepMind Ethics & Society 2017
129 CB Insights 2017
130 Turing 1951
131 Murphy 2016; Conner-Simons 2016; Hardesty 2013.
132 Vanian 2016
133 Pittman 2016
134 Petersen 2016; Wakefield 2016; Agence France-Presse 2016
135 McKinsey & Company 2017
136 Frey and Osborne 2013
137 Wakefield 2016b
138 Cohen et al. 2016
139 LaGrandeur and Hughes (Eds) 2017; World Economic Forum 2016, OECD 2016
140 EPSRC 2017
141 Baraniuk 2015
142 de Wargny 2016
143 Rehnberg and Ponte 2016
144 Wohlers Associates 2016
145 Gartner 2016
146 Wohlers Associates 2016
147 PwC 2016
148 Wohlers Associates 2016
149 Wohlers Associates 2014, p. 26
150 Rehnberg and Ponte 2016
151 Parker 2013
152 Based on author's calculation of the cost of an F-22 Raptor versus that of US Military Reaper and Predator drones. Flight hour costs are also an issue with drones operating at a small fraction of the cost of manned aerial vehicles. See Thompson (2013)
153 Author's interview with David Shim, October 2016
154 Author's interview with Andreas Raptopoulos, October 2016
155 Overly 2016
156 Kopardekar et al. 2016
157 NASA Traffic Unmanned Management 2015; Amazon Prime Air 2015
158 CRISPR stands for clustered regularly interspaced short palindromic repeat. See Cyranoski (2016)
159 Reilly 2017
160 Interview with Henry Greely
161 EY 2016
162 Lee and Kim 2015
163 Peplow 2015

164 Examples include chips grafted onto a brain or electrodes inserted into the skull; noninvasive electroencephalogram devices that monitor brainwaves and electrical signals from outside the skull or other noninvasive devices that can disrupt or trigger brain activity thanks to electric or magnetic signals; devices that interpret thoughts and intentions through physical signals and bodily movements, such as eye movement, heart rate, skin conductivity and blood pressure; chemicals that influence brain chemistry; devices that emit sounds or images that deliberately influence brain activity.

165 After spreading from Yemen and Ethiopia across the Islamic world in the 15th and 16th centuries, both coffee as a drink and the coffee houses in which it was sold were first banned by Governor Kha'ir of Mecca in 1511. While coffee-loving Pope Clement VIII "baptized" coffee in 1600, its introduction to Britain in 1637 threatened efforts to promote the consumption of tea (itself an effort against alcoholism), leading local authorities to prohibit takeaway coffee and King Charles II to issue a Proclamation for the Suppression of Coffee Houses in 1675. Frederick the Great of Prussia was sufficiently concerned about coffee depressing sales of beer, the country's national drink, that he employed "street sniffers" who fined those caught smelling of coffee, while Sweden prohibited the import of coffee in five different decrees between 1756 and 1817. Today, Nespresso not only allows coffee to be ordered via an app, but its Prodigio coffee maker connects to the internet to program coffee brewing remotely. See Juma (2016)

166 Constine 2017

167 World Economic Forum interview with Geoffrey Ling on 28 September 2016

168 Jones 2016

169 See, for example, EMOTIV at https://www.emotiv.com/

170 World Economic Forum interview with Nitish Thakor on 28 September 2016

171 Statt 2017

172

173 Neurotech 2016

174 World Economic Forum correspondence with Neal Kassell on 18 May 2017

175 Grillner et al. 2016; European Commission 2016

176 World Economic Forum 2016

177 World Economic Forum interview with Nancy Ip on 10 November 2016

178 Emmerich 2015

179 Oullier 2012

180 Ghosh 2015

181 Chafkin 2015

182 Zuckerberg 2015

183 Goldman Sachs 2016

184 The ancient Greek *techné* (τέχνη) is one of the roots of the word "technology" but is most often translated from ancient texts as meaning "art" or "craft" in the context of traditional arts, for example painting, sculpting or carpentry.

185 World Bank 2017

186 Kanellos 2013

187 Frankfurt School of Finance & Management 2017, figure 25

188 Ibid., figure 54, figure 1.

189 World Economic Forum interview with Cameron Hepburn on 28 September 2016

190 Tucker 2014

191 Woolford 2015

192 ITER (which means "the way" in Latin) is an energy project in which 35 nations are collaborating to build the world's largest magnetic fusion device.

193 Parry 2016
194 University of Texas at Austin 2017
195 European Commission 2017
196 United Nations, Department of Economic and Social Affairs, Population Division 2015
197 Stilgoe 2016
198 Pasztor 2017
199 Ibid.
200 IPCC 2013
201 Condliffe 2017
202 Neslen 2017
203 Pasztor 2017
204 de Selding 2015
205 Dillow 2016
206 Siceloff 2017
207 Thibeault et al. 2015
208 Carbon 3D 2017
209 See, for example, Vanian (2016)
210 McKinsey Global Institute 2017
211 AlphaBeta 2017
212 International Organization for Standardization 2017
213 International Organization for Standardization 2017a
214 This list draws gratefully from Maynard 2016
215 Hadfield 2016
216 Owen, Macnaghten and Stilgoe 2012
217 Sutcliffe 2015
218 Guston 2008
219 Mulgan 2017
220 Marchant and Wallach 2015
221 Thomas 2009
222 Rodemeyer, Sarewitz and Wilsdon 2005
223 World Economic Forum Global Agenda Council on the Future of Software and Society 2016
208 Carbon 3D 2017
209 See, for example, Vanian (2016)
210 McKinsey Global Institute 2017
211 AlphaBeta 2017
212 International Organization for Standardization 2017
213 International Organization for Standardization 2017a
214 World Economic Forum 2018
215 February 2001, "Manifesto for Agile Software Development", http://agilemanifesto.org/
216 The World Economic Forum Global Agenda Council on the Future of Software and Society issued "A Call for Agile Governance Principles" elaborated on the principles codified in the Agile Manifesto and reframed their application in the policy-making sphere. See http://www3.weforum.org/docs/IP/2016/ICT/Agile_Governance_Summary.pdf
217 World Economic Forum 2018
218 This list draws gratefully from Maynard 2016
219 See UK Government Policy Lab at https://openpolicy.blog.gov.uk/category/policy-lab/
220 Mulgan 2017
221 See CrowdLaw at http://www.thegovlab.org/project-crowdlaw.html

222 Hadfield 2016
223 Owen, Macnaghten and Stilgoe 2012
224 Sutcliffe 2015
225 Guston 2008
226 Marchant and Wallach 2015
227 Thomas 2009
228 Rodemeyer, Sarewitz and Wilsdon 2005
229 World Economic Forum Global Agenda Council on the Future of Software and Society 2016
230 See Civil Service College at https://www.cscollege.gov.sg
231 World Economic Forum 2017
232 The New Yorker 2017
233 See Fab Foundation at http://www.fabfoundation.org/
234 See Genspace at https://www.genspace.org/classes-alt/

62925218R00159

Made in the USA
Middletown, DE
27 January 2018